Michael A. Carella
255 West Santa Inez Ave.
Hillsborough, Calif.

75
5-97

Keep with
Books on Darrow
Rogers & John
Cow D'alene
the Rople & the Power
State of Colo"

Excellent acct
on
Earl Rogers
& Darrow
also; this of trial of
Calhoun; however does not
mention Election of New DA
who dropped case

The
Jerry Giesler
Story

BY JERRY GIESLER

AS TOLD TO PETE MARTIN

SIMON AND SCHUSTER · NEW YORK · 1960

First Printing

ACKNOWLEDGMENT

*My thanks to the Damon Runyon estate for allowing
me to quote from his column "The Brighter Side,"
copyright © 1941 by King Features Syndicate, Inc.;
to New York University Law Review for material
from their June 1954 issue; and to the St. Louis Post-
Dispatch for permission to quote from their edition
of March 1944.*

J. G.

Library of Congress Catalog Card Number: 60–8011
Manufactured in the United States of America
By H. Wolff Book Mfg. Co., Inc., New York, N. Y.

I owe much of whatever success I have had to the help I have received from my wife, Ruth Marie Giesler. There have been so many times when she has stayed with me into the small hours of the morning, giving me encouragement when I was preparing for a trial; so often she has allowed me to use her as a "guinea pig" so that I could better predict the reactions of the women jurors I was about to face. For all this and much more—thanks.

J. G.

THE BASIC FACTS OF THE CASE HISTORIES IN THIS BOOK HAVE ALREADY APPEARED IN PUBLIC RECORDS. I HAVE WITHHELD NOTHING EXCEPT THOSE "PRIVILEGED COMMUNICATIONS"—FROM CLIENT TO ATTORNEY—WHICH A LAWYER IS BOUND TO HOLD CONFIDENTIAL.

J. G.

Contents

"Get Me Giesler!"	1
For the Record	7
Alexander Pantages	14
The Little Fellow in the Attic	40
Margaret Ryan	72
Errol Flynn	94
Caress' Folly	148
The White Flame Case	159
Lili St. Cyr	177
Charles Chaplin	182
Ruth Etting and the Colonel	191
Garbo Talks	205
Norman ("Kid McCoy") Selby	210
The Case of the Fleeced Foreigner	215
The Perjured Witness	219
The Tokyo Club	225
The Missing Stomach	232
Benjamin "Bugsy" Siegel and Murder, Inc.	236
Edward G. Robinson, Jr., and Robert Mitchum	243

vii

Contents

Busby Berkeley   249

My First Murder Case   256

Divorce Cases I Have Handled   258

A Boy from Iowa   263

Earl Rogers and the Bar Examination   269

My Early Cases   281

Defending Darrow   285

Observations on the Law   289

Advice to Young Lawyers   298

My Courtroom Tactics   306

More of the Same   321

My Life Now   327

Index   333

PHOTOGRAPH SECTION FOLLOWS PAGE 6

The
Jerry Giesler
Story

I

"Get Me Giesler!"

FIRST I'd like to set this straight. The first syllable of my surname is pronounced to rhyme with "geese." It does not rhyme with "ice."

In the second place I'd like to tell who I am. Others have described me as "Jerry Giesler, the man who beats the rap," "Jerry Giesler, the man who handles the film capital's troubles from peccadillo to perjury, including pot shots at Pooh-Bahs." I have been called "the miracle man who invariably gets his clients off the hook," "the magnificent mouthpiece." These are only a few samples of the exaggerated, and often lurid, labels which have been pinned to my name.

What this means is that I am a criminal lawyer by trade. But even that phrase is wrongly worded. If a lawyer is a criminal, he should be clapped into jail like any other offender. What I really am is a defense lawyer.

One day I overheard a cynic say, "If it's murder, they call Jerry Giesler first. Then they call the doctor. Then they call the police."

That wisecrack was inaccurate. It reverses the almost invariable order of the doctor, the police, *then* me.

While of course he gets a fee for doing it, any lawyer who undertakes the defense of a wealthy or glamorous client is putting himself squarely on the spot. The fickle public (and juries are chosen from a cross-section of that public) places its celebrities on a pedestal, but it is quick to believe the worst of a figure it has idolized, to pull him down from his pedestal in a jiffy. One of my major tasks as a defense attorney is to try to make a jury see that regardless of the spotlight focused upon my client he or she is only an ordinary person who possesses the same emotions and problems any other human being possesses.

In March 1944 a St. Louis *Post-Dispatch* staff correspondent wrote me up. He began his summation of me as a lawyer by choosing the moment when the D.A. turns to the defense attorney and says, "Take the witness." The *Post-Dispatch* took me from there:

Giesler comes quietly to his feet, suave, poised, immaculate. He knows his stuff, but does not strut it. Small wonder that the courtroom is expectant. Here is the man who successfully defended old Alex Pantages, crippled Moe (The Gimp) Snyder, nervous Errol Flynn, the shattered Busby Berkeley, and now the distraught and aging Charles Chaplin, who is facing a morals charge and other legal entanglements which Giesler is seeking to unsnarl.

Why doesn't he begin? Because he is not ready. He begins when the jittery witness least expects it. The young accusing witness in the Pantages-girl-attack case made the jurors weep. Giesler made them think. As a result the witness writhed. . . .

Earl Rogers, who was Giesler's boyhood idol and early mentor, was flamboyant, spectacular; he dressed to kill. He wore long-tailed coats, some of them black, some brown, some gray, but all of them heavily braided. He wore spats, gay vests, he flourished a lorgnette—rather than the more conventional eyeglasses—at opposing counsel and under the noses of judge and jury. He hated to have anyone walk behind him when he was presenting a case. Yet he invariably stalked back and forth behind the prosecution, a parading which nettled his opponents. Rogers somehow managed to put the prosecutor on trial instead of his client. He quarreled and bickered. He ranted and wept, but he was a good lawyer.

Giesler is quieter, dresses more sedately, keeps his voice down, outsmarts the prosecution rather than behaving like a gamecock or small, irritating terrier. He never antagonizes a judge. If he detects an error creeping into the court's ruling, he does not bawl out the judge, as Rogers would have done. He bides his time. The next day, possibly three days later, he says softly, "If Your Honor please," then

2

adroitly places his finger on the error. Usually the court sees his point and undoes the damage before it's too late. The truth is Giesler likes to win his cases through acquittals. He does not really like court errors which lead to reversal, although he has obtained many of them in his time.

I'll settle for that.

I grew up with Hollywood. I worked in Los Angeles before there was a Hollywood. I've known Hollywood people for years, and they've known me. When they get into trouble, naturally they think of me—although many of my most intriguing cases have not involved Hollywood at all.

This is the reason why almost any feature writer assigned to write a series about me uses such an opening as: "If a Hollywood glamour boy runs afoul of the law, his first reaction is, 'Get me Giesler!'"

People who have read that and then happen to see me in the flesh often do a double take. I know why. Many criminal lawyers have been colorful-looking. I am not. I am, I hope, kindly-faced, my taste in clothes runs to conservatively cut suits, my hair is thinning, and when I read I peer through horn-rimmed glasses.

No motion picture producer or director would think of casting me as a criminal lawyer in a film; yet I have served some of the biggest stars in the business as a flesh-and-blood advocate, and, I might add, it's the hardest kind of work.

If I seem inclined to dwell upon many sex cases in my story, it's because sex is not only one of the facts of life, it's also—at least in my experience—one of the most prevalent bases of legal strife. However, I will not be telling these cases because of their sex content, but because they also involve interesting legal points as well as various aspects of court tactics and strategy.

I have been proud to have had at least one of my defendants, Robert Mitchum, found guilty and sentenced to serve time in jail. If anybody wonders why I regard that as a triumph, I think he'll understand before he's finished this story.

I was the advocate for the defense in a trial when the jury set a new record by staying out for ninety-nine hours. I was the defense

3

attorney when another jury set another record by staying out for exactly one minute.

I have acted for the defense when the district attorney failed to show up and the judge met the situation by wearing two metaphorical hats. First he wore his judge's hat, then took it off, did the examination, cross-examination and summing up for the prosecution. Then he put his judge's hat back on and delivered his instructions to the jury. I don't honestly expect anyone to believe this, but it happened.

Not all of my law practice has been criminal. I have been involved in some of the most sensational civil cases in southern California. I was in Shelley Winters' corner when she sued Vittorio Gassman for divorce. I fronted for Zsa Zsa Gabor in her suit against George Sanders. I represented Marilyn Monroe in her parting from Joe DiMaggio and Barbara Hutton in her lawsuit against Cary Grant. Not only did Miss Hutton retain me as her lawyer; she moved into my home for six weeks, with two chauffeurs, her personal maid and her private telephone.

I have defended clients I liked personally, such as Busby Berkeley, who killed three people and maimed a fourth with his auto, and Edward G. Robinson, Jr., who was accused by two cabbies of holding them up for money. I was able to win freedom for both of these men, although in the Berkeley case it took three grinding, grueling trials to do it and in the Edward G. Robinson, Jr., case it took a *bar mitzvah* ring that wouldn't come off to win my client's freedom.

I liked Norman Selby—otherwise known as Kid McCoy, a former world champion prize fighter—in spite of the fact that he did everything possible (as well as some things almost impossible) to land himself in the death chamber. I saved him from that, but I'm not sure he appreciated it. He was hoping the law would kill him to save him the trouble of committing suicide.

I have defended hoodlums and dipsomaniacs given to maniacal rages and men whom I didn't like at all. I have looked upon some of these clients with loathing, but I believe that every man has a right not only to be defended but to have a good defense. As Alex-

4

ander Woollcott said in his profile of the advocate Lloyd Paul Stryker, "The disposition in this country seems to imply that whereas even a Bruno Hauptmann is entitled to the services of a lawyer, when he is on trial for his life, he is surely not entitled to the services of a *good* lawyer."

When I went with Charles Chaplin to the Federal Building to have him fingerprinted, we got off the elevator and walked along a hallway toward the room where the fingerprinting was done. The hall was filled with women who shouted insults and obscenities at Chaplin, and there was the snakelike sound of hissing which, of all massed human sounds, is the most frightening.

Most of the cases against my clients have been conducted in an atmosphere of prejudice so thick it was stifling. I accept that as one of the hazards of being a defense lawyer. I defended one client, a woman, against a manslaughter charge in a little town where the feeling against her was so bitter that anyone who had anything to do with the defendant was subjected to scalding, explosive hatred. Once it was known that I was associated with her defense, the townspeople spat at my feet as I walked along the sidewalk.

At the opposite end of the spectrum is my defense of Lili St. Cyr against a charge of "indecent exposure" while she was working at her job as a stripper. I can honestly say I succeeded in having her case laughed into a not-guilty verdict. The laughter was stentorian, rollicking and so uninhibited that tears ran from the eyes of many of the people in that court.

There is a burden which rests upon a lawyer simply because he is a defense lawyer. I was lucky enough to wet my legal feet in the office of the great advocate Earl Rogers. No man was ever more generously endowed with legal brains than Rogers. No man ever gave more of himself fighting for his clients. In fact, he gave so lavishly that it burned him out and he died at an early age. To steal a phrase from Vachel Lindsay, "His valor wore out his soul in the service of men." Yet it has been written about Rogers that he was something of a charlatan and that his chief vocation in life was cheating the gallows of its legitimate prey.

I suppose that vague character, "the man in the street," believes that about me, too, although he lacks the courage to say it to my face. I'm sure millions of people have thought it and have said it about Fallon and Liebowitz, about Max Steuer and Ferdinand Pecora, even about Clarence Darrow, although in the years which have passed since Darrow's death it has become fashionable to think of him as having been pure of mind. I believed that of him before it became fashionable.

At the conclusion of one of my cases—a trial in which the tension had been almost unbelievable—one newspaper reported that when the jury came in I was weeping. That was true. I was not only weeping, I was completely exhausted. My preparation for that case had been so wearing that I was tired before I went into court for the first day.

But while I may seem sucked dry of energy during a trial, I'm *really* beat the day after. The stimulation of keeping up on my toes every moment sustains me during a trial, for the stakes in a criminal case are very high. Sometimes I become so closely identified with my client that I feel I'm on trial myself. I'm not unique in this; other lawyers have told me they feel the same way.

The criminal law is the triple-distilled brandy of the legal cellars. It is enormously stimulating; it also takes a lot out of those who are addicted to it. It puts an almost intolerable burden on the emotions, the brains and the bodies of those who learn to love it. It is my opinion (and I am not overdramatizing it) that being a criminal lawyer kills many of its practitioners early in life.

[ABOVE] Jerry Giesler shown with client Alexander Pantages, West Coast theater-chain magnate accused of raping a 17-year-old show girl. This is the case that made Giesler famous.

[RIGHT] "The Little Fellow in the Attic," Otto Sanhuber, who lived in a garret for almost twenty years, seldom seeing the light of day. He was a defendant in one the most fantastic crime cases of the century.

The two young complainants in the famous Errol Flynn rape case shown in court during the trial. Although the alleged rapes had occurred a year apart, the girls filed complaints with the district attorney's office only weeks apart. Peggy La Rue Satterlee [ABOVE, LEFT] holds a photograph of herself and Flynn taken aboard his yacht *Sirocco* at the time when he supposedly lured her down to his cabin to "watch the moon through a porthole." That neither Flynn nor Miss Satterlee could possibly have seen the moon from that particular porthole was a fact Giesler had no difficulty in establishing. Betty Hansen [BELOW, LEFT], the aspiring career girl from Nebraska who hoped to use Flynn's influence to break into the movie world. In this photograph, Miss Hansen's histrionic ability is viewed with doubtful appreciation by Policewoman Helen D. Stone. The youthful Flynn [ABOVE, RIGHT] talking with Giesler at the preliminary hearing. After the hearing Flynn was held on three counts of statutory rape—two for Miss Satterlee, one for Miss Hansen. Man in middle is unidentified. [BELOW, RIGHT] Leaving the Los Angeles court after his acquittal, Flynn is accompanied by his assistant, Buster Wiles, and a jubilant Giesler. [RIGHT] Seven years later, the not-so-young-looking actor hired Giesler again, this time to straighten out his costly alimony and child-support payments involving two ex-wives and three children. At the time, Flynn claimed to be in hock to the Government for $70,000 in back taxes.

Mrs. Margaret Ryan [LEFT], whom Giesler defended against a manslaughter charge in the small coastal town of San Luis Obispo. After a second trial, Mrs. Ryan was acquitted.

Les Bruneman [BELOW, LEFT, with Giesler], charged with complicity in the kidnaping of Los Angeles gambler A. L. (Zeke) Caress. Caress himself helped to exonerate Bruneman — with considerable help from the "magnificent mouthpiece."

Giesler confers with Paul Wright, who was charged with the double slaying of his wife and best friend when he found them *in flagrante delicto* in the living room of his home. The story made headlines as "The White Flame Case."

An unhappy Joan Berry [TOP] is cross-examined by an amiable Giesler during the Charles Chaplin trial for violation of the Mann Act. [BELOW] An equally sober-faced Chaplin as he pleaded Not Guilty to the charge in Los Angeles Federal Court.

A rare photograph of Greta Garbo taken in 1921 when she was attending the Stockholm Dramatic School with Mimi Pollack (seated). Astrakhan-hatted man unidentified. A few years later Miss Garbo allegedly incurred debts which eventually brought her and Giesler together for a memorable colloquy.

Ruth Etting, the early songbird of the air waves, as she appeared in January 1938 shortly after her divorce from Martin Snyder. She is shown here at the Los Angeles district attorney's office, where she asked for protection from "death threats" from her former husband.

UPI

UPI

In October of that year, Martin Snyder was indicted on three counts of attempted murder of Miss Etting, her musical director, Myrl Alderman, and his own daughter, Edith. He was also indicted on two charges of kidnaping as well as violation of the California gun laws.

Miss Etting came out of retirement to appear on a radio program of her own. Co-starring with her was Myrl Alderman, whom she married during Martin Snyder's trial.

Convicted on one count of attempted murder, Snyder receives condolences—and the promise of an appeal—from his lawyer.

Giesler faces his diminutive client, Norman Selby, during Selby's murder trial. The jurors took ninety-nine hours to reach their decision. Selby, better known as "Kid McCoy" (and also as "The *real* McCoy"), had once been welterweight champion of the world.

UPI

UPI

Lili St. Cyr hugs her lawyer after Giesler conducted on her behalf one of the most humorous defenses on record. In her left hand Miss St. Cyr holds the offending article of clothing which figured in the "indecent exposure" charge filed against her by an indignant D.A.'s office—her famous G-string.

Henry Talbot Devers Clifton, scion of a wealthy British family, dropped $150,000 on the turn of a card in a wild stud-poker game in a Long Beach hotel.

Lew Brice, one of the three other men in this game, screamed like a wounded stoat when Giesler, with a restraining order, showed up at the bank simultaneously with Brice and stopped payment on Clifton's checks.

Dr. George Dazey [LEFT], a Santa Monica physician, was accused of murdering his first wife. Giesler had to break down the testimony of one, possibly two, perjured witnesses to save Dr. Dazey from the gas chamber.

At the time of his murder trial, Benjamin "Bugsy" Siegel [BELOW, MIDDLE] was described as "one of the six most dangerous gangsters in the United States." Nevertheless, Jerry Giesler felt his client had as much right to a good defense as any other citizen. They are shown here with attorney Byron Hanna.

[RIGHT] Edward G. Robinson, Jr., with his famous father at young Robinson's trial for robbery. The senior Robinson helped prove without a doubt that his son could not have been culpable.

[BELOW] Giesler and Robert Mitchum in court after Mitchum surrendered to a grand-jury indictment returned against him for violation of the California Narcotics Act.

UPI

[RIGHT] Shelley Winters and Vittorio Gassman before The Rift. Giesler represented Miss Winters in her divorce action.

[BELOW] After the first Busby Berkeley trial for second-degree murder. The jury failed to agree. Here Berkeley is shown with his mother and Giesler (who also defended Berkeley in two subsequent trials).

UPI

[LEFT] Clarence Darrow on his 79th birthday.

[BELOW] Darrow testifying before a Senate committee in Washington.

Jerry Giesler and his "greatest helper."

2

For the Record

PEOPLE ASK ME, "Do any of your clients ever admit that they're guilty?" I answer, "With one exception, no." Once I decide my client is honest, my belief in him is so deeply ingrained it's a compulsion. I don't see how a lawyer can put his head, his heart and his back into a case unless he believes in it.

It is the jury's duty to decide whether an accused person is guilty, but it is my duty, in fact my ethical and moral obligation, to represent him if he wants me to. Even if his case seems hopeless there may be extenuating circumstances an attorney can bring out which will minimize a client's offense. I was once involved with a case which proves exactly that.

Some years ago a man came to see me. He began hysterically by saying, "I've just killed a woman. I'm guilty as hell." He had been traveling at a high rate of speed on a rainy highway when he skidded over a woman's body. When he pulled her from under his car, she was not only crushed to death but her blood was splattered on the underside of his car.

The dead woman had been a passenger in a car her sister had been driving on Alternate State Highway 101. The sister, behind the wheel, tried to pass a heavy truck loaded with asphalt. As she did, her car nicked the back of the truck. The door on the right-hand side of her auto flew open, and her passenger fell out on the highway. Seconds afterward my client skidded over her. The woman who had been driving also believed that my client had killed her sister.

7

My policy of digging for all the facts, not just *some* of them, paid off in this case, for, as it turned out, the facts didn't agree with my client's confession. He had been driving a Studebaker, yet the autopsy showed that the woman's body had been crushed to a width of twenty-two inches, including her head and the bones of her chest. I suggested to my investigator, "Measure the width of the wheels of the truck the sister's car nicked."

The owner of that truck refused to allow my investigator to examine it. However, we knew what kind of truck it was because the driver had stopped and had helped pick up the dead woman. So we took the measurements of a truck which duplicated the one we weren't allowed to measure. The width of one of its double-heavy-duty tires was exactly twenty-two inches.

When the dead woman fell out, a back wheel of the truck had run over her. She was already crushed and dead when my client's car had run over her body.

Let me repeat: That young man was absolutely convinced that he had killed that woman, yet the jury acquitted him.

No man is the best judge of his own guilt or innocence. It takes a special knowledge to know that—the kind of knowledge which recognizes mitigating circumstances of which the client may be ignorant.

Anyone who reads this story may find himself in deep trouble any day, any hour, any minute. The more prominent you are in your community and the more successful you are, the more your fellow citizens will indict you before you even come to trial if you get into a jam. There is a dash of sadism inside all of us which makes us secretly (and sometimes not so secretly) relish someone else's mistake. We believe that it will always be someone else who gets into trouble, especially deep trouble, not ourselves.

I hire an investigator for a case if I need one. When a lawyer can afford to assign an investigator to a case and keep him on it for four, five or six weeks and let him follow up every lead that comes his way, it's astounding what that investigation will uncover.

Usually I begin on the basis of information I get from my client. That's my first lead, and I build my case from there. I get other

For the Record

leads as I go along, sometimes in the most unexpected way and
from the most unexpected sources. One lead guides you to another,
and from that second lead a third lead comes. A lead can come
from the transcript of the preliminary hearing or the grand-jury
transcript. Study those, select a name, then tell your investigator,
"I suggest you talk to this person and see what you can find out."

A good investigator can make friends for you among potential
witnesses. In the Busby Berkeley case, when the accident which
killed three people occurred, the Pacific Palisades fire department
was called out, in addition to the police and the ambulances. I saw
to it that at least two of my investigators visited that fire station
and talked to the firemen. They found those firemen ferociously
hostile to Berkeley, but that didn't discourage my two investigators.
They went back to that firehouse again and again. In fact, they
dropped in two or three times a week. By the time they'd done
that eight or nine times, the fire company wasn't so hostile. The
reason why this is important is that when an investigator working
for me encounters hostility, if he can overcome some of it, little by
little the people he visits loosen up and tell him some of the things
they know.

My chief investigator, James Leahan, is one of the best in the
business. I can rely one hundred per cent on his reports. He not
only discovers things that will help me, he also finds out the things
I'm going to be up against and tells me about those, too.

While I try to be more than ordinarily thorough in my investigations, I can never be sure. There may be other lawyers who are
more thorough, but I'll say this: I'm as thorough as I can be. As
soon as I'm given a criminal case to defend, I start my investigating. Not tomorrow. Today.

I expect the investigator I employ to be so thorough that I'll get
both sides of the case from him. I want my investigator to pretend
he's working hard for the prosecution, too. If I know the best foot
the prosecution can put forward, I'll know how to step on its toes.
For instance, my investigator may uncover a neighbor who says,
"I didn't get home until five o'clock," when the crime being investigated took place at four-thirty. The prosecution subpoenas that

9

same man. He comes into court and swears that he was there when the crime occurred. If that happens, it's nice to be able to ask him, "Isn't it true that you told my investigator you didn't get home until five o'clock?" He has to admit that he did. Even if he's trying to be evasive, the very best he can do is say, "I don't remember whether I told him that or not." If that's the way things are, I put my investigator on the stand to testify that he interviewed the witness, and here's his report on that interview, made out at that time, in which the witness said that he didn't know anything about the crime because he didn't get home until later. At such a time I'm only human enough to wonder out loud why he's changed his story.

I recently had a case which involved such a switch. It concerned an automobile accident which happened on Wilshire Boulevard. One of my investigators talked to a witness who said, "I was riding down the street when I saw a car two hundred feet away coming at me. I had my wife in my car, and I wasn't paying any attention to such things as red lights or green lights because one of the cars which was involved in the accident was headed right for us and it kept right on coming. We pulled over to the side of the street and I stopped my car."

That same man turned up in court and testified that the client I represented was going down Wilshire Boulevard in spite of a red light staring him in the face. It must have been like that, he said, because there was a green light shining in his own eyes. His testimony became less valuable to the prosecution when I brought out the fact that he had previously told my investigator he had seen no traffic lights because he was interested in the safety of his own car.

I not only want my investigators' reports now instead of tomorrow, I want them to have their *t*'s crossed and their *i*'s dotted. I ask them to go back and call upon witnesses a second, a third and a fourth time, even if the witnesses tell them the same stories each time. I have known it to happen that after a second or third interview a witness remembers something he hasn't thought of before, but even if he doesn't, the chances are that if my investigator treats him politely and decently I'll have a friendlier witness on the stand facing me when the chips are down.

It is customary for old-timers to look upon the older ways of doing things as the good ways, even the best ways, but even if there are those who will mark me down as stuffy for saying so, I believe that the old methods of training and educating law students, which involved such practical training as working as runners and messengers, were better than the ones used today.

I mourn the thinning of the tribe of great criminal lawyers. Earl Rogers predicted the eventual death of the entire criminal-law profession. I'm inclined to agree with him. Clarence Darrow didn't die rich. Lawyers today are settling more and more into compartmentalized branches of the law. The criminal branch is the smallest compartment and it is rapidly getting smaller. This is the result of lawyers' devoting themselves more and more to business interests.

When the population of Los Angeles was 200,000, among its citizens it numbered some of the world's greatest trial lawyers. In addition to Earl Rogers, there were Stephen M. White, Henry T. Gage, LeCompte Davis, Paul W. Schenck, Horace Appel, Frank Dominguez. All of these are gone now, and few have come since to take their places. More and more lawyers are interested in personal-injury trial work rather than criminal trial work. The decline of the criminal lawyer is also caused by the establishment of the public-defender system. Most of the law students who graduate near the top of their class these days head for the lucrative field of corporation law.

I have received the permission of the New York University *Law Review* to quote from my review of Lloyd Paul Stryker's book *The Art of Advocacy* in its June 1954 issue. Perhaps it will throw some light upon my misgivings as I have watched the gradual extinction of the great advocates on America's West Coast and particularly within my sphere, which is Los Angeles. I wrote then:

> Gradually the giant advocates of the past have gone to their reward, leaving behind a field barren of contemporaries. I agree with

Mr. Stryker that the fault lies not with the lack of natural talent on the part of young lawyers; the finger of blame must point to the law schools which foster the barrenness by a total lack of preparation of a student for the active practice of his profession before the bar.

They are burying the American advocate beneath a mass of briefs, textbooks and casebooks, with him they are burying the future of the American bar. It is my hope that the challenge presented by this book will not go unanswered, but that it will contribute greatly to the reawakening of American educators in regard to stimulating the ambitions and latent talent of young lawyers. . . . Mr. Stryker's emphasis on the extensive and thorough preparation which must precede actual courtroom battle is worth the whole book. As I see it, preparation, both of the law and of the facts, constitutes seventy-five per cent of any law-suit. Stryker's dissertation on the perils of cross-examination is expertly done. Far too often the intemperate use of this potential weapon turned a rapier into a boomerang. . . .

The author makes an eloquent plea for the understanding and appreciation of the function of the trial lawyer. His feelings and thoughts may be summarized by the passage wherein Mr. Stryker states, "Throughout the ages man's inhumanity to man has become more manifest. Can anyone yet deny that now more than ever there is a crying need for the trained advocate; calm, willing, able and unafraid to stand between the accused citizen and the charges which society brings against him, as well as between the defendant and the embattled press, between the man under indictment and the public clamor of the moment. We have had such advocates in the past. Are we still breeding them or are they a dying race?"

. . . The author commends the duty of the American advocate to stand as a shield not between justice and his client, but as a bulwark against mob hysteria and resultant justice. The honesty and integrity of the advocate who rises to defend unpopular causes should never be questioned by the public. It is completely illogical to identify the advocate as the same caliber person the press claims the client to be. Upon the moral and ethical standards of the advocate in pronounced adversity brought about by mass hysteria whipped up by glaring newspaper accounts, rests the future of the American bar.

I could not agree with Mr. Stryker more if I had written his book myself. Eloquently he states thoughts which seldom occur to a reader who is largely concerned with the latest screaming headline and is clamoring for the blood of the latest (and usually the most famous) person the law has grabbed by the heels.

3

Alexander Pantages

Looking back, I'd say that the case in which my life turned its biggest corner was the second Alexander Pantages trial. If a single client can be said to have made a lawyer, Pantages made me. In my previous major cases I had been associated with Earl Rogers or I had played second fiddle to some other attorney. The second Pantages case was the first big one in which I was head man.

Alexander Pantages, a self-made man of Greek descent, was well along in years. He had parlayed a tiny Alaska gold mine into a chain of vaudeville palaces which extended across the western half of the United States. The flagship of his fleet of theaters was the Pantages Theater at Seventh and Hill streets in Los Angeles. Although he could neither read nor write, illiteracy, which might have proved a handicap to most men, failed to slow him down. He was a baffling combination of native common sense and imprudence. In his case imprudence verged upon foolishness. If he hadn't been foolish, he wouldn't have gotten into the trouble that led to his sensational trial.

The prosecution's case against Mr. Pantages was a crude and elementary one. It sounded like an early penny shocker of the "the villain still pursued her" school. The elderly showman was accused of having lured a seventeen-year-old girl, Eunice Pringle, into a room in his theater on the pretense of helping her to further her theatrical career.

From the moment Miss Pringle burst out of that room and ran out into Seventh Street with her clothing disarranged, claiming that she had been sexually outraged, public sympathy was aligned on her side. Among the pleasantest things an irate citizenry called Pantages was a "lecherous old goat."

My client said that he had tried to discourage Miss Pringle several times previously when she had urged him to book her act. Then, on August 9, 1929, she had begged him once more to talk to her about her theatrical ambitions. Wearily he had consented and had pushed open the door of the small mezzanine.

They sat down together. He wore no coat because the day was warm. Eunice Pringle was wearing a sophisticated dress which revealed more of her than was customary at the time. She also wore rouge and lipstick, a bit unusual for a girl of her age in those days. Once she was there, he was said to have made violent love to her, ending the interview by criminally attacking her while she fainted, after having madly fought off his advances.

In telling my story I plan from time to time to quote verbatim from transcripts of testimony given by the key figures before grand juries or in preliminary hearings, as well as direct testimony in the trials to which they were subjected, the cross-examination which followed and the redirect and the cross which concluded those trials. I will also quote from briefs prepared in an effort to persuade judicial bodies (or a judicial body) to reconsider decisions already taken.

I have noticed that in many books I have read which concern themselves with a "real" trial, the writers have been at some pains to do away with the Q-and-A aspect any trial involves. Apparently they have thought that such testimony will be more palatable if reduced to an ordinary narrative form. I disagree. To me, upon a rereading of the piles of such transcripts accumulated in my office storeroom, nothing is so well designed to take anyone interested in re-creating those trials back into the actual courtroom than what the simple, unadorned questions and answers reveal. Sometimes they are much more revealing than the person on the witness stand intended.

I don't pretend, nor indeed would it be possible, to give such testimony as a whole, but I have excerpted what, to me, seems most pertinent and the most absorbing bits of such testimony. I don't think I am overstating it when I say that such raw material (and some of it is actually, as well as figuratively, raw) affords deep insight into the personalities of those who are testifying; in fact, it renders a clear feeling of what kind of person a witness really is, far better than any effort on my part to take the testimony and rewrite it in the usual third-person fashion.

I thought I should explain this in connection with the next few pages, which will consist of just such a Q-and-A session—in this instance the testimony of Eunice Irene Pringle at the preliminary hearing in the Pantages case on August 14, 1929. I didn't appear in the case until later, and Mr. Pantages was represented by W. I. Gilbert and W. J. Ford. Miss Pringle was called as a witness on behalf of the people and was examined by Los Angeles County District Attorney Buron Fitts.

By Mr. Fitts:
Q. Have you any business or occupation?
A. None.
Q. How old are you?
A. Seventeen.
Q. When were you seventeen?
A. March the fifth, last.

❉   ❉   ❉

Q. Are you married?
A. No.
Q. Then I take it that Mr. Pantages, the defendant here, is not your husband?
A. Certainly not.
Q. Are you acquainted with Mr. Pantages, the defendant?
A. Yes.
Q. Just about, Miss Pringle, as near as you can recall, just when did you first become acquainted with him?
A. Somewhere near May first of this year.
Q. And under what circumstances?

16

Alexander Pantages

A. I went to him to see about booking my act.

Q. What kind of an act was it?

A. Musical sketch—singing and dancing.

* * *

Q. And as nearly as you can recall, that was approximately around the first day of May, 1929—around the first part of May, 1929?

A. Around the first part of May.

Q. That was the first time you ever saw Mr. Pantages, as far as you know?

A. It is.

* * *

Q. Then what conversation did you have with Mr. Pantages at that time?

A. I told him about my act, and he said that he would see it himself. The conversation was brief.

Q. Then what did you do, Miss Pringle?

A. I left the office.

Q. Did you see Mr. Pantages after that?

A. Yes.

Q. Under what circumstances?

A. He had told me to come to him again, so I did so.

* * *

Q. And where was that?

A. Pantages Theater Building, his offices on the second floor.

Q. Are you in a position to estimate the number of times, approximately, that you saw him there?

A. I really couldn't say.

* * *

Q. Now, Miss Pringle, let me direct your attention to last Friday, August ninth. Did you see Mr. Pantages on that day?

A. I did.

Q. And how did it happen that you came back to the office on that day?

A. That necessitates going back quite a bit.

Q. Just briefly.

17

The Jerry Giesler Story

A. I showed my act to Mr. Pantages, and he said he would book it. He assured me that he would send me to Fresno as a start on the circuit, and when I went to him for booking instructions, he told me that the manager of the Fresno house could not take me on the bill, and to come to see him again the next week, which I did. That was repeated several times, I can't say how many, and then he told me Sunday that it was too late in the season and to come to see him early next season.

❋ ❋ ❋

Q. Where did you see Mr. Pantages last Friday, August ninth?
A. In his offices, the second floor of the Pantages Theater Building.
Q. At what time?
A. Around three-thirty or a quarter of four.
Q. And when you went there, were you alone or was there someone with you?
A. I was alone.

❋ ❋ ❋

Q. Then where did he take you?
A. He took me to this small office off some of the landings of the stairs between the first and the second floor.

❋ ❋ ❋

Q. If I understood you correctly—this may be leading, but he told you that he would take you to his private office?
A. He said, "Let's go to my private office where we can talk."
Q. Now, when you got into this office was there any other person in the office?
A. No one.

❋ ❋ ❋

Q. Now, after he unlocked the door, what occurred?
A. We entered the room.
Q. You entered the room?
A. Yes, sir. He was very nice to me at first.

* * *

Q. What, if anything, did he do with reference to the door after you entered the room?

A. He merely closed it.

Q. Now, Miss Pringle, do you know what I mean by an act of sexual intercourse?

A. I do.

Q. Did Mr. Pantages, the defendant here, last Friday, August the ninth, at that place and in that office, in the Pantages Building, have and accomplish with you an act of sexual intercourse?

A. He did.

Q. Will you just state to the court now, from the beginning, if you will, just what occurred, how this act was accomplished from the moment that you and Mr. Pantages entered this room?

A. He entered the room. He closed the door. He began talking about my act. . . . He said it was a very good act, and in his conversation he also asked me if I had minded waiting for him and if I had minded the heat of the day. . . . He told me that he intended booking my act and then he picked up my hand.

Q. Let me interrupt, please, Miss Pringle. Were you seated or standing up?

A. Seated.

Q. And just in what position?

A. There were three chairs in the room, and I was seated in the chair farthest from the window and he in the chair next to me.

Q. Did you have your coat on or off?

A. During the first few minutes of our conversation I removed my little velvet jacket I was wearing, as it was very warm.

Q. You had a regular dress underneath that?

A. Certainly.

Q. And was his coat on or off?

A. Just after I removed my jacket he asked me if I minded if he removed his coat, as he also was warm.

Q. And during the time, then, that you were talking he had his coat off?

A. Yes, sir.

Q. Just go right ahead with your story, if you will?

A. He picked up my hand and he said I had a beautiful hand. He said he admired me very much, and I withdrew my hand naturally and I told him that had nothing whatever to do with business, and then he mentioned my act again and he said that I was a beautiful dancer and that the singer in my act had a wonderful voice. He told me again he intended booking me and then he put his arm around me.

Q. Yes.

A. And then he told me that I was wonderful, that he was crazy about me, and he said he wanted me for his sweetheart, that he would give me anything if I would be his sweetheart, and I told him that I did not wish any sweetheart, that all I was interested in was work, but he continued his advances. He told me again that he would give me anything if I would be his sweetheart. He said that he hated his wife and would I be his sweetheart, and I told him I was not in the least interested in his wife and would he please be a gentleman.

Q. All right. Go ahead, Miss Pringle.

A. He seemed to go crazy.

MR. GILBERT: We would like to have his actions described.

MR. FORD: We move to strike out the remark that he seemed to go crazy, as a conclusion.

THE COURT: Strike it out. State what he did.

Q. BY MR. FITTS: Just what he did, Miss Pringle?

A. He seized me very tightly, drawing me to my feet.

Q. Was he sitting down or standing?

A. He was sitting down and he arose to his feet as he pulled me to my feet.

Q. Now, what did he do?

A. He held me tightly and he said again he was crazy about me and he started trying to kiss me.

Q. Yes.

A. And I said, "Please be a gentleman."

Q. Where did he try to kiss you?

A. He started kissing me here. [*Indicating.*]

Q. Indicating the chin.

MR. GILBERT: The left side of the chin.

Q. BY MR. FITTS: What else?

A. Then he started to kiss my throat.

Q. Anyplace else?

A. That was all at that time, and I say—I asked him to be a gentleman and he continued and so I started to scream.

Q. And then what did he do?

A. He clapped his hand over my mouth.

Q. Which hand did he clap over your mouth?

A. His right hand.

Q. And how was he holding you at that time?

A. He was holding his right hand over my mouth.

Q. Just where was his left hand?

A. Around me, around my waist.

Q. Around your waist?

A. Yes, sir; holding me very tightly.

*   *   *

Q. All right. What next happened?

A. He was kissing me madly. He not only was kissing me, he was biting me.

Q. Where did he bite you?

A. He bit me here. [*Indicating.*]

Q. On your breast?

A. Yes, sir; and he pulled at me and bit me somewhere on my shoulder.

MR. FORD: Indicating the right shoulder.

A. He was sort of smothering me with kisses all over my throat and holding me very tightly and muttering how crazy he was about me.

Q. BY MR. FITTS: Yes. Go ahead.

A. And then he started pulling me down on the floor.

Q. Did he pull you down on the floor?

A. He did.

Q. In what position?

A. On my back.

Q. And what was the condition of your clothes at that time?

A. At that time when he started pulling me down on the floor he had been pulling and tearing— Oh, really, I can't say exactly what condition they were in.

Q. You say that he finally pulled you down on your back?

A. Yes, sir.

Q. Then what did he do?

A. He was holding me down with his right hand and the upper part of his body.

Q. You mean by that that he laid down himself.

A. Well, he was bending over me holding me down, rather sort of reclining on me.

Q. Now, describe that a little more in detail, Miss Pringle. It is not quite clear. Was he standing up, or stooping over holding you down?

A. No, sir.

Q. Then describe it a little more clearly to the court.

A. I guess the best way, he must have been on his knees. Anyway his chest was pressing against me right here.

Mr. Gilbert: You mean by "right here" on your chest?

A. Yes, sir.

*   *   *

Q. By Mr. Fitts: Now, then, while he was holding you down with his chest on you, what else, if anything, was he doing?

A. With his left hand he was fumbling at his trousers.

Q. What part of his trousers?

A. The front.

Q. All right. Then what happened?

A. He was working at them.

Q. Yes. After he finished working with them, Miss Pringle, what happened?

A. He pulled up my dress.

Q. Yes, go ahead.

A. And then he began tearing at my trunks.

Q. At your what?

A. Trunks.

Q. You were not wearing bloomers, were you?

A. No, sir.

Q. You were wearing these trunks that resemble the trunks that boys wear at the track meets at schools and colleges, regular men's trunks?

A. Like they wear in track meets, resembling them.

Q. How were they fastened?

A. By an elastic around the top.

Q. You had an elastic around the top?

A. Yes, sir.

Q. It was not necessary in order to pull them down that you unbutton them?

MR. FORD: I would prefer that you would let the witness testify.

MR. FITTS: You are right.

Q. BY MR. FITTS: What was necessary, then, in order to pull your trunks down?

A. Just pull at them.

Q. You say he was pulling at your trunks?

A. Yes, tearing at them.

Q. What did he do with the trunks?

A. He pulled them about around my hips, and I don't know how far.

*   *   *

Q. Now, what next occurred?

A. After pulling . . . my trunks he started forcing my legs apart.

Q. Did he succeed?

A. He did. I was struggling, but I was too weak for him.

*   *   *

Q. Then what happened . . . ?

A. I don't know, I fainted.

Q. Did you go completely out, Miss Pringle?

A. Yes.

Q. What next do you remember when you came to? Just where were you — May we have a moment's recess, your honor?

THE COURT: Yes. You want her mother to come over and stand by her? Do you want to rest a moment, Miss Pringle?

A. Just a second, please.

23

Q. By Mr. Fitts: All right. When you next remember anything, where were you?

A. I was lying on the floor.

Q. And what was the condition of your clothing?

A. I can't describe it exactly, except I felt exposed.

*　　*　　*

Q. Now, after you came to, was your clothing— You say your dress was up?

A. Yes.

Q. What was the condition of his clothing?

A. He also was exposed.

Q. What do you mean, he was also exposed?

A. His body.

Q. What part of his body?

A. I don't know whether you call it the central or lower part.

Q. Was that his private parts?

A. Yes.

Q. Were they exposed?

A. I didn't glance at him thoroughly.

Q. You just saw part of his body, bare skin exposed, saw the central part of his body?

A. Yes.

Q. Then just what took place, what happened, Miss Pringle?

A. As soon as I was conscious I struggled to my feet. I wanted to get away, and as I made a move to the door he said, "Don't go, I will give you anything or everything if you won't go, won't make any trouble."

Q. What did you do?

A. I told him all I wanted to do was to get away from him.

Q. What did you do?

A. I made for the door.

Q. Well, did you get to the door?

A. I reached the door, tried to pull it open, he grabbed me and pulled me back.

Q. You say you tried to pull the door open. Did you pull the door open?

A. I got it partly open.

Q. And did you, or did you not, go out?

A. I was in the doorway, tried to get out.

Q. Then what did he do at that point?

A. He grabbed me and jerked me back.

Q. And what happened to the door when he jerked you back?

A. I don't know whether it went clear shut or not.

Q. Now, then, during the course of this struggle, do you recall where Mr. Pantages was, what position he was in, and what part of your body he had hold of in his attempts to restrain you?

A. My main idea of it is just an awful struggle to get away.

Q. Well, did he have hold of you?

A. He did.

Q. Where?

A. I know one time he had hold of my left leg. I can't say just when.

Q. Just when?

A. When I was struggling to get up.

Q. During the struggle he had hold of your left leg. What part of your left leg?

A. The lower part, I think.

Q. I mean, up around the thigh, or knee, or ankle, or where, to the best of your recollection?

A. Somewhere between the knee and ankle.

Q. And when he had hold of your ankle—when he had hold of your left leg between your knee and your ankle, just insofar as you can recall it—what position was he in?

A. I really can't say. I was not looking at him. I was trying to get out. One time he was on his hands and knees, I remember.

Q. That is your best recollection?

A. Yes.

Q. By that you mean he was on his hands and knees when he had hold of your leg?

A. Yes.

Q. All right, did you finally get out?

A. Finally, yes.

Q. How?

A. Broke away from him.

Q. Then where did you go?

A. I rushed out into the street, anywhere to get away from him.

Q. And did you see anyone down there, talk to anyone?

A. On the street?

Q. Yes.

A. I was screaming and crying and struggling with him.

Q. And you met some people down the hall?

A. There were people down there.

Q. Did you know them?

A. No, I didn't know anyone.

Q. And later on you came back up with them in company with an officer?

A. Yes, with an officer.

Q. Let me go back for just one or two points: How were you dressed on this occasion?

A. I was wearing a red dress when I went up there, I had on a little red velvet jacket and I wore a red hat.

❀   ❀   ❀

Q. And I take it, Miss Pringle, that this act of sexual intercourse that occurred in the room between—on the part of Mr. Pantages and yourself—was against your will and without your consent?

A. Absolutely.

Q. You did not consent to it at all?

A. I should say not.

The following is the cross-examination of Miss Pringle during that same preliminary hearing. Most of the questions during this portion of the preliminary hearing were asked by Mr. Gilbert, one of Mr. Pantages' team of defense attorneys.

BY MR. GILBERT:

Q. Can you give the court, roughly from the first time you went in Mr. Pantages' office until August ninth, . . . give the court an accurate, or fairly accurate, estimate of the number of times you were there to see him?

A. Repeat that, please?

[*Question read by the reporter.*]

A. I am sorry, I cannot.

Q. Just your best recollection.

A. I cannot say with any degree of accuracy.

Q. Well, you were there on an average of every day or every other day, were you not?

A. You are mistaken.

Q. Well, if I am, how often were you there?

A. When I saw Mr. Pantages, as I have previously told, he was going to book my act, and he would say, "Come back next week, come back next week."

Q. I am merely trying to find out from you about how many times you were there.

A. I couldn't say.

Q. As many as twenty or twenty-five times?

A. I am not going to say.

Q. What is your best recollection as to the number of times you were there?

A. My best recollection would not be good enough.

Q. Give it to us and let the court pass on that, won't you please?

MR. FITTS: Do the best you can, Miss Pringle.

THE COURT: Answer the question.

A. I am thinking. I would say somewhere around ten, but that is with great reservations; I don't know definitely.

Q. Well, now, what was your idea in— Was it to get yourself on the stage or to get the Dunave act on the stage? Which was your major interest?

MR. FITTS: Objected to as incompetent, irrelevant and immaterial, not proper cross-examination.

THE COURT: Overruled.

A. Repeat, please.

[*Question read by the reporter.*]

A. My greatest interest was simply to appear on the stage in an act which I know was well suited to me.

Q. And that was the Dunave act?

A. That happened to be this act that I had been rehearsing.

According to Pantages, what had really happened was this: He had scarcely begun his conversation with Miss Pringle when she flung herself at him like a tigress—she was extremely agile and athletic—and yanked at his shirt, his suspenders and his trousers, while she screamed. She clung to the doorknob, and it was only by exerting all his strength that he was able to push her out of the room. Once he had gotten rid of her he returned to his office, and presently a covey of policemen descended upon him.

He swore that while Miss Pringle tore at his clothes and screamed he had sat there speechless and couldn't think clearly. "But," he added, "I did know this much; she was laying the groundwork to frame me."

There may be people who do not know it, but there is a difference between forcible rape and statutory rape. Forcible rape is self-explanatory. Statutory rape occurs if a man has intercourse with a girl who is under a certain age, known as the age of consent. In California that age is eighteen. If she is under eighteen and a successful attempt is made upon her virtue, she has been legally raped whether she has co-operated or not.

I do not claim to be an authority on such matters, but the girl who brought the charges against Mr. Pantages seemed to me to be a remarkably lush seventeen. Mr. Pantages was a scrawny little man, and while Miss Pringle weighed only about 115 pounds, she was an athletic, muscular girl who not only took hikes but could do the dance step called a full split.

When Eunice Pringle walked into the courtroom to testify at the first Pantages trial her curves were hidden under a schoolgirl disguise. She even wore a pigtail down her back. If a studio casting director had been looking for a maiden to type-cast as an outraged virgin, he could have found no one more suitable. However, there was something about Eunice Pringle which didn't ring true. I decided that it was the clothes she was wearing. She had elected to wear a blue dress with a Dutch collar and cuffs. As I have said, she was wearing her hair long, and it was caught with a bow at the back of her neck. She wore black stockings and shoes resembling the ones known then and now as Mary Janes. When she appeared on the stand she was carrying a little black bag and a pair of black gloves.

I can't swear that the D.A. suggested to her that she dress this way, but the unworthy thought did cross my mind. That didn't matter. What was important was that on the witness stand she looked about thirteen or fourteen.

Although, as I have indicated, this case was to become my responsibility later on, at the outset Mr. Pantages' legal team had been made up of Earl M. Daniels, W. J. Ford and W. I. Gilbert, whom I have already mentioned. When they asked me to join them, the understanding was that my contribution was to be the cross-examination of Miss Pringle, since cross-examination was thought to be my forte.

On the witness stand Miss Pringle's face seemed pale and drawn, but she didn't strike me as being particularly nervous. During the first hour of her direct examination she clutched a sodden handkerchief while she gave her account of the attack. During the rest of the day, beginning at 2:20 P.M.—at the conclusion of her direct examination, when I began her cross-examination—Miss Pringle told and retold her story with no further sobs. Apparently her weeping depended upon who was asking her the questions.

I inquired, "Did your studies in dramatic school include a course in memory training?" She said, "Yes," and I asked, "Were you taught to express your emotions dramatically?" Once more she said, "Yes."

My thought (a thought not too obscure to the jury, I hoped) was that although Miss Pringle had told her pitiful tale not once but several times to the press and to the law, she had scarcely varied a comma each time she told it.

In all, prior to the actual trial she had repeated her story eight or nine times without altering more than a few syllables. I pointed out in court that she had studied her lines and had not forgotten any of them, that her story seemed rehearsed as only a girl who was studying acting would have rehearsed it.

While Miss Pringle told her story, my client remained in his seat at the defense counsel table, all expression erased from his face. He seldom glanced at Miss Pringle. Once he took a small black note-book from his pocket and wrote something in it. Most of the time he just sat there and nibbled at his left thumbnail or sucked his little finger.

At the end of that day the headlines were particularly lurid. They seemed calculated to move the heart of a statue. They began in large type: "STORY SOBBED BY PRINGLE GIRL"; then in gradually diminishing size they described the proceedings (which, according to one reporter, had the jurors in tears), until they got down to the main body of the goings-on with the tidings: "Young Dancer Collapses at Climax of Account."

It seems to me useful to try to recapture that day as the press saw it. I've made a study of the clippings in my scrapbook and I'll try to paraphrase them, although it seems a shame to alter what seem the purest examples of sob-sisterese I have ever encountered. The printed words (and the tears) ran somewhat like this: "From the childish lips of Eunice Pringle, seventeen-year-old dancing girl, the chief prosecution witness against Alexander Pantages, millionaire theater owner, came yesterday her version of what happened in a little mystery room in the Pantages Theater Building on August 9th last, late in the afternoon." One reporter wrote that, accompanying Miss Pringle's bitter tears as she described her dishonor at the hands of the wealthy theater owner, "sobs echoed in the courtroom until women among the spectators broke down and cried." I wasn't aware of floods of tears other than the ones which flowed freely and at the most strategic moments from Miss Pringle's eyes, but I am not an accomplished reporter whose assignment is to cover the pitiful story of injured innocence ravaged by man's lust.

Fortunately for those present who might have had an attack of hysterics had things continued the way they were going, District Attorney Fitts completed drawing from Miss Pringle (albeit with some difficulty, since her face was half smothered with her tear-laden handkerchief) the facts relating to her age, her residence and her school life. She gave all of her answers in a clear, low voice which nevertheless carried to all parts of the courtroom.

The prosecution objected to the line of questioning I followed.

in my cross-examination as soon as I began to develop it, but in addition to such forensic parry-and-thrust I remember one other incident which occurred on that afternoon and afforded relief to a day filled with tears, sobs, protestations of innocence and other assorted drama. This lighter moment came when I was standing in front of the witness box during my cross-examination. Standing next to me was Chief Deputy District Attorney Stewart. In an effort to demonstrate just how Pantages was accused of holding Miss Pringle's mouth shut, I asked Mr. Stewart if he would let me use his face. With one hand planted across his mouth, I shot a number of questions at the witness. Stewart attempted to object to my line of questioning, but his efforts were made ineffective by the fact that I hadn't removed my hand. A series of grunts and gurgles was the best he could do in protest until Judge Fricke called my attention to the fact that the chief deputy district attorney was trying to say something.

Once my hand was removed, Stewart declared, "I was merely trying to object. I *still* want to object."

In my cross-examination I brought out that in all of Miss Pringle's previous visits to Mr. Pantages' office, some of which she had made alone at night, he had never made any improper advances. My next question was, "Is that the dress you were wearing the day you say you were attacked?"

She said, "No."

I turned to the judge and asked him whether I had the right to ask that Miss Pringle appear on the witness stand before the jury wearing the same clothes, the same make-up and the same hairdo she was wearing when my client allegedly violated her.

Following a protracted hassle, the judge granted my request. The next day when Miss Pringle came into court, instead of a schoolgirl's dress she was clad in a slinky red dress cut low enough to display quite a lot of her, and when she swung her hips up onto the stand she undulated.

There is no doubt in my mind that it was at that moment in that case the wheels of justice stopped grinding in one direction and began to grind in the opposite direction. As she sat there in her re-

31

vealing gown her story of outraged virginity was becoming absurd. But unfortunately for Mr. Pantages, it wasn't hilarious enough the first time around. One member of the press put it this way: "At 4:30 P.M. the little dancing girl left the stand, drooping somewhat from the day of testifying; her face pale and still tear-stained but her story left for all to read it on the pages of record against the man who lured her to his office, to do as he wished with her tender body."

In my cross-examination I also tried to bring out evidence of previous acts of unchastity on her part, but the court ruled that the matter of prior chastity or unchastity was irrelevant and immaterial. I dwelt upon the supposition that she had been living intimately with the Russian dancer Nick Dunave, but when I began to inquire into the possibility of her prior misconduct with him or with any other individual, the judge refused to let me pursue that line of questioning.

Looking back at it now from the vantage point of hindsight, it seems fortunate that my questions about Miss Pringle's prior chastity were objected to and that those objections were sustained in that first trial. The sustaining of those objections became the backbone of the brief I later submitted to a higher court of appeal.

In hindsight also it is clear that the longer the Pantages case dragged on the less clamorous were the yells for the scalp of "the wealthy old goat" and the demands that he be put into prison to stay until he rotted.

If an advocate can contrive to wait until the furor about his client has died down, both he and his client are much better off. Given sufficient time, a new sensation will come along which will take the heat off your client and give him a far better chance to stand trial as an ordinary human being rather than as the Central Figure in a Sordid Scandal.

The jury in the first Pantages trial had a chance to choose one of three verdicts: acquittal, guilty with a county-jail recommendation, or guilty with a penitentiary recommendation. They recommended the last, and Mr. Pantages was sentenced to serve fifty years in state prison. I headed the team of attorneys which prepared the

32

brief for his appeal to a higher court, seeking a reversal. In that brief we pointed out to the State Supreme Court that the lower court had erred in not permitting testimony concerning the pattern of immoral conduct previously followed by the complaining witness, Miss Pringle.

I contended that when the charge is rape by force and violence, the defendant is entitled to introduce evidence which tends to show prior unchaste conduct by the rapee, even though she is under eighteen and consent is not a defense. Evidence of previous acts of unchastity obviously tends to discredit her testimony that the defendant, in accomplishing his purpose, exerted force and violence. Moreover, from such evidence the jury has the right to infer that her entire story of the alleged occurrence was false and that no crime was committed by the defendant.

We also asked for reversal on the ground that the district attorney and his deputy were guilty of prejudicial misconduct in their arguments to the jury when they charged that the defense acted in "bad faith in not producing promised evidence that Miss Pringle was lacking in virtue." We had, of course, repeatedly tried to get such evidence in, but the prosecution's objections had been sustained by the trial judge.

The brief we filed was, and is, the most comprehensive treatise on statutory rape ever compiled. It contained hundreds of citations of cases and authority. It filled three volumes. It totaled 1,200 printed pages. The detailed index itself filled twenty-six printed pages. There were so many new elements in that brief that the final decision upon our appeal established precedent and authority not only in California but throughout the nation.

A section of the brief was titled "The Inherent Improbability of Prosecutrix's Testimony," and I will repeat only a small portion of it here:

> The story as detailed by the prosecutrix, first of all on direct examination, and then amplified upon cross-examination, of itself standing alone bears every imprint of improbability. . . .

Here was a young woman who on that day weighed in the neighborhood of 112 to 115 pounds, being between five feet two and a half and five feet three inches in height, who had since she was eleven years of age, and up until the date in question, at which time she claimed to be seventeen and a half years, been studying and practicing the art of dancing, preparing herself for the stage—including, as the evidence indicates, toe and full-split dancing, and, as the mother testified, acrobatic dancing, involving back flips, turns, side and back bends, which dancing she practiced several times weekly down to August ninth to keep herself in condition for her career—and whose story of what occurred in the little room indicated that during the greater portion of the time both her arms and her legs were free, and who testified affirmatively that she was kicking all of the time to the best of her ability and doing everything that she could with her hands, feet and legs to prevent the accomplishment of the act; and still with all that, as the evidence of the prosecution discloses, the defendant did not have a mark or scratch of any character or kind upon him after the act is alleged to have been consummated.

The girl's recital of how the defendant held her with her back upon the floor with his right hand over her mouth and his chest upon her chest and then accomplished all of the acts which she testified he did accomplish is not only improbable but to our minds impossible. She testified that while standing and before she was forced to the floor, as she claims, the defendant placed his right hand over her mouth and that it remained there from that moment and at all times thereafter throughout the entire struggle which she said occurred until she lost consciousness, and that all that he did do to her thereafter with respect to her clothing and to spreading her legs was accomplished with his left hand.

If her story is true and if defendant's right hand was over her mouth while she was lying on her back, then necessarily both of her arms must have been free for use throughout the entire remaining period. Yet there is no physical fact indicative of any kind or nature that she made use of them in any respect whatsoever. . . .

She testified further that while she was lying on her back on the floor and before he finally placed the lower portion of his body between her legs, the lower portion of his body was lying beside her, which would leave her legs free. Is it reasonable or probable that a woman trained in acrobatic dancing, who was capable of doing what is known as the full split, whose leg muscles must have been developed stronger than those of the ordinary woman of her age, could not, had she been in the predicament to which she testified, have been able to prevent a man, whether he weighed 128 pounds or 148 pounds, of the age of defendant, from accomplishing a completed act of sexual intercourse, particularly when that man's right hand was held over her mouth throughout the entire period of time to prevent her from making outcry? . . .

If we are to believe her story we have this picture—a man who has had many opportunities more propitious so far as time, circumstances and occasion are concerned, to have attempted to accomplish the act had he been so minded, for it will be recalled that the young woman admits that she had called at the office of defendant on a number of occasions at night, although not as late as other defense evidences indicates, but nevertheless at a time considerably later than the hour when she testifies this act did occur, and who, according to her own testimony, never at any time previously in any way made any improper advance toward her. Is it reasonable that this defendant would have selected such a time and place for the accomplishment of an act such as she pictures and in the manner she relates; five o'clock in the afternoon on one of the busiest corners in the city of Los Angeles, in a room with a window looking down upon Seventh Street and only halfway between the street and the second story—a room only half a flight below the floor upon which were many offices occupied by numerous people and within hearing distance of many persons?

. . . This does not ring true, nor sound reasonable, nor appear probable, bearing in mind that her charge is not one in which she voluntarily participated but one based entirely on violence.

Mr. Pantages was granted a new trial. That trial marked the beginning of the enlightened ruling which permits the defending attorney to go into the morals of a girl under eighteen in order to discredit the veracity of her testimony that she was criminally attacked.

By April 1931, when our appeal for a new trial was granted by the Supreme Court of California, the bitter public prejudice against Pantages during his first trial had begun to subside, although plenty of it still sloshed around, judging from these excerpts from an editorial in one California newspaper. (Remember that it was from among people like those who had read this that the jurors for Mr. Pantages' second trial were selected.)

That a conviction was secured in the first instance was a surprise to many because of the prominence and wealth of Pantages. But he got it and with it came a possible prison term of many years *if* he ever got around to serve it. True, he spent some time in the county jail, but was finally released on exceptionally high bail. Since then a battery of quick-witted and high-priced lawyers have been at work to secure a new trial for him. And they've succeeded. The court granted the same on the grounds of errors (so the court said) on the part of the prosecution and the judge who heard the case. Naturally District Attorney Fitts is going to fight this new court order, but how far he will get is problematical. . . .

At this time [this newspaper] does not care to pass upon the rightness or wrongness of the Appellate Court's action, or whether Pantages had a fair trial or not. Some are of the opinion that he was already a well-known bad actor along the lines charged. Be that as it may, it was a safe prediction made at the time that while the conviction of Pantages was as much a surprise as a Rockefeller giving away ten-dollar gold pieces instead of new dimes, it was also a safe bet that it would be a long time before he would don San Quentin garb, and that still goes. With a goodly sum in the bank to meet the checks that can be signed with a fountain pen that is never allowed to run dry, and with the many quips and quirks that astute lawyers can dig up when the financial reservoir does not fail and a man at his elbow to suggest new avenues of expenditures, Alexander Pantages is a long way from the final lock-up, no matter whether he merits acquittal or not.

When the second Pantages trial began in the fall of 1931 I was able to question Miss Pringle about her friendship with Dunave, but she steadfastly insisted that her relations with him had never gone beyond the bounds of propriety. When I tried to find out more about the link between them she told me that he was about forty years old, that he had accompanied her home after rehearsals several times, and that he had also gone along with her the first time she called on Pantages. Then she clammed up.

I called the Russian to the witness stand and questioned him, although I had a hard time getting him there. I had to subpoena him, but once I confronted him I brought out during my cross-examination—and out of Miss Pringle too—certain bits of information which suggested that the Pantages episode was designed to advance their careers in the entertainment world.

Under questioning she admitted that she had gone to see Mr. Pantages four times in all. Even now, as I look back on it after all these years, that strikes me as being a pretty intensive sales campaign merely to sell him a one-act play, unless some of her visits were intended to, shall we say, get to know him better.

One Los Angeles paper put it this way: "The defense built its case around the contention that Miss Pringle conspired with Nicholas Dunave and others to force Pantages to book her act, or, failing in this, to leave him in a compromising position." That wasn't very wide of the mark. The jury apparently accepted that theory and Mr. Pantages was found not guilty.

In acquitting him, the jury did a heartless thing. While waiting for the verdict, Mr. Pantages and I suffered agonies. But although the jurors had decided upon their verdict before dinnertime on Thanksgiving Day, they wanted to have dinner as guests of the county, so they decided not to tell the judge about their decision until the next morning. Perhaps to show their gratitude, the jury brought flowers to the judge when they came in to render their verdict. While I am not a vindictive man, I have never been able to forgive that jury their Thanksgiving dinner purchased at the expense of torture for Mr. Pantages and me.

One of my favorite documents is a translation of a story about me which was published in a French-language newspaper. It does such a fast and free-wheeling job of wrapping up my most famous cases that I cannot refrain from quoting from it, although it may repeat matters already touched upon:

The scene is Hollywood. The person who has committed an offense arrives late to a gathering. He tells his friends he was late because it was necessary for him to see Jerry Giesler. "Giesler," says the other. "In that case you must be in a fine pickle." "Not far from it," the other says. . . . When multi-millionaire Alexander Pantages was accused of attacking a seventeen-year-old schoolgirl, Eunice Pringle, Hollywood was outraged at the alleged revelation. It was a time when nude parties peppered [that's what the translation says] the road to success for shameless starlets, when drug-taking gave thrill-seekers new kicks from the morphine needle and opium pipe.

Eunice Pringle wrung the jury's heart. Dressed in simple school clothes, she shyly related how the rich and powerful tycoon had tried to despoil her in the cubbyhole of a room in a theater. She said when she had gone to see him, hoping to further her film career, she found not encouragement but rather an evil, lustful man. When she told how her protests were ignored while she struggled fiercely, women of the jury wept. The outlook for Pantages was black, but one man had no illusions about the girlish innocence of Miss Pringle. That man was Jerry Giesler.

Politely, Giesler began to cross-examine her. Speaking softly, as if regretting the necessity for arousing painful memories, he dug into her life. Under his deadly questions, Miss Pringle's composure began to crack. Yes, she admitted, she had done a dance number dressed only in a Spanish shawl and tights. And as other admissions were wrung from her, the picture of the innocent schoolgirl began to fade.

Then Jerry worked on the girl's vanity. Readily she agreed that she was a magnificent dancer. Yes, she could do a full split. How she was to regret this later, when Giesler pounced upon the point that an athletic girl, strong and agile, could easily have repulsed the unwelcome advances of an aging and undersized theater owner if she had so desired.

Then, having set the stage, Giesler pulled the master stroke that was to save Pantages. Giesler asked, "Please let the court see you in the dress you wore the day you went to my client's office." The prosecuting attorney leaped to his feet in protest, but Giesler had his way. Next day when Eunice Pringle took her seat in the witness box, she was wearing a dress of deep scarlet, the neck cut revealingly low to call attention to the far from schoolgirl body underneath. There were no sympathetic tears now in the courtroom, only subdued whistles.

Then Giesler switched his attack. Questions gushed from him about her relationship with a certain Russian playwright. The judge refused to allow the attorney to question her about her earlier morals. Patiently Giesler bowed to the rulings. With immense calm he heard a jury turn in a verdict of guilty. They had no alternative after the directions they had been given.

Pantages was shattered, but to Giesler the fight had only just begun. He prepared the machinery of appeal. Lights burned late in his book-lined office as the case went up to the Supreme Court. There, evidence about Miss Pringle's private life and conduct was admitted. Next he introduced into his case a well-laid conspiracy to frame Pantages. The charges against Pantages fell to pieces and the showman walked out of court, the sweet sound of "not guilty" ringing in his ears.

Giesler had scored a double victory. The case that had freed Pantages had made the lawyer famous.

4

The Little Fellow in the Attic

IN ALL MY LIFE I have never heard of a weirder case than the case of the Little Fellow in the Attic. I wasn't the only one who thought it fantastic. The press described the Little Fellow thus in screaming headlines: ATTIC HERMIT REVEALS SELF AS LOVE THIEF . . . ADMITS HE SOUGHT HEART OF MRS. OESTERREICH . . . SAYS GARRET HABIT GREW ON HIM.

Years have passed since the attic hermit (his real name was Otto Sanhuber) and Mrs. Walburga Oesterreich (her name was pronounced "o-strike") faced the bar of justice, but their tale is made up of so many wildly unbelievable details it still makes my brain whirl when I think about it. Although the names of the principals involved mean nothing to most people, the case was the most sensational I have ever had anything to do with.

The story of the Little Fellow in the Attic began in Milwaukee back in 1908, when Sanhuber, in his teens, struck up a friendship with Mrs. Oesterreich's son, Raymond. Sanhuber was uncertain who his own parents were; he had been left on a doorstep as an infant, and he was never sure of the date of his birth. Mrs. Oesterreich, an attractive, youthful-looking woman in her late thirties, treated him very kindly. He first met her when he visited her husband's garment factory to repair defective sewing machines. Occasionally Oesterreich sent him out to his house to repair his wife's sewing machine, which seemed to need more and more attention. Sanhuber reported later that he thought of Mrs. Oesterreich as his benefactress; that her loving kindness to him built up an overpowering loyalty and a silent devotion within him, so much so that he thought her—to use his own trite phrase—"the only woman in the world."

When young Raymond Oesterreich died, Mrs. Oesterreich's sorrow rendered her so distraught that Sanhuber continued his visits to her home to comfort her. She embraced him and told him that he made the loss of her son more bearable. Her emotional dependence upon him soon developed into a more passionate relationship. Mrs. Oesterreich was vital. Life's juices flowed freely within her. Seeking shelter one day from a sudden rain, they repaired to the small room where Sanhuber lived. There, swept by gusts of passion, they became lovers.

Walburga Oesterreich was fifteen to twenty years older than the Little Fellow, and she discovered hidden charms in this younger man. When I first saw him, his physical appeal was invisible. He was undersized. His skin was fishbelly yellow. He was weak and puny. Of course, I hadn't known him when he and the factory owner's wife began their affair. He might have had more appeal then.

Sanhuber began to meet Mrs. Oesterreich in her home when her husband was at work. On one such occasion, Oesterreich returned home unexpectedly. Sanhuber beat a hasty retreat to a small room in the attic and stayed there all night. After that interruption Walburga and Sanhuber determined that Sanhuber should make a permanent home in the cramped quarters under the eaves.

When Sanhuber later told his story to the grand jury, he admitted that he had lived in similar circumstances in six attics in Milwaukee and Los Angeles. Constant lying in concealment by day and emerging only at night turned his skin a sickly tallow. He didn't grow as big and strong as other men do who walk abroad in the sun's rays. He did, however, read murder mysteries obtained from libraries. Occasionally he slipped out of his cubbyhole to do what he called (I'm sure he was unaware of the possible double meaning concealed in his words) "helpful chores around the house."

Sometimes when the Oesterreichs were out and he felt sure they wouldn't come back for a while, he took a stroll after dark, and, he told the grand jury, he bought a revolver, "to make myself feel big when I walked at night."

Eventually he swapped his first gun for a smaller gun and purchased still another pistol, which he gave to Mrs. Oesterreich.

He was still living in the cubbyhole in her attic when Fred Oesterreich decided to move to California, taking his wife with him. The attic dweller was about twenty or twenty-one then. Mrs. Oesterreich sent him on ahead to wait for her until they could arrange another secret hiding place for him there.

For days on end he stood in a place close by the station in Los Angeles where he could watch the trains arriving. Finally he saw his beloved get off a train from the Midwest. He followed her to a hotel and watched her husband check in. Then, when the husband left, he called her on the phone and they went house hunting.

It was a peculiar house seeking, for any home she bought must have an attic. That wasn't easy, since the prevailing style of southern-California architecture doesn't run to garrets. But at last Mrs. Oesterreich found such a house. She was alone that day, so she sent for the Little Fellow to come and have a look at it. He approved.

He found a space under the rafters which he could make into a hiding place by putting boards over the two-by-fours. His new retreat had no bathroom. A bucket latrine served. His illumination was a single electric-light bulb. The wall itself had no obvious break in it, which made the door to his diggings invisible. There was no window. So they all moved in—Mrs. Oesterreich, her husband and the Little Fellow.

Fred Oesterreich's factory in Los Angeles kept him so busy that he lunched downtown daily, coming home only at night. The Little Fellow resumed his accustomed duties. One night there was an attempted burglary. Someone tried to break a window and enter, but the Little Fellow scared him away. After that, when the woman he loved went out with her husband he sat at the head of the stairs holding his two small guns in his hands, ready to blast any intruder. Clutching those weapons he dreamed of himself as Mrs. Oesterreich's protector.

Living so much alone, his mind peopled with phantoms, Sanhuber actually began to hope for a chance to rescue her. He continued his guard duty for a couple of years. Then one night, according to the story he told the grand jury, as he was poised restlessly at the top of the stairs with his guns, his mistress of ripe years came home with her husband.

The Little Fellow, sitting at the top of the stairs, heard the sound of scuffling on the first floor and a woman's voice calling out. Not realizing that what he was overhearing was the sound of his beloved slipping on a throw rug and crying out in pain, and thinking that someone was beating her up—perhaps that burglar who had tried previously to break in—something snapped in his mind. He rushed down the steps brandishing his two little guns and yelling.

For the first time in many years the husband saw him. Despite the changes sunless confinement had wrought, Fred Oesterreich recognized him. This was the boy—now grown older—who had occasionally worked for him in his Milwaukee factory. Like any other husband, Oesterreich's instinctive reaction was jealous rage. He started for the figure clutching the small guns. As he did so the Little Fellow pointed one of the weapons at him. The husband grabbed for it. There was a struggle, punctuated by hoarse breathing and strangled gasps. Then the gun went off repeatedly, killing Oesterreich.

With the pistol still in his hands, Sanhuber told Walburga Oesterreich to go upstairs and hide herself in a closet. He told the woman that he was going back to his cubicle and she was to scream and then hammer on the closet door with a shoe to attract the attention of neighbors. Once she was released, she was to say that a burglar had locked her in. After giving these instructions he locked the closet door from the outside, leaving the key in the lock. Then he went back to his cubbyhole.

An account of what the episode sounded like to an outside observer was contributed by two ladies who occupied the house next door to the Oesterreich home. The first of these called before the grand jury in April 1930 was Mrs. Cora N. Norton. She testified as follows when questioned by Los Angeles County Deputy District Attorney Costello:

43

Q. Where do you live, Mrs. Norton?

A. 1289 West Boulevard.

Q. Where did you live during the month of August, 1922?

A. I was the guest of Mrs. Rawson, I don't remember the exact number of the house, but it was the first house north of the Oesterreich house.

Q. The first house north or the first house east, was it north or east of the Oesterreich home?

A. North, wasn't it—no, east. I am wrong.

Q. Now, during the night of August 22, 1922, do you remember about what time of night you retired?

A. About eleven o'clock, if I remember.

Q. After you had retired, was there anything that awakened you?

A. Yes.

Q. Do you know what it was?

A. Apparently the wind blowing something on my dresser.

Q. And what did you do immediately after you were awakened?

A. I got up and went to the window.

Q. And who went to the window with you?

A. No one.

Q. And what did you do when you got to the window?

A. I heard a shot.

Q. How many shots did you hear?

A. One.

Q. And where did that shot appear to come from?

A. Straight across from me.

❀   ❀   ❀

Q. And what was straight across from you, what object—a house?

A. A house, yes, sir.

Q. Do you know who lived in the house at that time?

A. The Oesterreich family.

Q. Were you standing at the window at that time?

A. Yes, sir.

❀   ❀   ❀

44

The Little Fellow in the Attic

Q. Now, what did you see when you went to the window, over at the Oesterreich home, if anything?

A. Why, just a lighted house, that's all.

❀   ❀   ❀

Q. Will you describe now how it was lighted?

A. In the lower part of the house.

Q. Was there one light or two?

A. I don't know, I couldn't see the lights, I could only see the reflection of the lights. The curtains were drawn within about 30 inches of the floor, and I saw the lights of the house below that.

Q. Was the porch light on?

A. I didn't notice it at the time.

Q. Go ahead.

A. Right after the first shot, Mrs. Rawson came—I knelt down to the window, and Mrs. Rawson came from her room, and just as she came to the window, there was three shots in succession, and a scream, "Fred, oh, Fred."

Q. Then what did you observe, if anything?

A. We observed—we discussed the matter, we said there had been something serious happen at the house.

Q. Well, regardless of what you discussed, did you keep on observing the house at that time?

A. We were observing the house, we were kneeling at the window, the screen was up, and listening for further evidence, but between the shots, if I remember— You see, it has been eight years, and it is a long time to be exact.

Q. Go ahead.

A. I saw a shadow pass from the direction of the dining room across the living room. I don't know what it was, I didn't see the thing, but I saw a shadow and remarked that there was a shadow.

Q. Now, for how long a period of time did you and your lady companion observe the house?

A. Oh, about fifteen or twenty minutes, before we made any effort to call the police.

Q. You folks did call the police department?

45

A. Yes, yes. She [Mrs. Rawson] asked me what we should do next, and I said the first thing to do would be to call them over the telephone.

THE FOREMAN: Call the police?

A. No, call the house, and I said, "I will watch here at the window and listen, and you call the house, and I will see if there is any response to the telephone." She called them on the phone, and rang the phone steadily I think for what appeared to be about three or four minutes, and there was no response to the telephone, and then she asked what she would do next, and I said, "Well, you better call the police," which she did.

Q. BY MR. COSTELLO: Now, coming back to the scream you heard, was that the voice of a woman or a man you heard?

A. No, a woman.

Q. Calling, "Oh, Fred, oh, Fred"?

A. A woman's scream.

Q. Madam, did you hear any knocking over there or pounding?

A. Yes, later—oh, it must have been half an hour later when we began to hear knocking, after the calling of the police.

Q. Had the police officers arrived at that time?

A. No, sir.

Q. Can you describe that knocking, the best you can?

A. Well, it was just like the heel of a slipper on the—[illustrating by tapping on the arm of the chair]. Very distinct.

Q. Now, from the time you heard those shots and saw a shadow, did you observe anything about the lights going on or off?

A. Yes, the porch light snapped off; I hadn't observed the porch light previous to that.

Q. Did you notice any other lights go off?

A. Yes, there was a light snapped on in the upper portion of the house.

Q. Yes.

A. And a little to the south, you see, and then that was off again.

Q. Now, approximately how long after you heard all those shots, how long a time elapsed before the porch light went off?

A. I should say about fifteen minutes, as nearly as I can remember.

Q. And approximately how long a time from the time those shots were fired, that you saw the light go on upstairs and then go off?

A. I couldn't tell you.

Q. Well, approximately, Mrs. Norton, to your best judgment.

A. I should say twenty minutes, something of that kind.

Q. Now, did you keep observing that house until the police arrived?

A. Well, after calling the police, the second time, we went out onto the street and made an examination all around the house and went to Marshall Neilan's house, which was the next door west, and had no response, and then we went across the street and called the neighbors across the street and finally had a response from them.

Q. Did you see anybody leave or go into that house, that is, the Oesterreich house, until the officers arrived?

A. No, sir; no one did.

Q. What?

A. No one did enter the house or leave it.

Q. Did you go around the Oesterreich house yourself until the officers arrived?

A. Yes, sir.

Q. What did you do in that regard?

A. We just looked around and listened and called to Mrs. Oesterreich, or whoever was knocking, that help was coming.

Q. You didn't get any response?

A. We didn't know whether—we didn't know who it was knocking, but we just called, "Help is coming."

Q. That knocking was continuous, was it?

A. No, intermittent.

Q. For how long a period of time did you live at the house next door?

A. I was with her, I guess, about three weeks.

MR. COSTELLO: That is all.

I know the fact that in a house just across the way lived two women who heard four pistol shots rip their eardrums and that afterward they testified they heard a woman scream "Fred, oh, Fred!" reads like a tale told by Agatha Christie.

It likewise seemed to be pure Agatha Christie that one of the watching women told the other, "I will watch here at the window and listen, and you call the house and I will see if there is any response to the telephone." And the watching woman heard the telephone in the Oesterreich house ring, but no one answered. Then muffled and indistinguishable from within their neighbor's house came a sound of hollow pounding. Thereafter, as has been related, one of the women rushed to the telephone, rang the police and told them something queer was going on. The acting chief of police dispatched two detectives to the scene. The two women and the detectives attempted to open the Oesterreichs' front door. It was firmly locked, but they got in through the French doors which led from a porch to the living room. One officer turned on a light, which revealed Fred Oesterreich, dead.

Three bullets had entered his body. One of them had penetrated his heart. Another had entered his head a few inches above his left ear.

Naturally the cops wondered about Mrs. Oesterreich's whereabouts. The only answer was a noise of someone hammering on hollow wood. The group went through the house, trying to track the sound to its source, and so finally entered the rear bedroom. Unlocking the closet door, they found Mrs. Oesterreich crumpled on the floor. She seemed to be in a dead faint.

To the officers who threw water in her face she cried loudly, "Where's Fred?"

Presently Mrs. Oesterreich sat up and pieced together an incoherent story. The Oesterreichs had visited friends and had come home not long before midnight. According to her, when Fred Oesterreich let her in she had noticed a fur neckpiece on a chair, had picked it up, had gone upstairs and had just put the fur away in the bedroom closet. Then she heard unusual noises downstairs.

"I thought Fred had slipped on a rug," she said. "When I turned to leave the closet someone shoved me into it and slammed the door. I thought that perhaps Fred was playing a joke on me. Then I heard four shots. I took off my shoes and pounded on the door. I yelled, but no one came. After that I drew a blank."

Then she cried out frantically, "Something has happened to Fred. I know it has. Where is he?"

One of her women neighbors told her that the police had found her husband's body downstairs. For months that's all they did find. They found no cubbyhole in the attic with a putty-faced, runty Little Fellow living in it, and they accepted the conclusion that a burglar had done the killing. According to Mrs. Oesterreich, the burglar must have been after her jewels. As she told it, her wealthy husband had had what amounted to a mania for buying jewelry for her. He had given her adornment worth sixty thousand dollars.

Two officers dropped in to see Mrs. Oesterreich repeatedly after the coroner's inquest, hoping to pick up crumbs of information which had been swept into the corners of her mind and forgotten. One thing she was sure of, she said: there was no gun in the house that night; there never had been one. And one other thing that everyone was sure of: Walburga Oesterreich was an heiress. Her husband had left her a comforting sum exceeding $500,000.

Once the flurry of the investigation had died away, the widow continued to live in the house where the killing had occurred, and although there was no longer any danger of a husband suddenly confronting him, the Little Fellow stayed in his attic cubbyhole. He still continued to come down every day and do the housework. Mrs. Oesterreich had no other help.

Then the widow met another man and became interested in him. In the meantime she persuaded the Little Fellow in the Attic to break up his two pistols. He smashed them into bits, put them into handkerchiefs, tied knots in the handkerchiefs. The widow gave a male friend one handkerchief containing one of the broken guns— he said later he didn't know what was inside—and asked him to toss it into the La Brea tar pits on Wilshire Boulevard. Once it landed on that tarry surface it would sink out of sight forever.

Almost a year went by. Then, in mid-1923, Walburga Oesterreich and her new friend quarreled. Perhaps because conscience-stricken and perhaps induced by their quarrel, he went to the police and told them about the mysterious package he had thrown into the tar pits.

Dutifully the police listened, conscientiously they visited the tar pits. To their amazement the package was still there. It hadn't quite hit the tar. It had lain all that time only inches away from oblivion.

When the police opened the handkerchief, they found a jumble of broken metal inside. When they made this discovery, they arrested Mrs. Oesterreich, who by this time was forty-five years old. They still didn't know about the Little Fellow in the Attic.

The next day a second 25-caliber pistol, the property of Mrs. Oesterreich, was also found. A man who had been a close friend of the Oesterreichs for years told the detectives that after the coroner's investigation he too had been given a smashed pistol by Mrs. Oesterreich. She asked him to dispose of it, explaining that she feared the police might find it during one of their searches and accuse her of the crime. Thinking he was helping her out of an unfair situation, he promised to do as she asked. His wife helped him by tossing that handkerchief into an unused lot. It was those shattered remnants which were recovered.

Mrs. Oesterreich retained the services of two attorneys to defend her. I was one. The other was Frank Dominguez. I told the press, "This is a weak case for the prosecution. The fact that Mrs. Oesterreich happened to have two pistols, both the same caliber as the murder gun, does not prove that *she* murdered him. Moreover, would a guilty woman have given those guns away so casually instead of disposing of them herself? And what about the fact that she was found locked in a closet?"

In Mrs. Oesterreich's favor also was the fact that police tests proved that the gun tossed away by her friend of many years' standing was not the pistol used to kill Fred Oesterreich, and the pistol found at the La Brea tar pits was so broken and its parts had been so worked over with a file that tests made upon it proved fruitless. Nevertheless, the judge bound Mrs. Oesterreich over for Superior Court.

The wear and tear brought about by her arrest caused a deterioration in Mrs. Oesterreich's health, and she was in no condition to appear for trial. Accordingly, Mr. Dominguez and I asked for and obtained several postponements.

Although the district attorney labored mightily to accumulate sufficient valid evidence against her, in the end all he had was the finding of two broken guns whose rifling couldn't be matched with rifling marks on the bullets extracted from her husband's body. In addition there was the evidence that at the time of her husband's death she had been found in a closet, locked from the outside. The lack of evidence strong enough to convict her was so obvious that on January 16, 1925, eighteen months after her arrest, the D.A. dismissed the case and Mrs. Oesterreich was freed.

Another year passed. During that time she lived in the same house, with the Little Fellow still dwelling under the eaves. Then she fell under the influence of still another man. The latest entry in her personal sweepstakes was a Los Angeles lawyer whom she had known for some years.

Time went by, and Mrs. Oesterreich decided to buy a new home. Once more she made sure it had an attic where the Little Fellow could hide. He moved his bucket latrine, his collection of detective books and his bare electric-light bulb and took up residence in her new dwelling.

The lawyer friend was a constant visitor in the new house, but for some time he didn't see the Little Fellow. Finally one night he accidentally discovered him flitting about the house. Confronting Mrs. Oesterreich with his discovery, the lawyer told her that she must get rid of her batman. She agreed on condition that the lawyer drive the Little Fellow up to San Francisco and find him a job. This he did. He got Sanhuber a job as a janitor.

Mrs. Oesterreich was a woman of many emotional storms. After several years she quarreled bitterly with the lawyer, too, and he with her. When this crack in the picture window of their relationship appeared, he too decided to go to the police. In the spring of 1930 he showed up at the office of Buron Fitts, who was then the district attorney of Los Angeles County, and swore out an affidavit.

Although his affidavit sounded unbelievable, it was true. In a way he had known about Sanhuber for years. He declared that when Mrs. Oesterreich had been clapped in jail for the first time, in June 1923, she had told him that she was concerned about a "retarded" half brother, hidden in the attic of her home on North Beechwood Drive, and she had entreated him to make sure that the hidden one was supplied with food. She had added that her half brother would emerge from his hiding place only if someone scratched three times on the wall of the cedar closet behind which he was concealed.

The lawyer did that, and an apparition with a chalk-white face emerged and greeted him with these words, "I know you. I've been watching you visit here for a long time. I'm Otto Sanhuber." The lawyer's affidavit went on to say that the Little Fellow denied that he was related to Mrs. Oesterreich. He said instead that he had been her lover for a number of years.

Although the Los Angeles police were shockproof, the story was hard for them to believe. Nevertheless, they dispatched emissaries northward with the lawyer who had turned state's evidence. Together they located the former attic dweller and brought him back to Los Angeles.

He made a full confession to the grand jury concerning this strange upside-down life. He said that during many of the hours he had spent in his dim, slant-roofed cubicles, he had visualized enormously successful investment opportunities for the industrialist he was later to kill. According to Sanhuber, those imagined ventures bubbling to the top of his brain were relayed to Oesterreich by his wife; and he imagined that his financial suggestions made it possible for Oesterreich to expand his business to a point where he counted his fortune at close to a million dollars.

The Little Fellow testified that during the time he had lived in attics, Mrs. Oesterreich had occasionally given him small presents of cash. Sometimes she had given him twenty-five cents, sometimes as much as fifty cents. Out of this pinchpenny allowance he had managed to save $1,500. As the wages of such long-drawn-out sin, those dollars seemed paltry. He also went into the story of the two pistols. He said that he had bought them in Wisconsin, had used one of them to fire the bullets at Oesterreich and had erased the serial numbers from both guns with a file.

The strange confession made by Sanhuber to the grand jury was a multipage signed statement the length of a short story in a women's magazine, although far spicier. In talks with the press, he announced that during the months following Oesterreich's killing he had practiced to be an author. Crouched in his attic, he had developed a plot built up out of circumstances surrounding the slaying of Oesterreich. The hero of his tale, shining, noble and protective, was himself.

Somewhere along the way, Sanhuber had acquired a habit of twitching which almost amounted to a body tic. This convulsive shuddering was noticeable to all who saw him. And it made him seem even more pathetic.

Walburga Oesterreich took the Fifth Amendment when called before the grand jury in April 1930. (In those days the public was not nearly so aware of the privilege against self-incrimination as it is today, and witnesses were less articulate in raising it.) But as a result of Sanhuber's tale of his odd-ball existence in cobwebby, dusty attics, the grand jury indicted the Little Fellow and Mrs. Oesterreich for murder. Once more she employed me as her counsel. The Little Fellow retained another lawyer.

My next step was to go into court and seek a separate trial for my client. We argued my motion for severance before Judge Carlos Hardy in Los Angeles County Superior Court on June 6, 1930. Deputy District Attorney Costello strenuously opposed separate trials for the Little Fellow and Mrs. Oesterreich. His argument in opposition to my motion was a forceful statement of the people's contentions.

THE COURT: All right, I will hear you, Mr. Costello, what you have to say in opposition to this motion for a severance.

MR. COSTELLO: The facts are that we will contend and we will establish that away back in 1911, possibly previous to that time, that these two defendants met in Milwaukee, that Mrs. Oesterreich fell in love or at least started going around with this young man, who, we will establish, was about twenty years of age.

THE COURT: You mean Sanhuber?

MR. COSTELLO: Yes. And he was working as a sewing-machine repairman or mechanic; that at that time Mr. Oesterreich ran and owned an apron factory and had a great number of machines, and he came there and started to work for Mr. Oesterreich as a repairman on those machines. That he met Mrs. Oesterreich, and they started to go with each other, meeting each other at different times, unknown to Mr. Oesterreich. . . . That he [Sanhuber] wanted to leave Milwaukee and did leave Milwaukee, that she [Mrs. Oesterreich] went with him. They went as far as Chicago, and stayed in Chicago for a day or two, and then on to St. Louis, and stayed there for several days and finally came back to Milwaukee. We will establish that she persuaded him to come back from St. Louis to Milwaukee against his will, and finally he did go back there.

. . . That after this young man had got back to Milwaukee, he became very much afraid and frightened of Oesterreich, and that she took him, as a result of his fear and her desire to be with him, into her home, and arranged a place for him to stay in a garret in the two homes, two separate and distinct homes, in which Mr. Oesterreich lived. That he remained there during the balance of the time that they lived in Milwaukee, which was several years. That Oesterreich then made up his mind to come to California, and we will establish that this young man came to California with the money that she had given him from time to time, paid his own way, and arrived here several weeks prior to the time that Mr. and Mrs. Oesterreich arrived. We will establish that he stood on the bridge, the Elysian Street Bridge, and saw them get off the train. We will establish that he had knowledge as to where they were going, and that the next day, or possibly the same day that they arrived, that he called up that apartment house or hotel where they went to stay immediately after getting off the train, temporarily, and found out that they were there.

. . . That after a month or six weeks Mr. Oesterreich bought the home where this murder was committed. That before Mr. Oesterreich actually moved into the home, before his furniture was in there, that Sanhuber, with the knowledge and consent and acquiescence of Oesterreich's wife, built himself a place and cut a door leading into the attic, and was in the house several days, maybe two weeks or three weeks, before Mr. Oesterreich ever moved into it himself. We will establish that that attic, or the door leading into that attic, led from the bedroom of Mrs. Oesterreich. We will establish that she procured a lock to lock her bedroom door. We will establish that she refused to sleep with her husband or have any sexual relations with him at all. That she kept him [Sanhuber] in that attic, the door of which led out into her bedroom, up to and including the time several weeks after this murder had been completed.

We will establish that away back in 1911, in Milwaukee, this man bought two revolvers, purchased two revolvers, one of which was the revolver used in the murder of Mr. Oesterreich. We will establish that after the murder was committed that she took this young man out to another house which she had purchased, and had him there build another trap door leading into the attic there, and he stayed there up to and including the time that this woman was charged with the offense a year or two afterwards. We will establish that she had an understanding with this young man that if she ever went away from the house and stayed for a period of three days, that she would get him out of that attic and get him out of the way.

We will establish that after the murder was committed, her explanation to the police department and to the investigators' office were absolutely inconsistent with the innocence of that woman. We will establish that she denied all knowledge of having or owning a gun, or having a gun after the murder or previous to it. We will establish by two reputable witnesses that she took those guns and gave them to her supposed friends and asked them to destroy them. We will establish that the next morning or the next day after the murder was committed, that she had the gun under her pillow, and she made the declaration to one of her women friends that she almost suffered a stroke of apoplexy—it may be something else instead of that, those are my words—when Herman Cline [a police detective] was there questioning her about the gun, because the gun was within four or five feet of Herman Cline, under that pillow.

We will establish that she has stated that she was locked in the closet by the robbers and the burglars. We will establish that after the murder was committed, there was an agreement between Mr. Sanhuber and her it would be burglars. And that she would protect him. We will establish that it was not burglars that entered the

55

room, but it was Sanhuber [who] actually locked her in that room or closet. We will establish that she was present when the shot or the three shots were fired that entered this poor man's body, standing right there. We will establish that the reason that this man [Sanhuber] shot him was that there was a quarrel between the two of them that night, and he ran downstairs to take her part. And I say to you now it is an absolute impossibility to convict these two people or have any hope of giving the people of this state a fair hearing in this matter if you grant this motion of a severance.

The court, however, granted my motion for severance. It was decided to try the Little Fellow first.

When Sanhuber stood before the judge on June 11, 1930, to answer to a charge of first-degree murder, all of the witnesses who testified during the preliminary hearing of Mrs. Oesterreich in 1923 appeared again—if they were still available. But the things which had struck the investigators as mystifying then were much less mysterious now that the Little Fellow had been smoked out.

When Otto Sanhuber took the stand, his testimony followed the same path as the story he had told before the grand jury—as long as he was narrating his batlike life under the eaves. His lawyer, Mr. Wakeman, brought out the details of his client's strange existence as a member of the Oesterreich household.

Q. You were stating that there was an attic above the main part of the house, not the attic that was shown to the jury?

A. That is right.

Q. And the attic over the main part of the house was where you first went; is that correct?

A. Yes, sir.

Q. How long were you there?

A. About one month.

Q. And then where did you go?

A. Well, Mrs. Oesterreich then had a carpenter come and had him line up these sides here, because—

THE COURT: Indicating what room, for the purpose of the record.

The Little Fellow in the Attic

*   *   *

A. So then she had the carpenter line that up, and I was to go in there, just in there; she didn't say which side, or anything like that, you know; she left that to my own desire. Those little wishes she usually granted me. . . . So I—there were some extra boards left over, and so I opened up the section right behind the door here.

Q. Indicating the end of the partition, of the south partition of the trunk room next to the doorway between bedroom number one and the trunk room, is that correct?

A. Yes.

*   *   *

Q. Well, never mind. Go on with your statement.

A. I opened up a section about that wide [*indicating*].

Q. Indicating about a foot and a half. Yes.

A. And then I took those boards and the ones that were left there, and I fitted the door, a good door so that it would swing back up against the ceiling, you see, and so I just could crawl right in there and close it, and then I put window locks on the inside so I could lock it and I would be in my home then.

Q. How soon after the carpenters completed their work of building that ceiling, along on the two sides of what is marked "trunk room," did you do that?

A. Right away.

Q. You may sit down. Was Mrs. Oesterreich there when you did that?

A. Yes, sir.

*   *   *

Q. How long did you live there?

A. Until about the end of 1922, I believe.

Q. About December?

A. Yes, sir.

Q. And it was, as nearly as you can recall, 1918 when you began to live there, is that correct?

A. Yes, sir.

Q. Do you remember what month it was that you went in there to live?

A. No, sir.

Q. Did you have that space fitted up for your convenience?

A. Well, I had a place to sleep and to be.

Q. Describe it, and tell us where it was.

A. Well, I took the rest of that lumber that was left over, and I put it across the timbers, and then I laid my little mattress down on that, and the blankets, and whatever things I had, like books, and such things as that, and I put that in there. In clothes—I only had one suit. And shoes, and such things, well, I just had one pair of shoes.

Q. Where did you keep them?

A. And two hats, a straw hat and a felt hat. I kept them hung up against here, I think, somewhere in there, covered up nice, you know, so they would not get dirty and dusty.

Q. Did you have a light in there?

A. Yes, sir.

Q. An electric light?

A. Yes, sir. I tapped it from the wires that were running on the timber, and I knew by tapping them I could connect my lights, and the light hung just over the head of my—well, say bed.

Q. Now, how much of the time while you occupied that place did you spend there—for what part of the day or night did you stay there?

A. Well, just about all—may I say just about all my leisure time.

Q. Did you also work?

A. Yes, sir.

Q. What did you do?

A. Well, I had my work to do in the house. There was the scrubbing to be done and cleaning to be done, dusting, and each day I had service to do for Fred—Mr. Oesterreich.

Q. What was that?

A. Well, each morning I made up his bed for him, and each evening I would uncover it, you know, so it would be handy for him to go to bed, and then he usually took a bath almost every day, and he would shave himself; and Fred, he was a big businessman, he did not have time for such things, and when he would get ready in the morning he would throw everything right down. And I would pick it up and put it away, you know, and so I waited on him, and when he wanted a shirt or a collar or anything out of the neat drawers he would just throw out what was not needed and, of course, I would put them back again, and sometimes Mrs. O, she would say, in German, "Jesu, Marie and Josef, a tornado has struck this place."

Q. Now, when did you do that work that you are stating that you did?

A. Oh, it was a regular thing, sir, every day.

Q. Did Mrs. Oesterreich keep a servant?

A. No, sir.

Q. Never?

A. They had no servant in their house.

Q. Excepting just yourself?

A. Yes, sir.

Q. What other work did you do in the house for Mrs. Oesterreich?

A. Well, I made up the beds, and changed the linen about two times a week. They loved to sleep clean, and I made up the beds for them, and put away their clothes, and dusted Fred's clothes, because he had some beautiful things, and I would keep them in order for him and dust them, and dust his shoes, you know, so he would look neat always. And then I would wash the dishes if he wasn't home, and if he was home he would wash them, and Mrs. Oesterreich would dry them, because I couldn't then. And I would get the vegetables clean, and they *were* clean—everybody praised her, how clean her things were; and scrubbed the floor and kept it clean, and kept the floor neat, you know—she loved to have a beautiful floor—and dusted it, you know.

Q. Now, where was Mr. Oesterreich's bedroom at that time, during that time?

A. Well . . .

Q. Where did he sleep?

A. At first they slept in a beautiful bedroom in here [*indicating*].

      ❋   ❋   ❋

MR. WAKEMAN: Indicating Number Two bedroom.

A. In this bedroom here. Then she slept alone in this bedroom and he slept out here [*indicating*].

Q. Indicating bedroom Number Three.

THE COURT: Well, that does not make the record clear as to which one slept in Number Three.

A. Mrs. Oesterreich slept in bedroom Number Two, and he slept in bedroom Number Three.

MR. WAKEMAN: I think that is clear. How soon did they make that separation after they moved into that house?

A. Well, it wasn't really a separation. Mr. Oesterreich would read so late at night, and trot around, and keep her awake, so then she thought she would sleep in this bedroom here.

✿　　✿　　✿

Q. Take your chair. Now, was Mrs. Oesterreich home a good deal?

A. She was at first.

Q. That is, when you first moved in that house?

A. Yes, sir. She was home quite a bit then.

✿　　✿　　✿

Q. Well, did you see her when she was home?

A. Not always, sir.

Q. And was Mr. Oesterreich there always when she was home?

A. No, sir.

Q. Did you see her each day?

A. Oh, yes, sir.

Q. You saw her every day?

A. As best as I can recall, yes, sir.

Q. Did she indicate to you what work you were to do during the day?

MR. COSTELLO: Objected to on the ground it is immaterial.

THE COURT: Overruled.

MR. COSTELLO: Gone into, testified to.

THE COURT: You may answer whether she told you to do this work or not.

A. Well, at first she did, and of course the only time she would speak about the work is when she would find something that was not right, like if there was dust, you know, and she would speak about it to me; and of course I think it was my fault, because I didn't do it right. She would sometimes teasingly say, "I will have to talk to Fred about this," but she was only fooling. And sometimes when she would find—she was very neat and particular, and when she would find, oh, like a vase or something that was—or a tooth brush container—she was very particular about such things, and if there was anything in there she would hold it under my nose.

Q. Well?

A. She was a good housekeeper.

Q. Was there any particular time of the day that you usually did see her?

A. Yes, sir; in the morning, usually.

Q. About what time?

A. When Fred would go away to work.

Q. Before or after he would go away?

A. As a regular thing, it was after he was gone to work.

Q. Did she ever see you while he was still in the house?

A. Yes, sir.

Q. Frequently?

A. At first.

Q. Where would she see you then?

A. In that bedroom.

Q. Which bedroom?

A. In that little bedroom.

Q. The one that is marked Number One?

A. Yes, sir. Yes, sir.

Q. You say at first. You mean when you first moved over in that house?

A. Well, for a long time.

Q. Well now, tell us about that. What did you see of her? What conversation did you have, or what did you see of her? First, I want you to tell when you saw her, and tell us about your dealings with her. You say that at first you saw her sometimes before he went away, and later that you would see her usually in the morning, after he had gone, I believe. Is that correct?

A. As a rule, sir. Nothing went regular.

Q. Nothing was regular?

A. No, sir.

Q. Did you see her other times?

A. Yes, sir.

Q. When, what times of the day?

A. Oh, whenever—well I guess whenever I was willing and she wanted to see me.

Q. This morning you were telling us about living in her attic back East.

A. Yes, sir.

Q. And you told about a trip to St. Louis?

A. Yes, sir.

Q. With her?

A. Yes, sir.

Q. Did you and she have sexual relations on that trip?

A. Yes, sir.

Q. Did you have before that?

A. Yes, sir.

Q. How long before that did that sort of thing start?

A. Oh, I just can't place the time, Mr. Wakeman. It just was.

Q. Did anything of that kind happen around the factory?

A. Yes, sir.

Q. Was that where it started?

A. I think so.

Q. When, what time of day?

A. Oh, in the evening, at night.

Q. After everyone had gone?

A. Yes, sir.

Q. And did that sort of thing keep up during all the ten or eleven years that you were in her attics?

A. Well, there were periods—yes, with certain periods there were not.

Q. When were those periods?

A. When I was sick, and when I kept to myself and when I fasted.

* * *

Q. Were you sick quite a good deal?

A. Well, I was. I seemed to get so weak and sick, you know, sometimes I was terribly sick.

Q. Who would take care of you then?

A. Well, may I say it?

Q. Yes.

A. He who takes care of others who have no help, Jesus.

Q. Well, tell us about the times that you fasted.

A. Sir?

Q. Tell us about the times that you fasted.

A. It was a sort of defense. I had no other weapon. I did it deliberately. I would go in my attic and I would stay there, I would not come out except just when needful, and I would fast, I just wouldn't eat anything, that is all, and I had peace. Maybe it was foolish of me, but I did not—that was my best way of doing it—and she would begin to feel sorry for me, I think, and talk softly to me and bring me food, set it there. Well, now, like in that house, at that little door, you know.

Q. Outside of the door?

A. And then she would become, not disagreeable, but annoyed with me, and then I behaved myself.

Q. By "behaving yourself" you mean you did what she wanted you to?

A. Yes, sir.

Q. And did that have anything to do with sex?

A. Yes, sir, as a rule.

       ❀   ❀   ❀

THE COURT: Well, did he [Mr. Oesterreich] know that you were in the house after you left Milwaukee, so far as you know?

A. Not to my knowledge, sir.

Q. Did he know you were in the house in any of these attics, so far as you know?

A. No, not as far as I know.

But when it came to Oesterreich's death Sanhuber now contended that he hadn't departed from his hideaway at the time of the killing and that the fatal shot must have been fired by burglars. His lawyer made no particular effort to contradict Sanhuber's grand-jury testimony or to explain away the difference in the testimony. He was careful, however, to highlight the favorable aspects

63

of the strange little man's story. Among them was his suggestion that the biggest influence in Sanhuber's life had been an older
woman with a dominant will. Much also was made of his intense
desire to protect her.

Sanhuber stuck to his new version despite a grueling cross-examination by Deputy District Attorney Costello.

Q. Yes, then do I understand that you were telling the truth to the
grand jury?

MR. WAKEMAN: Objected to as indefinite.

THE COURT: Overruled. The witness can answer. If you understand the
question you may answer.

MR. WAKEMAN: No proper foundation laid as to time.

MR. COSTELLO: Oh, the grand-jury transcript, Mr. Wakeman.

THE COURT: The foundation is sufficient. You may make your answer
and make any explanation that you desire, Mr. Witness.

THE WITNESS: What was that question?

THE COURT: Read the question.

[*Question read.*]

A. Not all the truth.

Q. BY MR. COSTELLO: All right. Now, calling your attention to page
seven-six-three of the grand-jury transcript, I call your attention to
line twenty-three at page seven-six-three. Will you read that? [*Handing transcript to witness.*]

A. Surely, yes, sir.

✿   ✿   ✿

Q. This has reference to the night of the tragedy [*reading from transcript*]: "Q. You mean the key does? A. Yes, I locked it with that, and
I locked that trunk room door by— I had a big screwdriver and I just
locked that and all I had to do was to close the trunk room door and
just spring it a little bit and it went in. It wasn't very strong. Q. Then
you went into your cubbyhole? A. Yes, sir. Q. How long did you remain in there, Otto, before you came out? A. Well, I just stayed
there. Q. What did you do with those guns after you got in there with
them? A. Why, nothing at all. Q. Well, after you went back in there

you heard the police officers in there that night, didn't you? A. Yes, sir, and she pounded on the door and screamed, pounded on the door. Q. That is, you heard her while you were in your cubbyhole, pounding on the door? A. Forgive me, but I am trying to tell the truth and I don't want to tell what has been drilled into me." Did you so testify?

A. Well, I can't just recall the passage, but presumably it is there.

Q. Did you so testify as I have read to you?

A. It reveals my thoughts and my mental struggle there.

Q. Did I understand you to say this morning, in response to a question propounded to you by your attorney, Mr. Wakeman, that you never heard her scream that night?

A. Yes, sir.

Q. Did you say—you say you did not, didn't you tell him that this morning, or did you?

A. I said that I did not—I can't really recall whether she screamed before the gun snapped.

Q. Didn't you say here this morning that you did not hear her scream?

A. Yes, sir.

Q. When you answered, "Yes, sir, and she pounded on the door and screamed, pounded on the door," now, when were you telling the truth, was it this morning or was it before the grand jury?

A. This morning, Mr. Costello.

Q. And you were not telling the truth when you were before the grand jury?

A. You know it.

Q. Well, now, I don't understand that answer, Mr. Sanhuber—"You know it." Now, just answer it so that the judge and jury may understand it, and the reporter will read it to you.

A. Yes, sir.

THE COURT: Read the question.

[*Question read.*]

A. Not in part.

Q. BY MR. COSTELLO: Well, now, I want you, Mr. Sanhuber, to be good enough to state to this judge and jury whether or not you were telling the truth when you told the grand jury that you heard her scream and pound, or were you telling the truth this morning when you told the judge and jury that you did not hear her scream?

THE COURT: He has answered that question just a few moments ago.

A. I was referring to whether she screamed when she—right before the guns popped, or right after, but I had not arrived at the time when she pounded on the door.

✿   ✿   ✿

Q. And you stayed at home with your stepmother [in Milwaukee], did you not, until you got to running around with Mrs. Oesterreich, didn't you?

A. When I was with Mrs. Oesterreich I was staying at a rooming house.

Q. Previous to the time that you made your trip to St. Louis you were running around with Mrs. Oesterreich, were you not?

MR. WAKEMAN: Well, we object to the use of the words "running around," your honor.

MR. COSTELLO: May I suggest that you substitute a word for me?

MR. WAKEMAN: I would if I knew the object of your question.

MR. COSTELLO: All right. I will withdraw the question.

Q. You were going out with Mrs. Oesterreich before you left the city of Milwaukee to go to St. Louis with her, weren't you?

A. Yes, sir.

✿   ✿   ✿

Q. You would meet Mrs. Oesterreich away from her home and you and she would go out in Milwaukee many times before you finally went to St. Louis?

A. Well, I guess so.

Q. And she would come up to your room, or she would go to a room with you, isn't that true?

A. I don't know about that, but I know that she came up in my room once.

Q. And you were intimate with her before you left for St. Louis, were you not?

A. Yes, sir.

Q. And by intimate I mean in this sense, you and she were having sexual intercourse with each other?

A. Yes, sir.

Q. And that was at a time when you told this judge and jury that Fred was just a great big brother to you, wasn't it?

MR. WAKEMAN: Objected to as argumentative, your honor.

THE COURT: Overruled.

A. Well, Mr. Costello, I did not—I did not say when. I said he was like a big brother to me.

* * *

Q. And then, finally you started to go out with his [Oesterreich's] wife, didn't you?

A. Yes, sir.

Q. And at the time that you first started going out with her was he still like a great big brother to you?

A. Well, Mr. Costello—

Q. Won't you please answer the question now?

A. Sure.

Q. That can be answered Yes or No, and then you can make any explanation that you wish.

A. Yes, he was.

Q. And you felt that she was just like a great big sister or a mother to you, is that right?

A. Well, she took a personal interest in me.

* * *

Q. I see. Did he [Oesterreich] ever admonish you not to go out with his wife and remind you that he was happily married, and that he cared for his wife and didn't want you to interfere in his domestic or family affairs, prior to the time you left for St. Louis with her?

A. No, he did not use those terms.

Q. Well, in substance? Just use your own language in answering my question.

A. To the best of my recollection, when he talked to me he talked to me like as if it was a problem for us to work out.

❀   ❀   ❀

Q. And did you feel that it was quite a problem, too?

A. Yes, sir, I did.

Q. And at that time you were going out and having sexual intercourse with his wife?

A. Well, say off and on.

Q. Off and on, and you thought that that was quite a problem?

A. It was a problem to settle those things.

Q. And you quit your job with the Singer Sewing Machine Company on the day of the night that you left for St. Louis in company with Mrs. Oesterreich in 1911?

A. Oh, I went away—

Q. Will you answer my question?

A. Well, yes, sir.

Q. Well, you did go, didn't you, to St. Louis?

A. Yes, sir, I went.

Q. And Mrs. Oesterreich went with you?

A. That is it.

Q. And you were gone for a period of ten or twelve days to two weeks?

A. Well, I don't know just—

Q. Well, approximately?

A. Well, all right, yes.

Q. And you were sleeping with her every night, weren't you?

MR. WAKEMAN: Objected to as indefinite and uncertain.

MR. COSTELLO: Every night you were gone.

MR. WAKEMAN: At St. Louis? I am willing he should answer that.

Q. BY MR. COSTELLO: Will you please answer my question?

THE COURT: You may answer.

A. Yes— Wait. When we slept in a bed.

Q. BY MR. COSTELLO: I see. Well, you slept in the bed in St. Louis, didn't you?

A. I believe so.

Q. Have you any doubt about that?

A. No, sir.

Q. She slept with you?

A. Yes, sir.

Q. And then you returned from St. Louis to Milwaukee?

A. Yes, sir.

Q. You did not have the problem solved, did you?

A. No, sir.

Q. Did you try to solve the problem?

A. I had tried as best I knew.

My principal recollection of Otto Sanhuber is that at that point he was utterly forlorn. The jurors must have shared some of my feeling of pity for him; for while they didn't let him off entirely, after staying out for four and a half hours they brought in a verdict of manslaughter which carried with it a sentence of from one to ten years.

Now, while the crime of manslaughter is a part of murder, it is not wholly or legally murder. It is a separate offense. While there is no statute of limitations on murder, there is a three-year statute of limitations on manslaughter. Since the Little Fellow's offense had occurred more than three years before his indictment, the court had no choice but to dismiss the charges against him. And once having been put in jeopardy of his life on a murder charge, he could not be tried again. The judge granted his attorney's request for a stay of judgment and he was released.

Legally that took no heat off his paramour. The D.A. was still determined to prosecute her for murder. He didn't claim that she'd shot her husband, but he did claim that she had done what the law calls "procured murder to be done." However, the fact that the actual killer had gotten off free couldn't help but affect the atmosphere in which my client was tried.

So on August 4, 1930, five and a half years after the first charge against her had been dropped for lack of evidence, Mrs. Oesterreich was put on trial "for conspiracy, leading to the murder of her husband."

In general she told the same tale Sanhuber had told the grand jury. She said that she and Oesterreich had not quarreled; that instead, she had slipped on a small throw rug and had fallen to the floor, screaming in pain. "Then," Mrs. Oesterreich said, "I saw Otto. He thought Fred was hurting me. I heard him call out. Then I saw Fred start fighting with him. I hid my face. I heard shots and screamed, 'Fred, Fred.'" Mrs. Oesterreich then said Sanhuber shoved her into a closet and locked the door.

The D.A. put Sanhuber on the stand, but he made a very poor witness for the prosecution. He stuck to his "burglars must have done it" version of the killing and nothing would change him. He seemed amazingly naïve and childlike, and proudly described doing the housework "just the way she wanted it done."

One of the most pathetic moments in the trial came when the batman was asked what was the longest time he had ever been separated from Mrs. Oesterreich. "When I was away from my attic," he answered, "the time was so long I didn't measure it in hours. I was frantic until I returned."

Mrs. Oesterreich's story was that Sanhuber had come to her the day after the killing and had said, "Please help me dispose of my guns." Her instinct had been to try to shield the Little Man who had done wrong because he thought he was keeping her from harm. It was for this reason that she had asked her friends to dispose of the weapons.

My defense was that the fatal shot was fired during that dim struggle in the hallway and therefore the killing was accidental rather than criminal. Certainly, as the jury in the Sanhuber case had agreed, it hadn't been premeditated.

Both Mrs. Oesterreich's lawyer-lover and her former friend who had tossed the broken gun into the tar pits took the stand against her. Both of these onetime friends might have sent her to the gas chamber, but psychologically their turning against her did her more good than harm with the jury.

The papers called my cross-examination of the attic man "relentless." Whether it was or not, it drew from him the admission that it was he who had first sought the love of Mrs. Oesterreich in Milwaukee. It was he who had urged her to see him clandestinely in private meeting places, not the other way around. It was he who had induced her to spend one of the longest weekends on record with him. Mrs. Oesterreich had not compelled him to live in her attic. He had chosen such an existence himself to be near her.

The jury was deadlocked, the majority favoring acquittal.

Mrs. Oesterreich was never tried again. In December of 1930 the charge against her was dismissed.

Afterward one deputy district attorney was quoted as saying, "We are pretty certain the shooting occurred as Mrs. Oesterreich described it. We have been unable to discover anything additional which would have a tendency to show conspiracy. Accordingly, obtaining a conviction did not seem possible."

He added that he was certain there had been no miscarriage of justice.

5

Margaret Ryan

As with the Alexander Pantages case, the crushing weight of public prejudice confronting my client in the Ryan case was at first overwhelming.

Mrs. Margaret G. Ryan, a wealthy widow, shot and killed Leonard D. Ray, Jr., when he attempted to cross her eighty-acre Lopez Canyon ranch, near San Luis Obispo, on June 9, 1951. At the inquest Mrs. Ryan told the coroner's jury that she had shot Ray accidentally, while warning him to get off her property; he had ignored her orders to leave the ranch, she said, and also had threatened her with a rifle. However, by a seven-to-three vote, the coroner's jury on June 12 found the shooting "unjustifiable homicide," and a week later the county grand jury indicted Mrs. Ryan for manslaughter.

The circumstances leading to the shooting were these:

Mrs. Ryan, a stranger to the community, had purchased approximately eighty acres in the hills just outside the city of San Luis Obispo in September 1950. She was building her home on the highest point of the property, approximately a mile from the main highway. Immediately after acquiring the property she had had large printed no-trespassing signs placed at the gate to her home from the main road and on the fence along the highway.

Mrs. Ryan lived in a trailer while her new home was being built under her direction. The only other person living on the property was Evasio Piovera, the general hand, who had been employed by Mrs. Ryan since the 1920s. Mr. Piovera, who was called Henry, had his workshop and quarters down the hill from Mrs. Ryan's trailer.

On June 9, a Saturday, twenty-two-year-old Leonard Durvan Ray, Jr., was driven by his mother to a point on the highway at which she let him out to go through a fence up through the hills, where he had been accustomed to go some years before. On this occasion, according to her, he climbed over a barbed-wire fence, just as he had done the last time she had let him out there about three years earlier. Young Ray, who had been in the habit of hunting in the upland country beyond Mrs. Ryan's property, had with him a .22 rifle and his duffel bag with food and the like. In spite of the many no-trespassing signs, he went up the private road Mrs. Ryan had had constructed to the top of the mountain beyond her property. Halfway up the road he met Evasio Piovera.

At the closed grand-jury hearing, Henry testified that he was working near his workshop when young Ray appeared with his duffel bag on his left-hand side and a gun on his right-hand side and asked where he could get a glass of water. Henry, after giving him some water, asked him where he was going, and Ray said he was going fishing up in Lopez Canyon. Henry asked if he hadn't seen the sign on the highway and Ray said Yes, and Henry then asked him if he hadn't learned to respect other people's property, to which Ray responded—in an almost arrogant way, according to Henry—that he always went through that way and nobody was going to stop him.

Henry asked him if he would like anybody to go through *his* property, and the young man mumbled something that sounded like "The Germans ought to be here," and he started up the trail. Henry followed him a short distance and asked him again to leave the property. He told him that he was trespassing and that Mrs. Ryan did not allow trespassers without her permission. But Ray kept on going and did not answer. Henry repeated the order and then said he was going to call the police. He went into the workshop, believing that this action would cause the young man to go back. Instead, Ray started to run fast up the hill.

Henry testified that he then got very much worried because of

Ray's actions. He said that all the time they were talking Ray had looked straight at the ground, never raising his eyes; moreover, he had kept his gun on balance. When Ray dashed off up the hill on being told that Henry was going to call the police, Henry began to worry that the young man was up to something. Frightened, he ran up the road, calling to Mrs. Ryan to "please get your gun."

Henry testified that when he had told Mrs. Ryan about the young man she went to her trailer and he himself went back down the hill. He said that as he was going to his workshop he heard three shots. He had the impression that the shots were coming from somewhere between Mrs. Ryan's trailer and the slope. He went into his workshop to get his .32 rifle and when he came out with the gun he had to climb a steep hill to get to the path, and he didn't see Mrs. Ryan immediately. He did see the young man walking down the path toward the trailers. He recalled distinctly that the man had the rifle in almost the same position as when he was talking to Henry. Ray was carrying it right in the center and was playing with it.

When Henry got part way up the hill, he heard Mrs. Ryan's voice saying, "Now give me that gun." Then he looked up and saw young Ray turn in the path. At that time Mrs. Ryan was standing on the side of the road near Henry, and Ray was standing on the bank side of the trail.

Henry said that as he saw the young man turning swiftly to the right he actually could see the man's gun touching Mrs. Ryan. Then a shot went off. Henry jumped because he feared Mrs. Ryan had been shot, for the shot had come just about the same time that the young man had swung around with the gun.

Henry rushed up the steep hill to where Mrs. Ryan was. He heard her say, "I had to shoot him. I had to shoot him." Mrs. Ryan had Ray's gun in her left hand, holding it by the muzzle, and her revolver in her right hand. Ray had started down the hill. When Henry got up to Mrs. Ryan, she said, "I am afraid that I hit him badly." She said in French, "Go and call the police." Henry said he didn't see the young man, since his attention was centered on Mrs. Ryan.

Henry then dashed down to telephone the police. On the way

down the road he saw the young man lying on his back, but kept on running to call the police and an ambulance. After calling the police he went back and Mrs. Ryan asked him to get a pillow. Henry told her not to touch the man before the police came. Then he went down to the gate, which was about a mile away, to unlock it for the sheriffs.

In addition to Mr. Piovera, who was the only eyewitness of what occurred at the actual moment of the firing of the shot which killed young Ray, Mrs. Ryan herself testified at the grand-jury hearing. Her testimony was the same as that she had given at the coroner's inquest, although in greater detail.

She told the grand jury that prior to June 9, 1951, she had had quite a few trespassers, perhaps fifteen or twenty. For the most part they had been very nice. She believed some of them thought it was a government trail. She had spoken to them and explained that she lived alone there and that one of the big dangers was that of fire started by cigarettes; also, the topography of the land was such that if they shot at squirrels there was danger of hitting her or somebody at the house. One of her little donkeys was found shot in the neck about three weeks before, and she frequently heard shots.

Mrs. Ryan testified that there had been a few young men who tried to be belligerent. But no one really had caused her any trouble, and they seemed to understand. She said she asked them not to think of her as an ogre or someone unfriendly. She said she didn't feel that way and she didn't want to give that impression. She explained to them that now that she was building it really was different from what it had been before, when the property was part of a large ranch and nobody lived there.

Mrs. Ryan told the grand jury that she didn't object to people walking on her land. "I don't have the feeling that it's my land and nobody should put their feet on it," she said. "I simply don't want fire and don't want shooting up there. I am alone, but I have no feeling that the land should not be walked on by everybody. I have the feeling that that is the impression that has been given, and it hurts me."

Mrs. Ryan testified that on June 9 she had stayed overnight on the ranch. Henry was there that day. She said she was returning toward her trailer when Henry came running up the road, very much disturbed, and called to her. She couldn't remember his exact words, but, as nearly as she could recall, Henry was calling, "Mrs. Ryan, go get your gun. There is a man." Then he said, "Stop him," or "Watch him," or something like that. According to Mrs. Ryan, Henry was not of an excitable nature, but on this occasion he was very much distressed and excited and upset.

Mrs. Ryan said she ran into the trailer and got her gun, which she kept on a shelf over her bed. "As I came out," she said, "I could see the boy. . . . He was running up this steep bank with a gun, the rifle, in his hand."

She was not aware of what happened to Henry, because she was intent on the young man. She called out to him to stop as soon as she saw him. She didn't know what she said. She yelled to him once or twice. Then she fired some warning shots into the air and to the right; to the best of her knowledge there were only three such shots. She said the young man just kept running, or rather scrambling, because it was quite steep up there.

Mrs. Ryan was quite a bit behind him, but she ran after him until she couldn't see him any more. He seemed to dive into the underbrush. There was a curve in the road between them and she thought that protected her from any shooting he might be doing. "I knew he was strange," Mrs. Ryan said. "There was something very wrong about him." So she stopped where she would be protected by the bulge in the land.

She called to him to come out. There was no answer. She believed she called again, then waited perhaps a minute. Then he came out, but he didn't say a word. Mrs. Ryan told the grand jury, "He didn't say, 'I give up,' or 'I am here.'" He just came down the road toward her, "looking very peculiar." He stared right into her face, she said, and he didn't say a word, just kept on coming toward her.

She testified that young Ray was carrying his gun parallel to the ground, in his right hand. The rifle was balanced in the middle. He had a pack on his left shoulder, and he walked right up to her and passed in front of her. "As far as I was concerned, I was isolated out there on that road with that young man."

When he got opposite her, Mrs. Ryan said, "You will have to give me that gun," in a very firm tone of voice because "he was a dangerous man in some way and he was still armed, although he was walking toward me. I can honestly say that at the time, as he walked, I felt that the affair was over, he had come out—I felt he was surrendering. But I also felt that he was not rational, or was strange in some way, that he didn't speak—and a very peculiar look in his face."

Mrs. Ryan said the young man didn't stop when he got close to her. He didn't look at her, but looked straight ahead, although he had been staring at her until then. He was opposite her when she asked for the gun. He took a step or two past her down the hill "and suddenly swung on me, pointing the gun and pushing it right into the center of my stomach. . . . The gun hit my arm and my side and pushed in there. I have never been more scared in my life—I felt certain I was going to be killed."

She said she was aware of grabbing at his rifle with her left hand to try to shove it away, and at the same time she fired her revolver with her right hand. She was not aware of aiming her revolver at all. She said she simply had her hand on the trigger, as she had all along. The moment she fired, either the impact pulled the rifle from his hand or Ray loosened his hold. She found that his rifle was in her hand. "As I had been shooting to save my life, not to kill the young man, when the threat to my life was away from him and in my own hand, I stopped shooting. The danger was away—I had it in my hand and I stopped shooting."

She testified that when she reached over and grabbed his rifle, he seemed to swing around again in the same direction he had been going and continued walking down the road. Mrs. Ryan said she knew she must have shot the young man. She was stunned that he kept on walking without a word. He walked about fifty feet; then his pack slipped off his left shoulder and fell to the ground. From the moment the pack slipped off, he seemed to stagger.

77

Mrs. Ryan called to Henry and said she had had to shoot the boy. In French she told Henry that she thought she had hurt him badly and to "please call a doctor and an ambulance and the police right away."

The young man had fallen by the time Mrs. Ryan got to him. Then Henry came back from his telephone calls and she called to him to bring a blanket and a pillow, to look after the boy. She said it was pitiful, having him on the ground like that, but Henry told her not to touch him or do anything until the police arrived. She knelt down beside him and put her hand on his shoulder and told him to hang on. She stayed with the boy as he was lying there kicking in pain, asking him to hang on, telling him they had sent for help.

Mrs. Ryan testified that she had never seen the boy before; that she didn't know who he was or anything about him, except that his actions, if they weren't criminal, were definitely queer. She asked the grand jury to understand that Henry, whom she knew so well, would never have come running to her and asked her to get the gun if it hadn't been a very serious situation. She explained that she felt the young man was a dangerous person—that he didn't behave right; that he looked so peculiar; that he had a queer, blank, stary look; that he didn't speak.

She said, "My feelings have been that, through my last testimony when I was trying awfully hard to be collected and calm and answer questions, . . . I wanted to be accurate and calm and fair; I have a feeling that at the [coroner's] inquest I didn't get over . . . how completely sick I am over this. . . . I don't think that it's ever been stressed that I shot only under the circumstances to just save my life—to shoot a trespasser would never enter my thoughts; that I had never seen the man, that . . . even in the state of shock I was in after I knew he was dead, I never thought of calling a lawyer; that I never tried to confer with anybody; that I went openly to the district attorney; . . . that I didn't even dream of calling Mr. Brazil, who had done some little legal work for me in connection with my property, until the next day. . . . But I am stressing those points to show that my idea was not to kill him, and I feel that the fact that I only fired one shot into him when there still was some in the gun proves that I did not shoot him being mad, or vindictive, or haughty that he dared walk on my property, but that as soon as the danger to my life . . . was removed . . . , I had no further desire or wish or thought of going on shooting."

Young Ray's mother told the grand jury, "My son is gone and nothing could bring him back and I hold no bitterness in my heart to Mrs. Ryan. From the very beginning I have not, and I would like to ask the grand jury that they do not indict her."

Notwithstanding the charitable attitude on the part of the boy's mother, the San Luis Obispo County grand jury indicted Mrs. Ryan for manslaughter on June 20, 1951.

To appreciate what the defense was up against in defending Mrs. Ryan, it is first necessary to visualize a town like San Luis Obispo. I am not familiar with the town today, but I remember it as it was when I went there to defend Mrs. Ryan. It was a small community with a rural flavor. It had one or possibly two newspapers. It was a close-knit community where strangers were looked upon warily.

I was called into the case by San Luis Obispo attorney A. H. Brazil, who asked me if I would associate myself with him in Mrs. Ryan's defense. Our first move was to prepare a petition for a writ of prohibition. This is an order entered by an appellate court directing that the case be dismissed on the ground that there is insufficient evidence to justify prosecution. It seemed to Mr. Brazil and me that the testimony on which the grand jury based its manslaughter indictment was clearly insufficient even to create a suspicion of any criminal responsibility on the part of Mrs. Ryan, and that this was a clear-cut case of justifiable homicide.

In our petition for a writ of prohibition we contended there was nothing in the defendant's grand-jury testimony to cause it to be disregarded, nor was there any basis of impeachment or inherent weakness in it which detracted from the picture of justifiable homicide.

We argued that this was a clear-cut case of justifiable homicide, committed in lawful defense of the defendant, when there was reason to apprehend a design to do great bodily injury on the part of the decedent and an imminent danger of such a design's being accomplished.

We pointed out that the young man was a complete stranger to Mrs. Ryan and that there was no possible suggestion of any motive other than self-defense. As the California Supreme Court said in *People v. Weatherford,* 27 C (2d) 401, at 423, "the 'absence of motive tends to support the presumption of innocence'; it is 'a fact to be reckoned on the side of innocence.' "

Here there was no element of manslaughter. Certainly it could not have been voluntary manslaughter committed upon a sudden quarrel or in a heat of passion, for none of those elements was present.

We also argued that it could not have been involuntary manslaughter in the commission of an unlawful act not amounting to a felony, because self-defense is a lawful act, as recognized by Section 197 of the California penal code; nor in the commission of a lawful act which might produce death in an unlawful manner or without due caution and circumspection, for the reason that obviously self-defense is a lawful act, and under the circumstances depicted in the record before the grand jury the lawful act of the defendant clearly was not done in an unlawful manner or without due caution and circumspection.

We contended that the decedent placed the defendant in a position which justified her in acting as she did under the extreme circumstances presented. Looking at the situation from Mrs. Ryan's eyes under the circumstances which confronted her at the vital moment in question, it was clear that she had acted as any other reasonable person would have acted under the same set of circumstances. It was also quite probable that if she had not done so she herself might have been the victim.

But the California Supreme Court was not convinced. On October 8, 1951, the high court denied our petition for a writ of prohibition. Mrs. Ryan was required to stand trial for manslaughter.

When the Ryan case began, my associates and I were regarded bleakly in San Luis Obispo. The press was fiercely anti-Ryan. This was true not only locally but also on a state-wide basis. Vitriol was mixed with printer's ink. When a picture of the wife of the young man Mrs. Ryan had killed was printed in the Los Angeles and San Francisco papers, it showed her holding her small baby in her arms and standing beside her husband's grave.

No point was made of the fact that she'd been separated from her husband before he was killed.

Three out of every five potential jurors I examined in my effort to empanel a jury admitted to being prejudiced against my client and were excused. This proportion of admitted prejudice is the highest I have ever encountered. Because of this unconcealed bitterness, an inordinately long time was taken to obtain a jury, but one was finally empaneled and the trial began.

At this point I'd like to review some of the subsequent testimony. At the time of this story, an important segment of San Luis Obispo life was a branch of a religious sect which resembled the Holy Rollers. Ray was a prominent member of the sect. In the light of further testimony, it seems likely that he decided to go up into the hills above San Luis Obispo to pray, for he was unusually devout. It was offered as a fact (and it was not contradicted) that he had put a Bible in the pack on his back, had armed himself with a .22 rifle, and had started up into the hills through Mrs. Ryan's place. Apparently he planned to combine hunting and praying.

Newly arrived back in town from the Navy, he may not have got it clearly through his mind that Mrs. Ryan's hill was no longer open to outsiders. In any case, loading himself down with his Nimrod paraphernalia, he climbed over her fence and wandered up the private road Mrs. Ryan had had constructed to the mountaintop. He paid no attention to the fence, even less to the gate and the bell, and, ignoring the no-trespassing signs, he had trudged upward through Mrs. Ryan's property. It doesn't seem to have occurred to him that those impediments and warning signs applied to him, or, of course, it could have been that he just didn't care.

It was not a situation which tended to lend itself to cold analysis by the citizenry. Neither the fact that Mrs. Ryan was rich nor that she was from "someplace back East" endeared her to the townspeople. The fact that she had killed one of the town's young men who already possessed the town's sympathy "because his wife had taken his baby and left him" made Mrs. Ryan an ogress in the community's mind. People stood on street corners mumbling and muttering, "He wasn't doing anybody any harm, was he?" and, "She shot him in cold blood, didn't she?"

Shortly after Mrs. Ryan's indictment I had driven up to San Luis Obispo to take part in her defense. With me I took one of my associates, Rexford Eagan, who was then a youngster just out of law school. The feeling against Mrs. Ryan was running so high that we had to park our car outside the town and let Mrs. Ryan's San Luis attorney, Mr. Brazil, drive us the rest of the way. He had warned me that I would have to leave my auto at the airport. I thought he surely must be exaggerating. I found out that, if anything, he was understating the situation.

He explained that because my face had appeared in the papers in connection with other cases, my presence in San Luis would instantly be connected with the Ryan case. He suggested that to avoid unpleasantness I approach the town quietly and circuitously. I stayed in San Luis Obispo a day or two, then returned to Los Angeles.

In spite of the bitter talk against Mrs. Ryan, the fact that the young man had died had depressed her terribly. She was a very wonderful, very humane person, but the prejudice against her was so great that she didn't go into town at all unless it was absolutely necessary. After she testified before the coroner's inquest about what had happened, and had told her version of that story to the grand jury, she stayed away from San Luis until her case came to trial.

During the days which followed I was careful not to do anything, say anything or conduct myself in any way which would imply that I was a "slick city lawyer." I must have done a good job of living up to my favorite description of myself, "a Beverly Hills country lawyer," because one of Mrs. Ryan's friends who was sitting in the courtroom overheard one of the local people behind her say, "Wouldn't you think Mrs. Ryan would have hired a *smart* lawyer?"

That remark when it was repeated to me made me very happy. It was exactly the kind of reaction I'd hoped for.

About a week before the case went to trial I began to tighten up. I became jittery and nervous. I always do before a major trial. I have never stood up in a courtroom yet without having my knees shake with fear, stage fright, or whatever you want to call it. A young associate of mine once told me shamefacedly, "When I start a case I shake all over." I told him, "If you don't shake you're not up on your toes. If you ever lose that feeling, take a long vacation and pray for your nervousness to come back."

I chartered a plane to take my associates to San Luis Obispo for the trial itself. This time my secretary, Helen Fitzpatrick, and a former associate came along with me, as well as young Eagan. I wanted them at hand if I needed them. As it turned out, I did.

The shooting had occurred about four months before, but when we reached the town we were still given the deep-freeze treatment. Oddly enough, there was no for-hire transportation available to take us into town from the airport, and once more we had to call Mrs. Ryan's local lawyer for that.

I had engaged a suite, which I shared with Mr. Eagan, at the Anderson Hotel. Mrs. Fitzpatrick also had one down the hall. By another strange coincidence the elevator was always out of order when we wanted to use it. It was a break for us that we were only on the third floor.

I was made aware every second, every moment, that I was un-wanted and disliked. People glowered and muttered at me as I passed them on the street. I was literally spat at, although the spittle landed near my feet and not on me. But I can be determined when I want to be and I made up my mind to be oblivious to such things. I made no complaint, even on the morning before court opened when I tried to buy a newspaper—the news vendor saw me coming and his newspapers disappeared.

When I came downstairs and headed for the courtroom, because of my previous experience with the local taxi drivers at the airport I walked. The hotel had been too busy to send breakfast to my room and I stopped at a hash house to have breakfast served by a sullen waitress. Once more as I walked the block and a half from our hotel to the courthouse past dress shops, tobacco shops and poolrooms, people spat, not in my face but at my feet.

In the courthouse, waiting to represent the people against Mrs. Ryan, were a D. A. and an assistant prosecutor. Mr. Eagan told me afterward, "I knew you were in fine fettle and filled with competitive urge, for when you stood up as the attorney for the defense, I could see your knees shaking through the back of your pants."

Before that trial was over Mr. Eagan, as my temporary roommate, learned some of my other pre-trial symptoms. The night before a trial it is impossible for me to sleep. I lie awake all night, in the dark, thinking. Early in the morning before starting for the courtroom, I am sometimes nauseated.

The courtroom was packed, and those who couldn't get in made the air outside murmurous with their partisanship. The panel of jurors had been summoned from an area covering roughly eighty miles. Most of them were farming people who were distrustful of city people, with their smooth, slick ways.

I'll say this for San Luis Obispo. It is an honest community. It may hate, but if it does hate, it admits it. To get the necessary twelve we had to go through eighty-five jurors. However, once we had a jury, I felt it was a reasonably fair, honest, impartial one.

In spite of the fact that the boy's wife had left him, she now walked into the courtroom carrying her six-month-old baby son and sat with young Ray's parents in the middle of the front row in seats obviously reserved for them by the prosecution. They sat there through the selection of the jury, while the baby wept at strategic times, as if on command. During the recesses, when the courtroom was filled with the milling public, Ray's widow, a young and very pretty girl, would slowly rise to her feet and parade conspicuously with her baby to the water cooler to get a drink for herself and the child. Then she would march back to her seat. She did everything but wear a sign hung around her neck: "I've just been widowed by a murderess." It was in this atmosphere that the case was tried.

Not only was the emotional pressure intense but the temperature knocked the top off the thermometer. It was hotter in that courtroom than it had been in the Scopes trial in Tennessee when Clarence Darrow and William Jennings Bryan sat in their shirt sleeves and galluses and fanned their dripping faces with palm-leaf fans.

To digress for a moment, I bow to no one in my admiration for Mr. Darrow, and if he took off his coat or even his collar and tie in a courtroom I am sure it was a fitting and proper thing for him to do. I can only say that I've never taken my coat off in a courtroom, and I never will. I was brought up to believe that a man sitting in his shirt sleeves is a man who is getting undressed to go to bed or getting dressed in the morning. Consequently, I simply feel more comfortable with my coat on, no matter how soggy the atmosphere may be.

The first witness for the prosecution was the autopsy surgeon. He testified that he could tell from the position of the bullet's exit and entrance what angle the body had assumed when it was shot. That was obviously debatable. It is almost impossible to determine the position a man is in when a bullet is fired at him without any evidence of the whereabouts of the hand which fired that bullet.

At the coroner's inquest Mrs. Ryan had testified that as young Ray came down the path toward her, she was holding a .38 in her right hand, with her elbow on her hip. As he passed her on the narrow pathway she pivoted and said, "I'll have to ask you for your gun!" With that, Ray had swerved. The barrel of his .22 rifle had struck her right arm and had brushed across her stomach. She had grabbed the barrel of Ray's .22 with her left hand and had instinctively fired a shot with her other hand to frighten him away. It was the prosecution's theory that events couldn't have happened that way. It contended that the entrance and the exit of the wound indicated that the bullet had taken a downward path which showed that Ray was either prostrate or bending over, although Mrs. Ryan had sworn that he was standing upright.

The autopsy surgeon had had a dummy made—or perhaps the D. A. had had it made—in such a way that a school blackboard pointer could be thrust through and emerge on the other side, showing the bullet's path. All of his equipment was in the courtroom, together with the copy of the Bible which the dead man had carried up the hill. That Bible was prominently displayed.

The D. A. then called a local deputy sheriff to the witness stand and questioned him. Mrs. Ryan had told her story to the sheriff, she had told it at the coroner's inquest, she had told it to the grand jury. As I listened it seemed to me the D. A. was trying to interrogate that deputy in such a way that his questions would not bring out any statements he might have overheard Mrs. Ryan make when he arrived at the scene of the shooting.

Naturally the district attorney wanted Mrs. Ryan to take the stand herself and tell her story once more, because he had reason to hope that the sight of her and even the sound of her voice would inflame the local feeling against her even more. Although I purposely tried to convey the impression that I intended to call Mrs. Ryan in her own defense, the prosecution wanted to make sure that I did. By assiduously avoiding any reference to what Mrs. Ryan had said to the deputies when they arrived at the scene of the shooting, the district attorney hoped to force me into putting her on the stand to say that she had killed Ray in self-defense.

I hadn't made a final decision about that when the trial started. With San Luis Obispo sentiment following the Let's-get-Mrs.-Ryan line, I knew that the prosecution would try to beat Mrs. Ryan to a pulp with its cross-examination. On the other hand, if I *didn't* put her on the stand it would be pounced upon as an admission that she had something to conceal.

Moreover, some sixth sense told me that even if I did place her in the witness box the prosecution would try to prevent her from testifying about any conversation she had had with the deputies at the scene of the killing—if no such conversation was mentioned in previous testimony by anyone else.

There was only one out for me. I had to arrange it so that one of the deputies who had been there when the young man died *would tell the jury Mrs. Ryan's story for her.* Testimony of what Mrs. Ryan had said to a deputy shortly after the killing was, of course, admissable under the spontaneous-statement (*res gestae*) exception to the hearsay rule, since statements made under the stress of nervous excitement are not likely to be contrived, and the opportunity to cross-examine the declarent is of secondary importance.

Luckily for me—and for Mrs. Ryan—the D. A. made one mistake. One is all it takes. I tried to look impassive, but inwardly I was exulting, for when I cross-examined the deputy that one mistake gave me the right to bring out all of the conversation which had taken place on that hill prior to and immediately following the killing.

The prosecution's mistake began to take shape when the D. A. showed the local deputy who was on the witness stand a series of photographs taken at the scene of the killing while that officer was present. As a result, the photographs became a part of the testimony. But the D. A. had forgotten one thing. On two of the photographs someone had scratched a tiny x with a pin. Those photographs were passed on to me to see before they became a prosecution exhibit which the jury could examine later at their leisure.

I looked at those pictures, then handed them back, being careful to show no emotion. When the D. A. had finished with the deputy —and the witness undoubtedly figured that there would be no question from me because his testimony was cut-and-dried routine stuff—I picked up my glasses, put them on and looked down at my notes a minute. Then, carrying my glasses in my hand, I walked slowly to the witness stand, picked up the photographs, shuffled them, looked at one with an x scratched on it and asked casually, "What does this x mean, Sheriff?"

Before the D. A. knew I had even asked that question the deputy had replied, "That is where Mrs. Ryan told me she was standing when she fired the third shot."

I darted a glance from the corner of my eye at the D. A. He seemed in danger of having a stroke, for the moment that officer testified, "That is where Mrs. Ryan told me she was standing when she fired the third shot," the case had broken wide open and he knew it. The legal effect of his answer was to open up the witness's whole conversation with my client to questioning by me.

There was much heavy breathing, pointless objection and excessive sweating on the part of the prosecution, but according to the law I could now ask the deputy to recite his entire conversation with Mrs. Ryan, not just a portion of it, as it had taken place at the scene of the killing.

To the everlasting credit of the witness, he was honest enough to tell me the whole truth and nothing but the truth, in spite of the fact that it must have been clear to everyone in the courtroom that the prosecution would rather he had been stricken dumb. I got from this witness everything Mrs. Ryan had said, including the words vital to her defense, "I had to shoot him. He threatened me."

The prosecution's story had been that the dead man had merely been going up the hill to fish and commune with God; that Mrs. Ryan, a wealthy woman from the East who had bought up the whole mountaintop, had then killed the young man on the flimsy pretext that she thought he was a dangerous interloper.

Now the prosecution was desperate, for its own witness had helped me make out a case of killing in self-defense. Another deputy sheriff who had gone to the scene of the shooting was called to the stand.

Although there had never been any testimony that Ray had made a declaration just before his demise, I recognized the possibility that there might have been one, since the boy had not died until after the sheriff's deputies arrived. In preparation for testimony concerning such a dying statement, I had asked Mr. Eagan to spend night after night researching the law on dying declarations and their admissibility in evidence.

Time passed and I was beginning to think there was no possibility that the subject would come up. Then it happened. The second deputy testified that he had stood beside the wounded boy as his life ebbed. He said that a few moments after Mrs. Ryan had told his colleague, the previous witness, that she had shot the boy because he threatened her, the dying boy had whispered to him, "It's a lie."

At that point I turned to Mr. Eagan and said to him, "Please give me the file on dying declarations you have been working on."

Although Mr. Eagan had slaved endlessly in assembling that file, he didn't have it with him. Not anticipating my need for it, he'd left it back at the hotel.

He left the courtroom in a leap, knocking one newspaperman cleanly off his feet as he went. He ran down the stairs, across the street, over to our hotel and up to the third floor for the file, and in some miraculous fashion he was back in the courtroom before the D. A. had finished his direct examination of the witness. Mr. Eagan's remarkable performance earned for him the lasting nickname of Flash. Not more than two minutes had elapsed, three at the most, before he collapsed, exhausted, in the seat next to mine just as the D. A. turned the witness over to me and I stood up to engage in a legal tightrope performance.

Consulting the file Mr. Eagan had fetched, I found that the dying declaration which had just been testified to was very probably inadmissible as evidence, because the law governing this point rules that in order for a dying declaration to be admissible it must be established that the expiring party knows that he is in immediate danger of death, that he has no hope for recovery, and that what he is saying is being said in the presence of death.

In the testimony to which I had just listened, there was nothing which established that the deceased knew he was in imminent danger of death. However, I didn't want to argue that point too much. If I did it might well have been stricken from the record, and if it was left in the record it could conceivably be ground for granting a new trial to my client in the event the jury convicted. Stricken or not, I knew it couldn't be eradicated from the minds of the jurors.

Standing with one hand on the file Mr. Eagan had placed before me on the counsel table, I made up my mind. I said, "No questions."

With the boy's dying declaration in evidence, the prosecution apparently was convinced that I would be forced to put on a defense and to call Mrs. Ryan to the stand in her own defense. The district attorney decided to hold in reserve, and save for rebuttal testimony, a battery of scientific witnesses—including ballistics experts—to establish the fact that Mrs. Ryan could not have shot Ray in the manner she had twice described under oath, at the coroner's inquest and before the grand jury.

The prosecution rested after a short day and a half with only the skeleton of a case in the record. About all that had been established was that Mrs. Ryan had, in fact, shot the boy to death. It was late Friday afternoon. The judge recessed the court for the weekend. That night the town was packed with newspapermen from San Francisco and Los Angeles, as well as reporters representing papers in smaller communities. All of them were speculating on what kind of defense I was going to offer on Tuesday morning when the trial resumed.

I had already made up my mind what the defense strategy would be. I had settled upon it as soon as the deputy sheriff on the witness stand had revealed Mrs. Ryan's version of what had happened and that revelation had become part of the record—which meant that it would, in the end, be considered by the court and the jury.

I had decided *not* to put Mrs. Ryan on the stand. In fact, I was going to rest without putting on any witnesses at all.

My thinking behind that decision was that Mrs. Ryan's story had already been told by one of the prosecution's witnesses and if we based our case on that, how could the prosecution possibly object? However, I planned to keep the D. A.'s office off guard and off balance wondering what our next move would be. I didn't want the prosecution to ask permission to reopen its case on Tuesday morning.

I flew back to Los Angeles that weekend to work in my office, but I asked Mrs. Fitzpatrick and Mr. Eagan to stay in San Luis Obispo and keep the lights burning in my hotel suite late into the night. I also asked them to demand room service from the hotel, to order the morning papers sent up and to keep a typewriter chattering so that all who listened could hear it. I even instructed Mr.

Eagan to borrow a key to the local law library so that he could make a show of working there all day Saturday, as if preparing for a long and arduous defense.

Mentioning the newspaper and room service brings up a significant point. Those two services were gradually being offered to us as the days slipped by. Almost imperceptibly the town's bitter distaste for Mrs. Ryan and anyone connected with her had become less intense. No one spat in our direction as we walked the streets. Monday afternoon when I flew back to San Luis Obispo from Los Angeles, I was able to hire a taxicab at the airport for the drive into town.

I am given to special and peculiar diets while I undergo the strain of a trial, and, as I recall, the night before my final argument in the Ryan case my dinner consisted of a bag of popcorn eaten in a movie theater where I watched Fred MacMurray in a Western. After the movie I went back to my hotel, opened a can of pineapple juice, drank it and went to bed. In spite of this precautionary diet (or perhaps because of it) the next morning before I argued the case I had an upset stomach.

To get back to my decision: By the time the people's case was closed I knew that in bringing out the statement Mrs. Ryan had made to the deputy sheriff at the time of the shooting, before she had even talked to a lawyer or to the police, I had got everything into the record I could possibly hope for. Of course, I didn't disclose the way I felt. I pretended that I was a legal ammunition dump loaded with unexploded shells, but by not putting any witnesses on the stand I would make it legally impossible for the prosecutor to call any of the array of waiting experts whom he was saving to be his rebuttal witnesses.

My decision was a hard one to make, as all such decisions are. But unless the prosecution crossed me and called more witnesses, I was determined to close my defense without putting on any witnesses at all—neither Mrs. Ryan nor anyone else.

Tuesday morning the courtroom was once more literally packed. I don't think one other person could have been squeezed in. Everyone was waiting for the defense legal staff to send its witnesses into action. I could almost see the thoughts taking form and shape in the heads around the room: "What will Mrs. Ryan have to say?" "What defense will she offer?"

The San Luis Obispo papers still carried stories referring to the dead man as "our boy." "Our boy did this" and "Our boy did that." His widow, his baby and his family were still there in the front row.

The judge took the bench. The jury filed into the box. The judge asked, "Am I to understand that the prosecution has rested?" When he was assured that that was the case, he turned to me and said, "The defense may proceed."

That courtroom, which had been full of buzzing, suddenly hushed. I leaned forward in my chair and stood up. I picked up my glasses, nibbled briefly at their frames, looked at the judge and said, "Your honor, the defense rests." I added that I was content to base my arguments on the testimony I'd got from the deputy sheriff when I cross-examined him. Then I sat down.

There was a long moment of shocked disbelief in that courtroom. Not only the D. A. but the judge and everyone else sat frozen with their mouths gaping. Then all hell broke loose. Newspapermen shot through the door, clawing and scrabbling at each other. The prosecution huffed and puffed, but their huffing and puffing availed them nothing. They couldn't reopen the case.

The district attorney got to his feet and said, "But I am not ready to deliver my argument."

The associate D. A. dropped a book on the floor—he had a whole stack of them ready to refer to in rebuttal—and it was five minutes before the courtroom was restored to order. Then, despite the D. A.'s protestations, the judge directed that final arguments proceed after recess.

In my argument to the jury I was mean enough to wonder why the state had not called to the stand the ballistics experts it had kept waiting in court day after day. But for the most part my argument dealt with the testimony of the deputy sheriff and what Mrs. Ryan had said within his hearing. I went over it word for word, and I told the jury, "Remember this is what she said before any arrest

92

was made, before anyone had talked to her, before she had had a chance to consult her lawyer. Her story is the cleanest story it is possible to obtain from a defendant, since it is made up of her instinctive and spontaneous remarks, uninfluenced by anyone. On this testimony alone she is entitled to an acquittal."

The thought I kept constantly in the front of my mind while I presented my argument was that somehow, without belittling the dead boy, I must take the sting out of the prosecution's attack. I was trying to weaken the D. A.'s summing up by showing the jury exactly what had happened between my client and the young man who had been trespassing on her land, gun in hand.

The following day the district attorney and I summarized our closing arguments and the judge charged the jury. They went out late in the afternoon and were out eight hours. When they finally came in, they announced that they were hopelessly deadlocked, eight for acquittal, four for conviction. If the atmosphere in which that trial had begun is considered, that result was nothing short of a resounding victory.

To me one of the most absorbing things about the case was watching the local opinion slowly turn from hating the guts of anyone associated with the defense to a realization that it was possible that something might be said in behalf of Mrs. Ryan to justify what had happened. Watching public opinion in San Luis Obispo reverse itself was like watching a glacier in motion. It was almost imperceptible, yet it occurred.

That switch may have had something to do with the fact that after her second trial Mrs. Ryan was acquitted. By that time the back of the anti-Ryan feeling had been broken and after testimony almost identical with that in her first trial she went free.

Her second trial began on February 27, 1952. I wasn't worried about its outcome. I saw no need for Mrs. Ryan to be put to the expense of two sets of lawyers for her retrial, so with the consent of her local lawyer, Mr. Brazil, who assisted in the first trial, I withdrew from the case.

6

Errol Flynn

Errol Flynn also went to trial with a crushing burden of public
opinion upon him.

If Los Angeles was ever in danger of losing its franchise as a setting for sensational trials (and there has never been a real threat of
that) the Flynn trial in 1942-43 would have restored the city to its
good standing.

Flynn's troubles began when he met Miss Betty Hansen at the
home of a friend in Bel Air. Miss Hansen was only seventeen, but
her youthfulness did not keep her from being ripe physically, a
quality which Mr. Flynn somehow noticed. Miss Hansen, in turn,
was impressed with Mr. Flynn's charm and his stellar position in the
Hollywood firmament. Until the day of his death these two patterns,
lubricated by copious portions of alcohol, shaped his life.

Betty Hansen had traveled west from Nebraska to visit her sister
in Los Angeles. Her visit must have been an eventful one, because
her sister reported to the police that Betty had not been home for
some time and would they please run a fine-tooth comb over the city
to see if they could find her.

Los Angeles is a vast, sprawling city, but locating a pretty missing
girl from Nebraska seemed no trick at all to the police. They found
her registered in a Santa Monica hotel and brought her in for questioning. Their queries dredged up a story of amatory adventuring.
Although some of it may have been the product of the girl's imagination, she did produce Flynn's unlisted telephone number to back up

her story that not only had she met him but he had committed statutory rape upon her.

When the grand jury failed to return an indictment against Flynn in October 1942, after hearing Betty Hansen's story, the district attorney's office had its investigators root around for further evidence against Flynn to bolster its case. In pursuit of these investigations they dug up the fact that the mother of a girl named Peggy Satterlee had once come to the sheriff's office to complain that her child, who, she said, was fifteen at the time, had been twice seduced by Flynn on his yacht during a pleasure cruise off Catalina Island. The incidents in question were said to have taken place while the yacht, the *Sirocco*, lay at anchor off Avalon. According to Miss Satterlee, at one point Flynn had suggested that she leave the deck and visit his stateroom with him to see the moon through a porthole, and as a result of her moon-gazing she had been violated.

The sheriff's office had investigated that charge but hadn't taken it seriously. Now, however, the police did their fine-tooth-comb trick once more. This time they discovered the same Peggy Satterlee, now a full-bodied, sixteen-year-old night-club dancer.

The Hansen and Satterlee charges were combined in a single district attorney's complaint, and a preliminary hearing was set for November 2 before Los Angeles Municipal Judge Byron J. Walters. I represented Flynn at the hearing, assisted by Robert Ford.

As I studied the two complaining witnesses at the preliminary hearing, I made up my mind that whether Flynn had known them slightly or well, the two busty ladies listed as complainants against him were not as unversed in the ways of the world as the district attorney's office would have the public believe.

One thing which struck me immediately was that although the alleged two victims claimed that the offenses had occurred almost a year apart, their charges had been filed within weeks of each other. That seemed overly coincidental to me, and there was no doubt in my mind that the district attorney's office was doing its best to pile it on, hoping to strengthen its first charge against Flynn with a second one.

Deputy District Attorney Thomas W. Cochran called Betty Hansen to the stand first. He established that she had turned seventeen on September 21, 1942, and that she had attended a party at a Bel Air home a week later with a newly acquired male friend. Miss Hansen testified she arrived at the party in the late afternoon and was introduced to Mr. Flynn, who was also a guest. She had a drink with Mr. Flynn in the den and sat on his lap. Five of the guests, including Flynn and Miss Hansen, stayed for dinner.

Mr. Cochran questioned Miss Hansen about the post-dinner events:

Q. And after the dessert, what if anything was done by those persons present, what did everybody do after the dessert had been eaten?
A. Talked.
Q. At the dining table, or did they go somewhere else?
A. They talked a lot at the dining table and then left the room.
Q. Where did they go?
A. I went out with them to the den.
Q. Who else went into that same room with you?
A. All of us.
Q. Was Mr. Flynn there?
A. Yes.
Q. After you had gone into this other room, was there any conversation had between yourself and Mr. Flynn?
A. I don't recall.
Q. Do you recall feeling somewhat ill?
A. Yes.
MR. GIESLER: Pardon me. I think, your honor, I may suggest: I don't think there should be, I know there is nothing intended, but I don't think there should be anything leading.
THE COURT: I think that counsel will be aware of the suggestion.
Q. BY MR. COCHRAN: Oh, of course. I am trying, of course, Mr. Giesler, not to lead her at all.
Q. Do you recall, about that time, Mr. Flynn saying something to you?
A. No, I don't.
Q. Did you go anyplace with Mr. Flynn?
A. Yes.

Errol Flynn

Q. Where did you go?

A. Upstairs.

Q. Just before you went upstairs do you recall anything that was said by yourself or Mr. Flynn?

A. I don't recall what was said, but I know something was said.

Q. By whom?

A. Flynn.

Q. What is your best recollection, if you have any recollection, as to what he did say to you?

A. I do not know the words, but that he was going to take me upstairs and lie me on the bed for a nap.

THE COURT: Will you please keep your voice up as much as possible, so that all can hear.

Q. BY MR. COCHRAN: After that had been said by Mr. Flynn, what was the next thing that happened?

A. I went upstairs.

Q. And when you got upstairs, where did you go?

A. The bedroom.

Q. Do you recall whether or not the door was locked or unlocked?

A. Locked.

Q. I mean before you got in?

A. It was unlocked.

Q. Was the door—did the door remain unlocked before you got in, or was some change made in it?

A. It was unlocked when we went in.

Q. After you got in?

A. It was unlocked.

Q. Was the door subsequently locked?

A. Yes.

Q. By whom?

A. Errol Flynn.

Q. All right, now, after you got into this room, was anything said by Mr. Flynn to you or by you to Mr. Flynn?

A. Yes.

Q. Relate the conversation in full that you can now remember.

A. I believe he told me to lie down.

*   *   *

Q. Tell the court what transpired from that time on, and what was said. Just go ahead and relate what was done and said.

A. Well, Flynn took me in there and sat me down.

Q. Where?

A. On the twin bed, the first one.

Q. All right.

A. And I believe he told me to lie down, and I told him I did not want to take a nap, I could go back downstairs, and I do not know what he said or anything. He went out and locked the door and came back.

Q. Went and locked the door?

A. Yes.

Q. All right. Then what happened?

A. I had an act of intercourse.

Q. Before you had this act of intercourse, was anything done about your clothing or his?

A. Yes.

Q. Tell the court what was done in that respect.

A. He undressed me and then he got undressed.

Q. How were you dressed on that occasion?

A. I had slacks on.

Q. What else?

A. That is all.

Q. Did you have on panties?

A. Yes.

Q. When you say he undressed you, what of your clothing did he take off?

A. All of them.

Q. And of his clothing, what was taken off?

A. Everything except his shoes, I believe.

MR. COCHRAN: I did not hear that.

A. Everything except his shoes.

Q. You stated you had an act of sexual intercourse with Mr. Flynn there on that bed . . .

A. Yes.

Q. And was such an act performed by this defendant upon you in that room?

A. Yes.

Q. Now, after this act had been completed, what, if anything, did you hear?

A. A knock at the door.

Q. And what else did you hear besides a knock?

A. That is all.

Q. Did you hear anything said by Mr. Flynn or any other person?

A. He said something about a shower.

Q. Tell us what you heard Mr. Flynn say.

A. I recall somebody knocked at the door, and I believe Flynn said we were taking a shower.

Q. That is, Mr. Flynn said that?

A. Yes.

Q. Could you hear what the person on the other side of the door said?

A. I believe she wanted to use the telephone.

Q. Did you hear a woman's voice?

A. Yes.

Q. Did you recognize the voice?

A. Yes.

Q. Whose voice was it?

A. Lynne Boyer.

Q. She said something about the telephone?

A. Yes.

Q. Do you recall anything else that was said by either Mr. Flynn or Miss Boyer at the time?

A. I believe Flynn said, "There is a telephone downstairs."

Q. After Mr. Flynn said something about you and he taking a shower, what, if anything, did you do or say?

A. I don't know. I believe we were dressed when Lynne knocked at the door.

Q. Where were you at the time in the room—in where the twin beds were, or in the bedroom, or where?

A. I don't recall where we were. It might have been in the bathroom.

Q. Did you go in the bathroom after this act of intercourse with the defendant?

A. Yes.

Q. Now, after the episode of the door and the knock at the door, what was the next thing that happened?

A. He put some hair oil on.

Q. I did not hear that.

A. He was in the bathroom and he was putting hair oil on.

Q. What else do you recall that happened there?

A. I think he asked if I ever used it and I said no.

Q. Anything else?

A. Not that I recall.

Q. During any of that time was there any conversation about telephone numbers?

A. I believe he took my address down.

Q. What is your recollection on it? Don't say you believe.

A. I am sure he did.

Q. Did you give him your address?

A. Yes.

❖   ❖   ❖

Q. All right, now, after you had dressed, what was the next thing you and Mr. Flynn did? Did you stay there or did you go out of the room?

A. I believe we were combing our hair in front of the mirror, and I asked him if he was married.

Q. What did he say?

A. Yes, he was.

Q. What else, if anything, do you recall was said between you and the defendant?

A. I believe he said he had a divorce.

Q. I cannot hear you.

THE WITNESS [repeating]: I believe he said he had a divorce.

Q. Did you leave that room?

A. Yes, we did.

Shortly thereafter Mr. Cochran turned Miss Hansen over to me for cross-examination. By going into her background and motives to the extent the court would permit, I hoped to persuade Judge Walters that Betty Hansen was unworthy of belief and that Mr. Flynn should not be held for trial. I also wanted to bring out all the details of her story so that the defense could be fully prepared if Judge Walters was not so persuaded.

First I questioned Miss Hansen about her early life in Lincoln, Nebraska, her arrival in California to stay with her sister, and her leaving her sister's house to live in a hotel. I tried to go into the details of her relationships with the boys and men she said she went out with, but I was stopped by the court. Judge Walters ruled that, since the prosecution did not claim force and violence were used by Flynn in criminally attacking Miss Hansen, evidence of prior acts of unchastity was inadmissible under the holding in the Pantages case.

I turned to the matter of Miss Hansen's motives in going to the Bel Air party. She admitted that she had been told Errol Flynn would be there and that she had in mind the hope that he might help her to get a job with the movies. She admitted that Armand Knapp, the young man who took her to the party, had given her some advice as to how she might improve her chances. Miss Hansen said that Knapp told her to play up to Flynn. The questioning continued:

Q. BY MR. GIESLER: And in talking about playing up to Flynn, did he say anything about intercourse?
A. No, he did not.
Q. He did not mention intercourse at any time?
A. No, he did not.
Q. Now, then, for the purpose of refreshing your recollection, Miss Hansen, I will ask you, do you recall, do you remember your testimony you gave before the grand jury up on the fifth floor, or down on the fifth floor, of this building?
A. Yes.

Q. That was some little time ago?

A. Yes.

Q. I show you your testimony—page twenty-four, Mr. Cochran, parts of the page, referring back to line eighteen. We are talking about Armand Knapp. That is the same young man?

A. Yes.

Q. [*reading*] "Did he say anything to you about going to introduce you to Errol Flynn? A. He said how I should act and play up to him. Q. Tell us about that? A. He said play up to him and drink with him and he even said to have intercourse with him." Do you remember so testifying? This is your—

A. No, I don't.

Q. So there won't be any mistake, your name is Betty Hansen, and you start here over on page one and the next witness after you is on page seventy-five, and I will show you page twenty-four, line five.

Mr. Cochran: Will you go as far as twenty-five?

Mr. Giesler [*reading*]: "Did Mr. Knapp tell you to have intercourse with Flynn? A. He said to be sociable and do anything he asked me to do." That is true?

A. Yes.

Q. And so you testified—what you testified to is true, then?

A. Yes.

Q. Pointing out line one, she says she doesn't remember this, where she says, "Even have intercourse with him." She does not remember that. You might have got that wrong, you might have said that?

A. Yes.

Q. As a matter of fact, you did say it, didn't you?

A. Yes, but I might have meant something else.

Q. You think you might have meant something else about what you testified to here today?

A. No.

Q. Well, now, after having talked with Mr. Knapp along that line, you still went on out to the house, did you?

A. Yes, I did.

Q. And you had hopes by doing that, meeting Mr. Flynn and being nice to him, he might get you a job, isn't that true?

A. Yes.

Q. You knew he was in pictures, didn't you?

A. Yes.

Q. And you liked him in pictures, didn't you, before this Sunday, didn't you?

A. No, I never did.

Q. You never did? In Lincoln, did you go and see his pictures?

A. Once in a great while.

Q. And back there, didn't you kind of like his acting?

A. Not so good. He don't act like a gentleman, I will tell you.

MR. GIESLER: I move to strike that as not responsive.

THE COURT: Motion granted—the last sentence.

I cross-examined Betty Hansen extensively about the events in the upstairs bedroom after dinner:

Q. And you went to that room, and you say that Mr. Flynn undressed you?

A. Yes.

Q. You are sure of that?

A. Yes, I am, because I remember him throwing my slacks on the twin bed.

Q. He took off your clothes?

A. Yes.

Q. You are quite sure of that?

A. Yes.

Q. Don't you remember telling the officers over at Juvenile Hall that Mr. Flynn was over there and that you had undressed before?

A. Yes, I remember saying that I undressed myself. I remember.

Q. But now you say he undressed you, is that it?

A. Yes.

Q. All the rest you told the officers was the truth, wasn't it?

A. Yes, it was.

Q. And when you told them that you undressed yourself it wasn't the truth, was it?

A. No, it wasn't. I was sticking up for him.

MR. GIESLER: I move to strike that out as not responsive.

MR. COCHRAN: I resist that motion to strike because it is very definitely explanatory of the answer.

MR. GIESLER: I think it is not responsive to the question which I asked.

THE COURT: Motion denied.

Q. BY MR. GIESLER: At the same time you said you had intercourse with him, didn't you?

A. Yes, I did.

Q. You were not sticking up for him then, were you?

A. No.

Q. And you also said he locked the door at the time, didn't you?

A. Yes.

Q. You were not sticking up for him then, were you?

A. No, I wasn't.

*　　*　　*

Q. And when he told you to lie down on the bed, did he tell you what he wanted you to lie down for?

A. No, he did not.

Q. Did you have any thoughts of what he wanted you to lie down for?

A. No.

Q. When he locked the door did you have any thought why he locked the door?

A. Yes, I did.

Q. Did you say anything?

A. Yes, I believe I asked why he locked the door.

Q. What did he say?

A. I don't recall.

Q. Did you tell him you objected to his locking the door?

A. Yes, I did.

Q. What did you say?

A. I don't know, but I do know I objected.

Q. Did you object to lying down on the bed?

A. Yes, I did.

Q. What did you say?

A. I told him I wasn't feeling all right and wanted to go downstairs.

Q. Didn't you have any idea about what he wanted you to lie on the bed for?

A. No.

Q. You never had any idea?

A. No.

Q. Even though Armand told you to have intercourse, you never thought of what that was?

A. No.

Q. Nevertheless you did lie down on the bed yourself?

A. Yes.

Q. Did you talk about shop lying down?

A. I don't recall.

Q. You talked in the room about shop?

A. Yes, in the other room.

Q. Which room was it you talked about shop?

A. When we first came in.

Q. When you first came in you talked about shop?

A. Yes.

Q. What did you say about shop?

A. I believe I recall him asking where I had been working and where I lived.

Q. What did you say about shop?

A. I do not know what he said.

Q. What did you say?

A. What did I say? I don't recall.

Q. Did you say you would like to have a position?

A. Yes, I did.

Q. Or did you tell him you wanted to get a position?

A. I believe downstairs before we went up he asked what I could do, and I believe I told him I could type and I used to work as a waitress or something like that.

Q. Did you talk about acting at all?

A. No.

Q. Or singing?

A. Not that I recall.

*　　*　　*

Q. And now, back in the room, after your clothes were off and Mr.
Flynn's clothes were off with the exception of his shoes, and you being undressed with the exception of your stockings and sandals,
which bed did you say the act was performed on?

A. The first one when you come in to the twins. There are twin beds, but
the first one you come to.

Q. It was not on the double bed, the large bed?

A. No.

Q. And it was on a twin bed?

A. Yes.

Q. And did you lie down yourself? After your clothes were off?

A. I don't recall.

Q. Did you stand up as your clothes were being taken off?

A. No, I did not.

Q. You were lying down when they were being taken off?

A. Yes.

Q. Did you assist in taking the clothes off?

A. Well, I did not think very much of it.

Q. It did not mean much to you?

A. Yes, it did. I had no idea what I was going upstairs into.

Q. I am talking, after you were upstairs on the bed, lying down and your
clothes were being taken off, did you assist in taking off your
clothes?

A. No.

Q. Not at all?

*　　*　　*

Q. Then I believe you said you had some sport shirt?

A. Yes.

Q. Did that button or zip?

A. Buttoned.

Q. Did you help him on that?

A. I helped him.

Q. You did not know then what was going to happen?

A. No, I did not know exactly.

Q. What did you think was going to happen—just going to take a nap?

A. Yes.

Q. That is what you thought, and you were made more comfortable so that you could take a nap better?

A. Yes.

Q. And then you had on, I believe—in answer to Mr. Cochran's question I believe you used the word panties—you had some panties on?

A. Yes.

Q. How did they fasten, pull, or zip? I do not know how they do.

Mr. Cochran: Maybe they don't do that.

Mr. Giesler: Maybe they don't. I don't know. Do you remember how they were?

A. Just slip them on.

Q. You don't pull or zip?

A. No, they don't.

Mr. Giesler: Mr. Cochran knew more than I did.

Mr. Cochran: I just made a better guess, is all.

Q. by Mr. Giesler: Did they have elastic band or not?

A. Yes.

Q. Were they tight around your waist?

A. Yes.

Q. Did you help take them off?

A. Not that I recall.

Q. May you have had to help take them off?

A. I might have.

Q. Did you still not know what was going to happen?

A. Maybe he took my clothes off to go to bed. Don't you take your clothes off to go to bed?

Mr. Giesler: Maybe I do. That is what you thought you went up there for?

A. Yes.

Q. When did you come to the conclusion that something was going to happen?

A. When he went and locked the door.

Q. Your clothes were all off when he went to lock the door?

A. I believe they were.

Q. When he came back from locking the door, what happened?

A. So, I knew.

MR. GIESLER: I am not doing it to embarrass you.

A. As if you had not. I had an act of intercourse with him.

Q. Did he lay on the bed beside you?

A. Yes, he did.

Q. Did he immediately commence to have this act of intercourse with you?

A. Yes.

Q. He didn't talk to you about it first?

A. No, he did not.

Q. And then you knew what an act of sexual intercourse was at that time?

A. Yes.

Q. You had heard of that before?

A. Yes, I have.

Q. And when he lay down beside you and commenced to have the act of sexual intercourse, then, of course, you knew what he was trying to do?

A. Yes, I did, and I objected.

Q. What did you say?

A. I know I objected. I told him I wanted to go downstairs.

Q. You told him you wanted to go downstairs. Did you push him away?

A. No, I did not.

Q. Did you use your hands on him in any respect at all?

A. Not that I recall.

Q. Did you kick him?

A. No.

Q. Well, I would not know, I would like to know. Did you scratch him in any way?

A. No, I did not.

Q. What objection you made was merely an expression or statement from your mouth?

A. Yes.

Q. You don't know exactly what that was?

Errol Flynn

A. No.

Q. Except you would like to go downstairs?

A. Go downstairs.

Q. By that you knew he was trying to have an act of sexual intercourse with you?

A. Yes, I did.

Q. And from what I understood you to say, you did not want it to happen?

A. No, I did not.

Q. You did not have any desire to have an act of sexual intercourse with him?

A. No, I did not.

Q. Even if it would help you get a job?

A. No. Armand just told me to play up to him.

Q. By playing up to him, you thought you had played up far enough?

A. Yes.

Q. How had you played up to him at that time?

A. Just laughing and talking, and I drank with him.

Q. How many drinks?

A. One.

Q. And that was the extent of it, was it?

A. Yes.

Q. And as a matter of fact, Miss Hansen, you knew what you were going to do when you went up there, didn't you?

A. No, I did not.

*   *   *

Q. And before Flynn left [the house], I believe you testified, in answer to Mr. Cochran this morning, he kissed you?

A. Yes.

Q. Did he kiss you or you kiss him?

A. He kissed me.

Q. You did not kiss him?

A. I kissed him back, I mean just one smack.

Q. Just one of those quickies [*snapping his fingers*]?

MR. COCHRAN: I think that is objected to as calling for speculation.

MR. GIESLER: I will withdraw it.

Q. BY MR. GIESLER: It was not a lingering kiss, anyway?

A. That's right.

Peggy La Rue Satterlee's story, as related at the preliminary hearing, was to me even more preposterous than Miss Hansen's. She had gone aboard Flynn's yacht, the *Sirocco*, for a weekend cruise at midnight on Friday, August 1, 1941. Also aboard were Flynn, his friend Buster Wiles, another girl and a crew of three. Peter Stackpole, a photographer, joined them Sunday to take pictures of Mr. Flynn spear-fishing. According to Miss Satterlee, Flynn had had intercourse with her twice—the first time early Sunday morning after they returned from spending Saturday evening ashore.

The complete story was brought out on both direct and cross of Miss Satterlee. In my cross-examination, I asked Miss Satterlee what had happened after Mr. Flynn and his three guests returned to the *Sirocco* early Sunday morning.

Q. So what time did you get back on the boat?

A. Well, I remember they were closing things up around there. I guess it was two o'clock or after.

Q. When you got back on the boat did you go right to your room?

A. No, sir.

Q. Where did you go?

A. We had some milk or something before we went to bed.

*   *   *

Q. Anything in this milk?

A. No, sir.

Q. This was straight milk?

A. Yes, sir.

Q. And how much of that did you drink? Just a glass?

A. I don't remember if I finished it or not, but after that we went to bed.

Q. Then you went into your cabin?

A. Yes, sir.

Q. That was on Saturday night or Sunday morning?

Errol Flynn

A. Early Sunday morning.

Q. About two or three o'clock?

A. Yes, sir.

*   *   *

Q. Did you at that time wear a nightgown or pajamas?

A. No, I wore a slip—slept in my underskirt.

Q. You did not take any pajamas?

A. No.

Q. Or nightgown?

A. No.

Q. You were in the habit of sleeping in pajamas or a nightgown?

A. I was in the habit of sleeping in nothing.

*   *   *

Q. So you went down then—now we are getting back to Sunday morning for the moment—and we are going to bed?

A. Yes, sir.

Q. And when you went into your room you took off your blue denim?

A. Yes, sir.

Q. Took off your shoes?

A. Naturally. I mean, yes, sir.

Q. You did take them off, or didn't you?

A. Yes, sir.

Q. Took off your stockings? Or did you wear stockings?

A. I did not wear stockings. I think I brought some socks.

Q. You did not have any on, did not wear them?

A. I had pants on, so naturally some socks and other shoes.

Q. So you took your socks off too, and you wear those— What do you
call those things?

MR. COCHRAN: I haven't the slightest idea.

MR. GIESLER: Brassière?

A. Yes, sir.

Q. Did you take that off?

A. No, sir.

Q. You did not take that off?

111

A. I mean yes, sir.

Q. Which was it?

A. I took it off.

Q. Before you went to bed?

A. Yes, sir.

Q. And you put your slip on? Was it already on?

A. No, I took my slip off and took my brassière off, and then put the slip back on.

Q. Did your slip cover your brassière? Before you took it off, did it cover it?

A. Yes, sir.

Q. Then, after you took it off, your slip covered your bare skin where the brassière had been?

A. Yes, sir.

Q. And did you—I believe you testified, in answer to Mr. Cochran, you had on a pair of panties?

A. Yes, sir.

Q. Had you had those on under the denims?

A. Yes, sir.

Q. Had you taken those off, or leave them on?

A. I left them on.

Q. Did they pull on, zip, or what?

A. Elastic.

Q. Elastic. Were they silk or rayon or cotton?

A. I cannot remember.

Q. You don't remember?

A. No, sir.

Q. The slip was rayon?

A. I would not swear to it, but I believe it was.

Q. Did the slip have a sash around it, or anything?

A. No, sir.

Q. Rope to tie it up with?

A. No, sir.

Q. And the slip was loose, was it, or did it slip on?

A. I put it over my head.

Errol Flynn

Q. So you put that on and got in your bed. Did you put the light out?
A. After I got in bed, yes, sir.
Q. And were ready to go to sleep?
A. Yes, sir.
Q. And you heard a knock on the door?
A. Yes, sir.
Q. You had not gone to sleep yet?
A. No, sir.
Q. When you heard the knock on the door, did you hear somebody say something?
A. They did not wait long enough to say anything. They just came in.
Q. When they came in did they say anything?
A. I said something first.
Q. Something about it being kind of late, or something, or what?
A. No, sir, I noticed he walked in before he said anything. I said, "You should not be here," and he said, "I just want to talk to you," and I said, "You should not be here, because it is not nice to come in a lady's bedroom when she is in bed."

* * *

Q. He came over by the bed?
A. Yes, sir.
Q. And did you have the covers on?
A. Yes, sir.
Q. Was it cold that night?
A. I do not know.
Q. What?
A. Not particularly, no.
Q. There was a porthole open?
A. I cannot remember.
Q. Any other window in there besides the porthole window?
A. No, sir.
Q. What covers did you have on? Do you remember?
A. No, sir.
Q. Did you have a sheet?

113

A. I had a blanket.

Q. A blanket?

A. I mean also.

Q. A sheet and a blanket?

A. I think so.

Q. Did he sit on the side of the bed?

A. Well, he did not sit there.

Q. He stood there?

A. He stood in the doorway a while talking, and then he said to me, well . . .

Q. Go ahead and tell us what he said. I would like to have everything he said.

A. Well, he said to me he just wanted to talk to me, and I told you a while ago what I said, and he said, "Let me just get in bed with you and I will not bother you. I just want to talk to you." And so I said, "Why do you have to bother a nice girl?" And I don't remember what he said after that.

Q. You said?

A. Yes, sir.

Q. And did you say anything, did he say anything, about bothering you about what, or just about getting in bed?

A. That is right.

Q. Just about getting in bed?

A. That's right.

Q. How was he dressed then?

A. In pajamas.

Q. What color?

A. They had stripes in them.

Q. Shoes on, or did he have anything on his feet?

A. I did not notice his feet.

Q. Did he have a robe on then?

A. No, sir.

Q. Did the pajamas have a sash around them?

A. I don't remember.

Q. Were they buttoned in the shirt?

Errol Flynn

A. I don't remember.

Q. Were they stuffed inside the pajama pants or on the outside of the pants?

A. I am sorry, I cannot remember how his pajamas were.

❋   ❋   ❋

Q. Let's go back to the bed. He was over by the bed and said something, oh, "All I want to do is, if you would let me get in bed and talk to you," that is all? He wanted to get in bed and talk with you?

A. Yes, sir.

Q. Did you let him get in bed?

A. No, sir.

Q. Did he get in bed?

A. Yes, sir.

Q. Did he pull the covers down off you, or did he push them down?

A. He pulled them down.

Q. Up to that time had he said anything about sexual relations?

A. No, sir. I cannot remember what he said because I was too frightened.

MR. GIESLER: Move to strike the last portion as not responsive.

MR. COCHRAN: I think it certainly is responsive.

MR. GIESLER: It is a conclusion, and not responsive.

THE COURT: Motion granted.

Q. BY MR. GIESLER: Did he say anything to you about sex before he got into bed?

A. No, he just said I asked for it so I would get it.

Q. That is, after he had asked to get in bed and you said no, it wasn't nice for him to come in the room where a lady is in bed?

A. Yes, sir.

Q. And then he said, "Well, I won't be nice to you," or did he say that?

A. That is when he said, "I wanted to be nice to you, but you asked for it so you will get it."

Q. When he said that, what did he do?

A. Well, he just walked over to the bed, pulled down the covers and pulled up my slip and pulled down my pants.

Q. Was the light on?

115

A. I don't remember.

Q. Pulled up your slip?

A. Yes, sir.

Q. Did he tear it?

A. No, sir.

Q. He pulled down your pants?

A. Yes, sir.

Q. Did he tear them?

A. No, sir.

Q. How far down did he pull your pants?

A. I cannot remember.

Q. How far up did he pull your slip?

A. Up to my shoulders.

Q. Above your bosom, or below?

A. Above.

Q. Above your bosom?

A. Yes, sir.

Q. And as far as the pants are concerned, you do not know how far down?

A. No, sir.

Q. They were not torn?

A. No, sir.

Q. And after he did that, what did he do? You tell us what he did. After he pulled up your slip and pulled down your pants, what did he do?

A. As I say, he completed an act of sexual intercourse.

Q. Did he say anything at that time before the act of intercourse?

A. Not that I recall.

＊　　　＊　　　＊

Q. Did you fight him then?

A. Not very much, no, sir.

Q. Did you fight at all?

A. No, sir, I cried.

Q. You just cried?

A. Yes, sir.

Errol Flynn

Q. Did you kick him in the nose?

A. Well, I might have slapped him in the nose.

Q. Did you slap him in the nose?

A. I believe so, yes, sir.

Q. All right, then. You did fight to that extent?

A. Yes, sir.

Q. Did you scratch him?

A. No, sir.

Q. Did you try to scratch him?

A. No, sir.

Q. Did you scream out?

A. No, sir.

Q. Do you recall kicking him at all?

A. I did not kick, sir.

＊　　＊　　＊

Q. What is the first thing you did after he completed the act?

A. I got up.

Q. Where did you go?

A. I did not go anywhere, I was just standing.

Q. What did you do?

A. I pulled my pants up, and my underskirt down.

Q. Where were your pants then, down at the knees?

A. They could have been down to my ankles, I do not remember.

Q. They were simply between your thighs and ankles?

A. No, sir, they might—could have been—might have been off.

Q. Were they off?

A. I cannot remember.

Q. What is your present recollection?

A. I cannot remember. They could have been off or on.

Q. They may have been on and they may have been off?

A. Yes, sir.

Q. And did you— What is the next thing you did after you put on your pants?

A. I just stood there, and by that time he come back.

Q. Had he gone out?

A. Yes, sir.

Q. As soon as he completed the act, did he leave?

A. Yes, sir.

Q. Left the room?

A. Yes, sir.

Q. And then you got up immediately, did you?

A. Yes, sir.

Q. Put on your panties?

A. Yes, sir.

Q. And what else did you do before he came back?

A. Just pulled my slip down, and he came back with the robe.

Q. Did you go out? I believe you went out after he brought you the robe?

A. Yes, sir.

Q. And you went on deck?

A. Yes, sir.

Q. And had a glass of milk?

A. Yes, sir.

Q. Was there any rum in that milk?

A. No, sir.

Q. You stayed on deck until almost morning?

A. Yes, sir.

Q. What time was it you went back down?

A. I do not know.

Q. He went down and left you on deck?

A. Yes, sir.

Q. You did not go down until later?

A. Yes, sir.

Q. Anyone else up there with you?

A. No, sir.

Q. Did you see any member of the crew up there?

A. No, sir.

Q. Any time you were up there?

A. Not that I can remember, no, sir.

Q. After you went back down, what did you do?

Errol Flynn

A. I went back to bed.
Q. Went to sleep then?
A. I might have dozed off.
Q. What time did you get up?
A. I don't remember.

* * *

Q. BY MR. GIESLER: Miss Satterlee, we are at Sunday now, the day-
time.
A. Yes, sir.
Q. And did you have breakfast on the boat that morning?
A. Yes, sir.
Q. Who had breakfast with you, do you recall?
A. The girl and Mr. Flynn, I think. Mr. Wiles wasn't around too much.
Q. Was Mr. Stackpole there at the time you had breakfast?
A. Yes, he was, yes, but I don't think he ate breakfast with us.
Q. Where did you have breakfast?
A. On top of the . . .
Q. On the deck?
A. Yes, sir.
Q. How were the three of you dressed?
A. Not three of them.
Q. How were the three of you dressed? You said you and the girl and
Mr. Flynn?
A. I believe I put my bathing suit on that morning.
Q. You had your bathing suit on for breakfast?
A. I believe so.
Q. How was the girl dressed?
A. I think she had a bathing suit on. I am not sure.

* * *

Q. You said earlier in your testimony you could have—a person could
swim to shore from the location of where the boat was. When you
went up on deck that night or morning you did not try to get off the
boat, did you?

119

A. No, sir.

Q. You did not scream out from the top of the boat to the girls' school or anyone on shore, did you?

A. No, sir.

Q. Did you tell the girl on the boat there with you folks anything about it?

A. No, sir.

Q. Did you tell Mr. Wiles when he got up?

A. No, sir.

Q. Did you go to the captain of the boat or the crew?

A. No, sir.

Q. Did you scream out so the crew or the captain could hear you?

A. No, sir.

Q. And on the same Sunday afternoon Flynn had the intercourse with you against your consent, and after you tried to resist him, you had your pictures taken with him?

A. Yes, sir.

Q. And you had your pictures taken with him and were right close to him there?

A. Yes, sir.

Q. You had your pictures taken in various positions around the boat?

A. Yes, sir.

Q. And decided to stay on board and come back to Los Angeles on this same boat?

A. Yes, sir.

Q. Stay all night again?

A. Not all night again.

Q. You intended to come back to Los Angeles on the same boat?

A. Yes, sir.

❊　　❊　　❊

Q. When you got through [having intercourse], why didn't you go up on deck and jump off?

Mr. Cochran: That certainly is argumentative.

Mr. Giesler: Withdraw the question.

Errol Flynn

Q. BY MR. GIESLER: When you did get up on deck you did not get off and swim, did you?
A. I cannot swim very well.
Q. You did not scream out, did you?
A. There was no one around. Everybody was asleep.
Q. But you did not scream?
A. No, sir, because I did not want to embarrass myself along with everybody I did not know.
Q. You did not want to embarrass yourself with the crew, anyway?
MR. COCHRAN: Just a minute. Object to that as argumentative. The form of that question is argumentative.
THE COURT: It may be removed from that conduct, but it was suggested by the previous answer. I think under the circumstances it should be overruled.
Q. BY MR. GIESLER: You did not want to embarrass yourself with the crew, did you?
A. When it was happening I did not care whether I screamed or not, but after it was over I felt very ashamed.

*   *   *

Q. I am talking about when he is raping you. Did you think then about being embarrassed?
A. In a way, yes.
Q. You did not feel embarrassed in doing such a thing? You did not want to protect your honor, did you?
MR. COCHRAN: That is objected to as argumentative.
MR. GIESLER: To which I think the district attorney would not try to interpose any objection to questions of that kind.
MR. COCHRAN: I am not objecting to any questions propounded to the witness in a legal manner, nor will I do so, but I submit the form of that question is indefinite.
THE COURT: Objection overruled.
[Question read by the reporter.]
MR. COCHRAN: There is an objection to that question, in the form of the question, as being definitely argumentative.

THE COURT: I ruled once, before this question was restated, and I will rule again: Overruled.

Q. BY MR. GIESLER: Did you, Miss Satterlee?

A. After that I did not count my honor, because I had no honor anyway after he was finished.

MR. GIESLER: Yes, I am talking now about while he was trying to rape you.

A. That is what I mean.

Q. Did you, during the time he was trying to rape you, as you have told us today—did you at any time feel embarrassed to the extent you did not want to call out to protect that honor?

A. Yes, sir.

❀　　❀　　❀

MR. GIESLER: The three reasons why you did not scream out: the first is because it might embarrass you, the second because of the crew and third because they were friends of his. Those reasons did not prevent you from resisting him and fighting him to the very bitter end, as far as you were concerned, did they?

A. No, sir.

Q. Had you tried fighting him to the best of your ability?

A. Yes, sir.

Peggy Satterlee's story became even more unconvincing as the cruise progressed. After spending Sunday with Flynn and his guests posing for photographs, watching aquaplane races and spearfishing, Miss Satterlee permitted herself to be lured below by Flynn to see what the moon looked like viewed through a porthole. According to her testimony, she was violated again. This is how she told it on cross-examination:

Q. BY MR. GIESLER: Now, then, we are coming toward home, after dinner Sunday night. How far out were we from shore when you spoke about the moon?

A. It wasn't too far, because—

Q. I do not know how far too far was, but how far out were you, in your judgment?

A. Well, after we got up it was about thirty minutes before we came to shore, that is before we went down.

Q. About thirty minutes?

A. Yes, sir.

Q. And you were on deck, were you?

A. When I was talking about the moon?

Q. Yes.

A. Yes, sir.

Q. Whom were you talking with?

A. Mr. Flynn.

Q. Who else was up there?

A. I don't remember.

Q. Was anyone else up there?

A. There probably was.

Q. You were the one that volunteered about the moon, were you?

A. Yes, sir.

Q. Was the moon back of you or in front of you?

A. Naturally, I was facing it.

Q. I appreciate that, but where was it? Going ahead or back of the boat?

A. I don't remember.

Q. Was it a full moon?

A. I don't remember that either.

Q. You do not know whether it was full or not?

A. No, sir.

Q. And you referred to the moon, and he said it looked better from the porthole, did he?

A. Yes, sir.

Q. Did he carry you downstairs?

A. No, sir.

Q. Did he pull you downstairs?

A. No, sir.

Q. Did he then take hold of your arm and lead you downstairs?

A. He might have taken hold of my arm on the way down the steps, but I do not remember that he pulled me.

Q. Did he tell you where he was going to take you?

A. No, sir.

Q. Do you know where the portholes were down there?

A. Yes, sir, he went in first.

Q. And you went in?

A. Into Mr. Wiles's room.

Q. When you went around that boat, you had seen that same cabin?

A. Yes.

Q. Did you follow him in?

A. Yes.

Q. Why?

A. Because I wanted to see the moon through the porthole.

Q. So, then you wanted to see the moon through the porthole?

A. Yes, sir.

* * *

Q. So you followed him in the room and looked at the moon?

A. Yes, sir.

Q. Did you look through the porthole?

A. Yes, sir.

Q. Which side was it?

A. The right side.

Q. The right side as you came toward San Pedro?

A. As they came toward the dock.

Q. On the right side?

A. Yes, sir.

Q. Could you see the moon?

A. Yes, sir.

Q. Where was the moon? Was it up above the boat, or where was it?

A. I don't know. Naturally I guess it was that way, because I saw it.

Q. Did you see it clearly?

A. I did not see much. I did not have time to look at it too long.

Q. Did it seem to be on the water?

A. I do not remember that either.

Q. Did you see the silvery surface?

A. I don't remember.

Q. As you looked through the porthole what happened?

A. Mr. Flynn sat on the bed for a minute, and then he come up and said since he had . . . He did not say it in exactly these words, but said since he had possession of me once, naturally why wouldn't I let him do it this time.

Q. Is that the way he approached you?

A. Yes, sir.

Q. He just said, "Seeing as I had possession of you once—"

THE WITNESS [interrupting]: He didn't say it in those words.

MR. GIESLER: I mean in effect he said he could not see why he could not do it again, in effect?

A. Yes, sir.

Q. That was his approach?

A. Yes, sir.

Q. Didn't he say anything about having sexual intercourse? Did he mention sexual intercourse?

A. No, sir.

Q. Did he use any vulgar term that referred to it?

A. No, sir.

Q. He just referred to it as possession, is that it?

A. He did not say those exact words. I don't remember what he said.

Q. What did you say?

A. Naturally I started to go immediately, to leave.

Q. You started to leave?

A. Yes, sir.

Q. Was the door open?

A. I don't remember.

Q. When he went in the cabin ahead of you, did you say, "Put the light on?"

A. I believe the light was on already.

Q. And you came in following him. And when you started to go, what did he do?

A. He pushed me on the bed.

❋   ❋   ❋

Q. What did you say when he pushed you on the bed?

A. I cannot remember.

Q. Did you say something?

A. Naturally I must have said, "Let me go," and when I tried to get up a few times—

Q. This time you were mad?

A. Yes, sir.

Q. Already mad, were you?

A. Yes, sir.

Q. Do you get pretty mad?

A. Yes, sir.

Q. And when you got mad you fought, didn't you?

A. Yes, sir.

Q. And you fought pretty hard, didn't you?

A. Yes, sir.

Q. How was he dressed?

A. I cannot remember. He had on slacks and a jacket of some kind.

Q. Did he have shoes on?

A. I don't remember.

Q. Stockings?

A. I don't remember.

Q. Did he take off his clothes?

A. Yes, sir.

Q. Where did he take off his clothes?

A. After he pushed me down he would take off something, and then I would try to get up and he would push me down again.

Q. He took off his clothes before any of yours were off?

A. I think he just took his pants off.

Q. Before he touched you?

A. Yes, sir.

Q. And when he did that you did not jump up and try to run out the door?

A. I told you he was pushing me down every time I got up, and the door was closed then.

Q. Who closed it?

A. Mr. Flynn.

Q. When did he close it?

A. After we looked through the porthole.

Q. And you started to leave, you said, when he mentioned about having possession of you, and why should you object?

A. I started to. I was standing away back in the front, and as I got up he pushed me down.

Q. How high was that bed above the floor?

A. I do not know. It is off the ground. My feet would not still touch the floor.

Q. Would you say it is about the same height as the bunk in the other room?

A. No, sir, I believe it is a little higher.

Q. Well, how much higher?

A. I would not say. I don't know.

Q. What did you do, just step from the floor into the bunk?

A. You cannot just step, you kind of have to jump.

Q. You have to jump?

A. Not jump, you just kind of . . .

Q. What do you mean?

A. Haven't you ever jumped up on something that is high and put your hands back and scoot up like that?

Q. Is that the way you got up?

A. Yes, sir, as well as I remember.

Q. When did you jump up?

A. When he said, "Look at the moon," and I did.

Q. You were on the bed looking at the moon?

A. Yes, sir.

Q. And I mean when he asked you this other thing that you did not think was right, you started for the door?

A. I got off the bed.

Q. More than one time?

A. Maybe one time, but he kept pushing me back.

Q. When you got off that one time, how did you get back up?

A. He pushed me.

The Jerry Giesler Story

Q. You got back up on the bed?
A. Yes, sir.
Q. From the floor?
A. Yes, sir.
Q. You did not jump up yourself?
A. No, sir.
Q. He did not lift you up?
A. No, sir.

✢   ✢   ✢

Q. What did he do about your clothes? You said something about your clothes?
A. He did.
Q. What did he do?
A. He pulled my pants down.
Q. What about the belt? Did he loosen the belt?
A. It was loose—it would get loose by itself—and I suppose he loosened it up the rest of the way because he got them down and I did not do it.
Q. While he was trying to get your pants down did you fight him?
A. Yes, sir.
Q. Did you kick him?
A. Yes, sir.
Q. Under the eye, or was the swelling above it, please?
A. I do not know.
Q. Are you sure that you kicked him at all?
A. No, sir.
Q. How far did he pull these pants down?
A. I don't remember, but they would not come clear off.
Q. You don't think he took them off?
A. No, sir.
Q. Did he unbutton them?
A. No, they were too big. He did not have to unbutton them.
Q. What about your own panties?
A. He pulled them down.
Q. How far?

128

Errol Flynn

A. I don't remember.

Q. He didn't take them clear off, did he?

A. I don't think so.

Q. And with reference to your shirt, what did he do?

A. He didn't bother my shirt.

Q. But you loosened it part of the way yourself?

A. Yes, sir.

Q. And the sweater, if you had a sweater on?

A. Yes, I had a sweater. Whatever I had under it, whether it was a shirt or not, I don't remember.

Q. So he did not bother the jacket or the shirt?

A. No, sir.

Q. At that time did he have his trousers clear off?

A. I think so, yes.

Q. And did he have his shoes off?

A. I don't remember.

Q. What about your shoes?

A. I had mine on.

       ✻   ✻   ✻

Q. Did you scratch him?

A. Not that I know of.

Q. Did you try to?

A. I don't remember what I did.

Q. Why didn't you scream? You were mad then, weren't you?

A. Yes.

Q. Why didn't you scream?

A. I was too interested in fighting then.

Q. The reason you did not scream this time was you were too interested in fighting, is that it?

A. Yes.

Q. When you got through fighting did you have any bruises on you?

A. Not that I remember.

Q. Did he fight back?

A. He pushed me back, but he did not hit me or anything.

Q. Did he hold his hand to your mouth?

A. He held his hand here, and I was sore there.

Q. On your left breast?

A. No, on my bosom.

Q. Did he hold his hand over your mouth?

A. No, sir.

Q. He had one hand on your bosom, where was his other hand?

A. His whole arm was like that.

Q. Where was the other arm?

A. I don't remember.

Q. Where was the other arm?

A. I do not know.

Q. Did he complete the act with you?

A. Yes, sir.

Q. Did he— You testified yesterday to Mr. Cochran you knew what it meant for a man's privates to be inserted in a woman's privates?

A. Yes, sir.

Q. Did he direct his privates into you?

A. Yes, sir.

Q. How did he do it, do you know?

A. No, sir.

Q. Did you observe how he did it?

A. No, sir.

Q. Were you on your side all the time?

A. Yes, sir.

Q. Were you trying to turn around on the bed?

A. Yes, sir.

Q. You were not kicking your feet around all the time?

A. Yes, sir.

Q. Were you kicking around all the time?

A. Yes.

Q. Fighting to the best of your ability, is that it?

A. Yes, sir.

Q. And yet he completed the act?

A. I beg your pardon. May I finish?

MR. GIESLER: I was through with that question. Go ahead and tell us.

A. After I fought for a long time, he said, "If you relax I won't hurt you," and then I did.

Q. Did you consent?

A. I did not, but he—

Q. He had completed the act; then he let you alone, didn't he?

A. Yes, sir.

Q. The act was completed when he left you alone, according to your testimony?

A. Yes, sir.

Q. What did you do when he completed the act—what did he do?

A. He got up and dressed and went out.

Q. Did you see him dressed?

A. No, sir, because I was getting up.

❀   ❀   ❀

Q. Did you become pregnant?

A. No, sir.

Q. You were not pregnant after either one of these acts?

A. No, sir.

❀   ❀   ❀

Q. When you got upstairs on deck, did you go beside Mr. Flynn and talk to him?

A. I kept away from him for a while, and then talked to him a while afterwards.

Q. You did talk to him a while?

A. I sat on a bench and he talked to me.

Q. What did you talk to him about?

A. I cannot remember.

Q. Anything said about the act?

A. I don't remember.

One surprise at the preliminary hearing was the revelation that my client had a system of verbal shorthand, consisting of initials strung together. Two of Flynn's abbreviations were J.B. and S.Q.Q. During my cross-examination of Miss Satterlee concerning the alleged ravishments by Flynn I noted that in quoting portions of Flynn's conversation she used those initials.

When I asked her why she hadn't mentioned them in her direct testimony she said that she hadn't thought them significant until a policewoman had asked her the night before if Flynn knew how old she was when she boarded his yacht. Miss Satterlee said she had told the policewoman that she hadn't given it much thought, but she assumed Mr. Flynn did because he called her J.B.

"Did you know what that meant when he said J.B.?" I asked.

"It means Jail Bait," Miss Satterlee told me.

"What did you understand it to mean?" I asked.

"That if a man was having an affair with a girl under such an age and attacked her, then that would be it," she replied.

"Did Mr. Flynn say what S.Q.Q. meant?" I persisted.

She said that Mr. Flynn had told her that those initials meant San Quentin Quail. She remarked that if you thought of them in conjunction with J.B., she supposed S.Q.Q. meant that if a man was intimate with a girl who was under a certain age he would end up in San Quentin.

I found the next two sentences in my exchange with Miss Satterlee fascinating. "And you felt, from what Mr. Flynn said to you, that if you had an affair with him, a sexual affair with him, he might go to San Quentin?" I asked.

"Yes, sir, but I did not think of it that way," she said.

When Betty Hansen and Peggy LaRue Satterlee were through testifying at the preliminary hearing, Judge Walters held Flynn for trial on three counts of statutory rape—two involving Miss Satterlee and one involving Miss Hansen.

The popular concept of a successful criminal lawyer is that he gets his results by a combination of hocus-pocus and legerdemain. The truth is that a dull word, thoroughness, is responsible for the noteworthy victories won in any court. (Not that there was anything outwardly dull about the Flynn trial.) Consequently the defense was well prepared when Errol Flynn's case was called for trial early in January 1943 before Judge Leslie E. Still and a jury in Los Angeles County Superior Court.

I managed to get nine women on the jury, believing that they would be more kindly disposed than men toward the boyishly hand-some screen actor.

Betty Hansen was the first of the two complaining witnesses to take the stand for the people. Her direct testimony was substantially the same as that she had given at the preliminary hearing. If any-thing, her testimony on cross-examination was a little more gamey.

Q. BY MR. GIESLER: Miss Hansen, the act itself lasted about how long, please?
A. About fifty minutes.
Q. About fifty minutes?
A. Yes, that is right.
Q. And during the entire time he was on top of you?
A. That is right.
Q. Did it pain you?
A. Yes, it did.
Q. You did not scream?
A. I did not.
Q. You did not cry at that time?
A. I did not.
Q. Did it hurt you very much?
A. No.
Q. Did you take part in the performance of the act yourself?
A. Explain that some to me, please.
Q. I am asking you if you took part in the performance of the act your-self. Did you respond to him in his performing the act with you?
A. I did.

❊   ❊   ❊

Q. During the time he was having the act with you, did he say anything to you?
A. Yes, he did.
Q. What did he say? Do you remember?

A. I do. He said I have a nice pair of breasts.

Q. Anything else?

A. Yes. And I had a nice fanny.

Q. Anything else?

A. Not that I recall.

Prior to her alleged affair with Flynn, Miss Hansen had been apprehended engaging in some rather unusual sexual practices and had so admitted to the grand jury. She had not been prosecuted for the crime, although the young man who had been involved was. After something of a hassle, I was able to get this fact before the jury as tending to show her motive and state of mind in testifying against Flynn. We believed she was being overly co-operative with the district attorney's office in the hope of avoiding prosecution herself.

With this testimony before the jury, it seemed almost certain that they would have substantial doubts about Miss Hansen's credibility as a witness against Flynn. I saw no reason to prolong the cross-examination.

Miss Satterlee too testified for the people much as she had at the preliminary hearing. Her testimony continued to be that Mr. Flynn had used force in twice criminally attacking her aboard his yacht, the *Sirocco*. A point of law I had established in the Alexander Pantages case put us on solid ground in exploring into her past moral conduct on cross-examination. The California Supreme Court had decided that where the rape is alleged to have been committed by force, even though the girl is under eighteen, evidence of her prior acts of unchastity is admissible for the purpose of showing the nonprobability of resistance on her part and—under certain circumstances—the probability that the crime was not committed at all.

I'd like to go into this again, for it is most important. Let's assume that a girl under eighteen is testifying about improper relations forced upon her by a man, and that during her testimony she glibly describes lewd conduct upon the attacker's part. The defense may well argue, "This girl couldn't possibly testify like this unless

134

her experience is based upon a wider experience than the single occasion about which she is testifying."

It follows that if it can be brought out in cross-examination that
she has had previous sexual adventures, a strong jury argument
can be made that her testimony is unworthy of belief and that the
rape never occurred.

The cross-examination also brought out that Miss Satterlee, her
mother and her sister were accustomed to hitch-hiking across the
country, from California to Texas and from California to St. Louis.
The prosecution objected when I started on this line, but the court
ruled that the moral character and the moral fiber of her parents,
as well as of the complaining witness, should be presented to the
jury in this type of case.

While preparing a major case I make sure that all of my phones
are open to take calls at all times. My secretaries and my switch-
board operators have instructions to put through all calls for me,
nutty or sensible—even anonymous—while a noteworthy trial is in
progress. My operators never ask, "Who's calling?" The chances are
such a question won't be answered, or, if it is, that it won't be
answered truthfully. This way I gathered some information about
the Errol Flynn case which helped my defense enormously. A
strange voice told me over the phone that if I would go to a certain
funeral parlor and ask a certain attendant certain questions, I
would find out things which would interest me. The voice was right.

At that funeral parlor I dug up some gruesome and damning
knowledge. Peggy Satterlee had visited the place with a Canadian
air-pilot boy friend, who worked as a technical advisor on Hollywood productions involving military flying. She had gone with him
into the room where the cadavers were laid out on slabs and had
frolicked about, pulling sheets from the naked bodies and peer-
ing at them.

It was important for me to get this information into the court
records, but I wasn't sure I'd get the opportunity. The trouble was
I couldn't question the pilot unless the prosecution placed him on
the stand of its own accord as a prosecution witness, thus making it

possible for me to cross-examine him. In that way I could also show by implication what the probable relations had been between the flier and Miss Satterlee, for a mutual inspection of dead naked bodies didn't fall into the classification of playing pat-a-cake.

I injected the name of the forty-two-year-old Canadian flier, Owen Cathcart-Jones, into the cross-examination of Miss Satterlee at every opportunity. I wanted to make it appear that there was a mysterious connection between the girl and the flier, and I hoped that the D. A. would put him on the stand in an attempt to blow away the smog I had thrown up about Miss Satterlee's association with him.

I brought out that Miss Satterlee had taken trips with Mr. Cathcart-Jones; that he had bought her some slacks on one trip and perhaps other wearing apparel at other times; and that Miss Satterlee and her sister lived in his apartment during his absence in July and August 1941. I asked Miss Satterlee about pet names given her by Mr. Jones:

Q. Now, pardon me, Miss Satterlee, for asking you, but did Mr. Jones have any particular pet name that he knew you by—that he applied to you?

A. Oh, he had quite a few of them.

Q. Quite a few?

A. Yes, sir.

MR. COCHRAN: Pardon me. I am sorry. I was talking to counsel.

[*Record read.*]

MR. COCHRAN: That was Mr. Jones, you say?

MR. GIESLER: Mr. Jones.

MR. COCHRAN: That is objected to as immaterial—what nicknames Mr. Jones may have used.

THE COURT: Objection will be overruled.

Q. BY MR. GIESLER: What was the particular one? Do you remember, Miss Satterlee?

A. Rather silly names, but Scrumpet, Bitchy Pie, and so forth.

MR. GIESLER: May that be read, your honor? The jurors did not hear.

Error lynn

THE COURT: All right. Will you read the answer?
[*Answer read.*]
Q. BY MR. GIESLER: Scrumpet, Bitchy Pie, and so forth?
A. Scrumpet.
Q. Did you say Scrumpet or Strumpet?
A. Scrumpet or something. It is an English name for crumpet or . . .
Q. Well?
A. I know it was something.
Q. You know it sounded something like Scrumpet?
A. Yes, sir.
THE COURT: I understood her to say Strumpet.
MR. COCHRAN: No, it is a little cake, I think.

To my almost gasping relief, just before the prosecution closed its case Deputy District Attorney Cochran called the Canadian flier to the witness stand to prove that there had been nothing improper between him and Miss Satterlee. He didn't know it, but he had handed me my opportunity on a golden platter.

Mr. Cochran first questioned Captain Cathcart-Jones on direct examination, about his pet names for Miss Satterlee among other things:

Q. BY MR. COCHRAN: Did you ever call Miss Peggy Satterlee any pet names, as we might say it?
A. Well, I called her a kind of an English idea of what a ragamuffin is, which is Scruppet.
Q. How do you spell it? You know we have had some considerable controversy over this thing.
A. [*spelling*] S-c-r-u-p-p-e-t.

My cross-examination followed:

Q. And shortly after you got back Peggy visited you, didn't she?
A. After I got back from Canada?
Q. Yes.

37

A. No, I went up to Santa Barbara to visit her.

Q. But after you had been back—when you came back to Los Angeles —she came down to visit you, isn't that correct?

A. Well, she came to Los Angeles.

Q. She visited you here, didn't she, down here?

A. Yes, she visited me here. Yes.

Q. And that was in the month of August?

A. Yes.

Q. And you were still living at the Alto Nido Apartments?

A. Yes.

Q. And she visited you at the Alto Nido Apartments?

A. Yes.

Q. And she had visited you at the Alto Nido Apartments before you went to Canada, had she not?

A. Oh, yes.

Q. She had visited you up there alone at times, hadn't she?

A. Yes.

Q. And she visited you while—just after you came back from Canada, didn't she?

A. Oh, yes.

Q. And she visited you quite frequently up there alone, didn't she?

A. Oh, yes.

Q. Both before and after you went to Canada?

A. Oh, yes.

Q. And she visited you up there alone in the evening sometimes, did she not?

A. Oh, yes.

         *   *   *

Q. Didn't you call Peggy Bitchy Pie?

A. No.

Q. You never did?

A. No.

Q. Did you ever call her bitch?

A. No.

Q. You are sure of that?

Errol Flynn

A. No. Absolutely.

Q. You are sure that you never called her Bitchy Pie?

A. Absolutely.

Q. As a matter of fact, you used to call her Grummet?

A. No.

Q. Do you know what that means?

A. It is a rope that you throw on a quoit.

Q. It is a rope that you throw on a what? Well, maybe we better—

THE COURT: Well, have him explain it, have him explain so that we can understand what he means.

MR. GIESLER: Yes.

A. The English, I think, of "grummet" is a piece of vertical rope which you throw along the deck of a ship.

Q. BY MR. GIESLER: And doesn't it have any other English expression?

A. Not that I know of.

Q. Now, you have gone other places with Peggy other than the Coleman ranch and to Arrowhead, have you not?

A. Oh, yes, I have been all over places with her.

* * *

Q. Never alone?

A. No.

Q. Who was with you there?

A. Her sister June.

* * *

Q. Well, you also were with her down to a mortuary down here in Los Angeles, were you not?

A. Yes.

Q. And she was kind of playing hide-and-seek around the corpses, wasn't she? Do you remember that night?

A. Yes.

Q. Do you remember she showed you—opened it up and showed you— the body of an elderly lady?

A. Yes.

Q. And pulled the sheet down in the mortuary on a Filipino who had been crippled across his center?

A. Yes, I remember that.

Q. And then went back to where they inject the veins of corpses and there opened and looked down at an elderly man lying there, and her head was pushed down against the man's face. Do you remember that?

A. Yes, I remember that.

THE COURT: Keep them quiet out there, Mr. Bailiff.

The witness was obviously shaken by my line of questioning, which included his admission that his young companion had lifted the sheets which covered the dead and had peered under them. During this part of the testimony the jury's faces were a study, especially those of the women jurors. I saw them wince and I knew I had them. It was plain to everyone in the courtroom that the jury had made up its mind about the quality of the "innocence" Miss Satterlee might have had while studying the moon through a porthole in Flynn's yacht.

When Miss Satterlee flung her charges at Flynn, she had claimed that one of the two affairs took place under the moon-watching circumstances already described. Apparently it had never occurred to her to wonder why the moon couldn't just as easily have been seen from the deck. Obediently she had scampered below to scan the heavens.

It was important for the prosecution to prove that there had been a moon that night and that it could have been seen. If those two things weren't true, the reason Miss Satterlee gave for going below would seem even less believable. In proof of these matters, the prosecution summoned to the stand a professor of astronomy, who successfully established that the moon had actually been out that night and that it had not been obscured by clouds. It did not require much intelligence on my part to foresee his testimony and to realize that it must be coped with, and I was prepared.

A reporter present wrote that "a sense of hushed expectancy pervaded the courtroom when the counselor for the defense rose from his seat, for The Great Mouthpiece was in a tough spot." I hate to spoil the effect of that purple prose, but I was not in a tough spot. As a part of my preparation for Mr. Flynn's defense I had delved into such heavenly matters as the position of the moon in relation to the yacht when Miss Satterlee said she had been rudely surprised while gazing at it. The tide and the way the vessel swung at its anchor had everything to do with whether she could have seen the moon from the porthole in that particular cabin at that particular moment.

I recalled the government meteorologist for questioning. "I will now draw you a map of the heavens," I told him.

I walked to a blackboard I had brought into the courtroom, picked up a piece of chalk and began to sketch the position of the celestial bodies as they appeared on the night when Miss Satterlee said she had been polluted.

"This," I said, as I chalked in a star, "is Sirius."

A wryly cynical newspaperman who was covering the trial quoted one woman juror as whispering to another, "It certainly is. Too many people take these things too lightly."

Engaging the astronomy professor in a discussion, I said I was very much interested in establishing the position of the moon in the skies that night in relation to the *Sirocco*'s portholes. I chalked in a few more celestial bodies. Then I summoned a harbormaster and two sea captains to the stand. My questions and their answers demonstrated that in view of the position of the moon and the way in which the yacht had been anchored on the night in question, Miss Satterlee couldn't have seen the moon when she said Flynn was sullying her good name. For one thing, the moon was on the other side of the boat. If Miss Satterlee had obtained a glimpse of the moon while "under a flank attack" (as one member of the press put it), she must have been able to see through steel bulkheads.

The answers Mr. Flynn gave on cross-examination by the prosecution were enough to make any sane man wonder if he and Miss Satterlee were talking about the same voyage on the same boat, or even whether it had traversed the same body of water.

Mr. Flynn was asked what he and Miss Satterlee had discussed while on shore at a night spot having some refreshments before repairing to the *Sirocco*. Flynn answered, "Well, I would say trivialities. I do not know anything specific I discussed with her."

Q. You did not have interest in exploring the girl's mind or finding out what she was interested in or anything while you were sitting there for four hours?

A. Well, I cannot remember what I spoke to her about.

Q. In other words, you were not interested in her?

A. No, not inordinately, no.

         ✿   ✿   ✿

Deputy District Attorney Cochran then questioned Flynn about events back aboard the *Sirocco*:

Q. Well, the girl has said here that she had some milk with rum in it. Do you recall that?

A. I recall her saying it.

Q. You do recall her saying it?

A. Yes.

Q. But does that refresh your recollection in respect—in any respect whatsoever?

A. No, it just strikes me as a very peculiar thing to drink.

         ✿   ✿   ✿

Q. Did you say good night to the young ladies?

A. Yes.

Q. And you kissed her good night, didn't you?

A. No.

Q. Lightly, as she said?

A. I neither kissed her lightly nor heavily.

Q. You did not put your arm around her, either lightly or heavily, either?

A. No.

Q. At any time while you were on this trip?

A. Yes.

Q. You mean when you assisted her from the paint locker near the
   harbor entrance, is that it?

A. Yes.

Q. But not at any other time?

A. No.

Q. You never called her any endearing terms?

A. No.

Q. Did she go immediately below into her cabin after you came back
   from the Hut?

A. It is my recollection that the two young ladies went immediately below.

Mr. Flynn was also cross-examined concerning his farewell to
Miss Satterlee following what—according to her, at least—had been
a fairly active weekend:

Q. It is your testimony that when you got to the dock and she went
   home she said that she had a wonderful time?

A. She said that she had had a wonderful time and that it had been like
   a dream.

Q. And she left you at what time?

A. She left very shortly after the boat docked.

Q. Was she crying when she left the boat?

A. No.

Q. She seemed to be all right, did she?

A. She seemed to be perfectly all right.

Q. Didn't give any evidence of emotion whatsoever?

A. No, except that she seemed to be very grateful for having had a very
   nice time.

Q. Very grateful to you?

A. Yes.

Mr. Flynn's version of the Bel Air party, which was brought out
on direct examination, was also poles apart from Miss Hansen's. In
answer to my questions, he testified that he had not requested
anyone to bring Miss Hansen or any other girl to the party, and that

he had no knowledge that Miss Hansen or any other young lady was going to be there. My questioning continued:

Q. Before your departure, at any time that evening after dinner were you upstairs in that house?

A. No, I was not.

Q. Did you say to Betty Hansen after dinner down on the porch, "I am going to take you up and lay you down?"

A. No, I did not.

Q. Did you take her upstairs?

A. No.

＊　　＊　　＊

Q. At any time that night did you see Miss Hansen upstairs?

A. No.

Q. Did you go into the room and undress her?

A. No.

Q. And thereafter did you lock the door?

A. No.

Q. And thereafter did you get into bed with her and have and perform an act of sexual intercourse?

A. No, I did not.

Q. Thereafter did you go into the bathroom with her?

A. I did not.

Q. Do you use hair oil?

A. Very little.

Q. Do you use it at all?

A. I try to avoid it. I do not think I use it. No, I am not sure—sometimes they put it on out at the studio, but I do not use it myself.

Q. That's what I had in mind. Did you that night use any hair oil?

A. No.

＊　　＊　　＊

Q. Did you give her your telephone number that night?

A. No.

Errol Flynn

Q. Did you take down her address?
A. No.

✿   ✿   ✿

Q. Did you at any time or place, Mr. Flynn, ever have an act of sexual intercourse with Betty Hansen?
A. I never at any time had an act of sexual intercourse with Betty Hansen.
Q. Did you at any time or place have an act of sexual intercourse with Peggy Satterlee?
A. I never did.

In my argument before the jury I did my best to analyze the girls' motives in testifying against Flynn. I pointed out that Betty Hansen wanted to leave Juvenile Hall, a place where underage delinquents were detained, and that in exchange for appearing for the state in the Flynn case she undoubtedly hoped not to be prosecuted for immoral acts she had admitted.

I mentioned that Miss Satterlee had confessed under oath in court that she had consented to have an abortion performed upon her. I tried to place my mind inside her mind and to imagine what she was thinking. It seemed likely that she had told herself that if her testimony pleased the authorities no charge would be brought against the man who had caused the abortion and no penalty would be exacted of her for having submitted to one.

I also said that the whole setup gave off a strong smell of "fix." Here were girls who had everything to gain by playing ball with the law; it was to their benefit to point a finger at someone else instead of having a finger pointed at them.

There was a certain amount of scorn in my voice as I described Miss Satterlee's arising on the *Sirocco* on that Sunday morning a few hours after, according to her testimony, she had been "forcibly raped." I asked the jury what was the first thing any decent girl would have done. Obviously she would have poured out her shameful story to the others on board, would have asked them for help and would have blistered Flynn's ears with her accusations.

145

"What did she actually do?" I asked. "She ate a happy and peaceful breakfast with Flynn, and later that day she was photographed smiling joyfully."

Flynn was a good witness. He was good because he answered forthrightly everything asked of him. He didn't change his pace between his direct examination and his cross-examination. In too many cases a witness is alert, responsive and convincing on direct examination, but as soon as the cross-examination begins and he is asked, "Where do you live?" he begins to look evasive and says, "I'm afraid I didn't quite get the question." Flynn wasn't like that.

In his charge Superior Court Judge Leslie E. Still reminded the jury that there can be no mitigating circumstances in statutory rape involving minor girls. But he added, "You jurors, of course, are not required to believe anything as jurors that you would not believe in the ordinary walk of life. And I must insist that you have an abiding conviction before you reach any decision."

In taking up the first count of Miss Hansen's charge, that she had been seduced by Flynn at a home in Bel Air, the judge said, "Even if Miss Hansen consented, that is no extenuating circumstance in this case." But on behalf of the defense he added that the fact that there had been an opportunity for a criminal attack was legally not enough to insure the probability that such an attack had actually taken place.

He went on to add—and I was overjoyed to hear him say it— that the California law takes into consideration the fact that in such cases there is always a chance that a personal reason, such as vengeance or malice, has bred such a charge.

In the portion of his remarks touching upon Peggy Satterlee, the judge reminded the jury of testimony which was brought out during the trial that an abortion had been performed on her a year after Flynn allegedly had attacked her. He also mentioned the fact that under California law abortion is a felony. Judge Still instructed the jury, "If you believe Miss Satterlee is guilty of such an act, then you have the right to take into consideration her state of mind while she was testifying in this court. Also, if you believe that Miss Hansen engaged in an illegal act with a man, you may consider the effect upon her mind and her statements. You may consider that both girls were hoping for leniency."

Pointing out that statutory rape is a charge easily made and difficult to disprove, he continued, "You must look upon the testimony of Peggy Satterlee and Betty Hansen with great care and deliberation. If you are not satisfied with the defendant's guilt beyond a reasonable doubt, you may acquit him."

Judge Still also reminded the jury that birth certificates do not conclusively prove age—in this case, that the girls were minors. "A birth certificate is not conclusive," he said. "It is only prima-facie evidence. If you entertain a reasonable doubt in your mind as to the ages of the witnesses, you should give the defendant the benefit of the doubt."

The Flynn case went to the jury at 11:19 on the morning of February 6, 1943. The jurors spent what seemed to me an interminable time debating my client's guilt, before acquitting him.

I still feel good when I remember that when their finding was announced Judge Still told the jury, "I think you have arrived at a proper verdict," for Flynn had gone into that trial with the dice of public opinion loaded against him.

7

Caress' Folly

THE NEXT CASE I'd like to talk about is a sharp departure from the Errol Flynn trial. For one thing, it has no sex angle. The Flynn case had its moments of boudoir humor, but the humor in the Les Bruneman case had a Damon Runyon touch. It involved a kidnaped gambler, E. L. (Zeke) Caress, who sincerely believed that he was worth the ransom the snatchers demanded for him and who, consequently, wrote out checks for that sum himself.

My client in this case, Les Bruneman, who was well known in Los Angeles gambling circles, was indicted for taking part in Caress' kidnaping. When the indictment was handed down, Bruneman was not around to be arrested, but six others who had taken part in the snatch were unlucky enough to be within the state's jurisdiction and were taken into custody. Five of them were tried and convicted of kidnaping. The sixth, James Gatewood, alias Jimmy Doolen, turned state's evidence and testified against the other defendants.

Bruneman was not in town for their trial; in fact, he wasn't even in the state. He was unfindable and couldn't be served. Later, when he decided to surrender, he got in touch with me, and I made the arrangements. Before carrying out those arrangements, I familiarized myself with the evidence and the legal questions involved in the case. I sent an associate to bring me the decision of the people versus the defendants, as well as the decision of the District Court of Appeals affirming the five convictions.

The facts were these: In December 1930 a man named Zeke Caress, his wife and his Japanese chauffeur had been kidnaped. The snatchers had demanded a ransom. Caress was a big wheel in L.A. gambling circles, but, as I have mentioned, apparently nobody thought he was worth a ransom of $50,000 except himself. He didn't have that much cash, so he gave the snatchers four checks for the amount.

This confronted the kidnapers with a dilemma. Slips of paper worth thousands of dollars were burning their hands, but who was going to cash them? Caress wasn't the one to do it, for even with a couple of snatchers standing on either side of him he might blurt out his predicament to a bank teller.

Some suggested that because Bruneman knew Tony Cornero Stralla, who ran the gambling barges which then plied their trade off the coast of Lower California, Bruneman might be a suitable go-between to persuade Stralla to act as cashier. The kidnapers got hold of Bruneman, and, accompanied by three of them, he attempted to take their hot checks out to one of Stralla's gambling boats for cashing. They were stopped by Long Beach police, and after a wild, mixed-up gun battle the ransom checks were recovered by the law. The Caresses and their chauffeur were released by the other kidnapers around that time and were questioned by the police, who then pieced together the story on which the indictments were handed down.

In May 1934 Les Bruneman went to trial for his participation in the abduction of Zeke Caress. Once more Jimmy Doolen, confessed member of the kidnap gang, appeared as the major prosecution witness. Doolen testified that Bruneman had participated in the entire plot and had agreed to assist the kidnapers in abducting Caress. He said that he had discussed with Bruneman the names of wealthy men in the Los Angeles area who might be kidnaped for ransom and that the name of Caress had met with Bruneman's approval.

The contention of the defense was that Bruneman had had no part in the kidnaping of Zeke Caress and was an innocent go-between used to cash the ransom checks, and selected for the job by Caress himself. At the trial Caress supported our contention. On cross-examination of Caress, I had him relate his conversations with the men who held him, his wife and his Japanese chauffeur prisoners at a secluded house outside Los Angeles in December 1930. Caress testified that he had been told by his kidnapers that he was "in a pretty tough spot." My cross-examination continued:

Q. And they told you you would have to pay some money to get out with your lives, you and your wife and the Japanese, is that right?

A. Yes, sir.

Q. And they told you, did they not, on Sunday, that it would be necessary for you to find some contact man, some person who could cash checks for you?

A. Yes, sir.

Q. Now, then, as I understood your testimony this morning, they mentioned some names to you on Sunday, and I desire to ask you at this time, Mr. Caress, to read your testimony given at Long Beach back in the early part of 1931, which was a period of only a few months after the happening of the occurrences, when your memory no doubt was much fresher than today, after this extended period of time. Calling your attention directly, first, to volume twenty-two, Mr. Veitch.

MR. VEITCH: Volume twenty-two, yes.

Q. BY MR. GIESLER: Page 1810, and I will ask you to read from line twenty on that page, Mr. Caress, down to and including line twenty on page 1811, if you will, please [*handing transcript to the witness*].

Deputy District Attorney Veitch suggested I read the testimony aloud so that both the witness and the jury would know what was being talked about.

Q. BY MR. GIESLER [*reading*]: "Q. Tell us what conversation, all the conversation you had there. A. Well, they just—just simply told me it was up to me; it wasn't up to them at all. As soon as I could pick up somebody that could—or name them somebody that could— help me, it would be over. So I finally thought of a name and . . . Q. Did they mention what would be over? A. They would release me.

Q. Did they mention some names to you? A. They asked me if I knew a man named Walter McGinley. I told them I did, and they wanted to know if he could cash my checks, and I told them I didn't think he would. Q. Did they mention any other names? A. I think they mentioned a party named Stuttering Sam and asked me if I had heard of him and if he would cash my check, and I told them I didn't think he would. Q. Were there any other names? A. I don't know if there was. Q. Was Farmer Page mentioned? A. I believe they might have mentioned his name. Q. What was said about him? A. Well, the remark was that he was in jail. Q. Well, did you mention any names? A. Yes. That brought up a friend of mine that I had known for several years, so I asked them if they knew a man by the name of Les Bruneman, and they said no, they didn't. Well, I said, he would answer for me; if they could go and find out about him, or hear anything about him, why, he would be very satis- factory to me. Q. Did you mention any other names besides that name? A. No, I don't believe I did. Q. That was the only one you mentioned? A. Well, I happened to think of him after they followed . . . after they mentioned . . . We was talking about Farmer Page and then Les Bruneman came to my mind." Now, do you recall so testifying?

A. Yes, sir.

Q. Does that refresh your recollection, Mr. Caress?

A. Yes, sir.

Q. The only name that you did mention at any time out at that house was Les Bruneman, the defendant here?

A. I think that is correct.

Q. Yes, sir, and you were the person who mentioned Les Bruneman's name, were you not?

A. Yes, sir.

Q. They didn't mention Les Bruneman's name to you, did they?

A. No, sir.

Q. You had known Les Bruneman for a number of years, ten years at least, up to that time, here in Los Angeles, had you not?

A. Yes, sir.

Q. And you had confidence in him?

151

A. Yes, sir.

Q. And you and he— He had at one time worked for you?

A. Yes, sir.

Q. He had handled, during that time, large sums of money for you?

A. Yes, sir.

Q. And you knew you could trust him?

A. Yes, sir.

Q. At that time you believed yourself to be in a very precarious position, did you not?

A. Yes, sir.

Q. And you believed that it was necessary for you to have someone who was capable of going through with that matter, didn't you?

A. Yes, sir.

Q. And so, because of the fact that you wanted someone in whom you had confidence and could depend upon to represent you in the matter, after his name came into your mind on that Sunday afternoon you suggested his name?

A. Yes, sir.

Q. And when you talked to him on the telephone, you impressed upon him, did you not, that it was your urgent desire that he should act for you?

A. Yes, sir.

Q. And you asked him not to turn you down, didn't you?

A. Yes, sir.

Q. In other words, more or less pleaded with him not to turn you down, not to turn down your request?

A. Yes, sir.

Q. The story which you told him as to the purpose for which you needed the money was one originating entirely in your own mind, was it not?

A. Yes, sir.

Q. It was not suggested to you by those persons there in the house?

A. No, they told me to create my own story.

Q. You then told him the story which you related here this morning, over the telephone, as to the necessity for this money at that time, on your part?

A. Yes, sir.

Q. And you likewise told him in that conversation, did you not, after he had told you that he didn't know where he could raise any such sum as ten thousand dollars or twenty thousand dollars on Sunday in Hollywood, you suggested to him going down to the gambling ship off Long Beach, did you not?

A. Yes, sir.

Q. And your purpose in doing that, Mr. Caress, was that you believed that was about the only place you knew of where they would have that amount of cash on a Sunday night, isn't that true?

A. Right.

Q. And you asked him then to go down to the gambling ships off Long Beach, for the purpose of trying to cash these checks and deliver [the money] to the persons whom he was to meet on the street corner, is that right?

A. Yes, sir.

Q. And these gentlemen, as you testified this morning, who had you there in prison, told you to tell him to meet them at Sixth and Spring streets. Is that right?

A. Yes, sir.

Q. And they likewise directed you, did they not, to obtain a description from him over the telephone, of the kind of car he was driving?

A. Yes, sir.

Q. And in response to that request on your part he told you he was driving a Nash sedan?

A. Yes, sir.

Q. And that he would be there at the corner of Sixth and Spring streets on the corner in a Nash sedan, and that they could identify him in that way. Is that true?

A. Yes, sir.

Q. Now, so much for the house at Alhambra; one more question about that. After you told them or suggested his name, they went out, apparently at least; they said they were going out to see if they could locate Mr. Bruneman, is that right?

A. Yes.

Q. And they were gone approximately two hours, were they not, Mr.

Caress, before they came back and talked to you again about the matter?

A. I am not sure; an hour or two hours.

Mr. Caress, after his recollection had been refreshed by previous testimony, acknowledged that the men who held him prisoner returned about two hours later and reported that they had located Les Bruneman and that Bruneman would be acceptable to them. Mr. Caress then told about writing the checks:

Q. And the checks were written by you and made out to Les Bruneman?
A. Yes.
Q. Your handwriting?
A. Yes.
Q. Four checks?
A. With his name on the face of the check, each of the four checks.
Q. The name of Les Bruneman?
A. Yes.
Q. Two of them for ten thousand dollars each and two for fifteen thousand dollars each?
A. Yes.
Q. Those were the four checks, delivered to these parties at that house?
A. Yes.
Q. At the time you signed those checks, you had previously arrived at an agreement with them that you were only to give them twenty thousand dollars, had you not?
A. Yes, sir.
Q. But when it came to writing the checks, they forced you to write checks to the extent of fifty thousand dollars?
A. Yes.
Q. They are the checks you have already testified to?
A. Yes.
Q. And now when they returned that night, and awakened you in the middle of the night, and got you up, and dressed you and your wife and the Japanese, and took you down to Alhambra Boulevard, or rode, or whatever it was, and released you, at that time the party

who had you in tow and told you that your present deal was all off—

A. Yes.

Q. —told you to have no fear at all?

A. Yes.

Q. Nothing was said by them at that time that they would come back and request you to pay that twenty thousand dollars in the future?

A. No.

Q. You were told simply to the effect that that transaction was at an end, and you could go, you had no fear, and nothing to worry about. Is that right?

A. They told me to take care of Les Bruneman.

Q. Yes, to take care of Les Bruneman. That was because Les Bruneman — They said, didn't they, something had happened, some shooting?

A. Something.

Q. Now, at the time you returned home that night— After your release out there, you returned to your home, did you not?

A. Yes.

Q. Your wife was with you?

A. Yes, sir.

Q. In the morning, the next morning—which would be a Monday morning, wouldn't it?

A. Yes.

Q. Monday morning, you and your wife went to the Hollywood police station?

A. No, when we got home the Hollywood police were there, and they held us. They would not let us go in the house, and took us down to the Hollywood police station.

Q. They took you down to the Hollywood police station?

A. Yes.

Q. Because of the fact they had found checks in Long Beach?

A. Yes.

Q. In a shooting affray, with your name signed to them?

A. Yes.

Q. And they took you to the Hollywood police station and held you until lengthy explanations were made?

A. They held us until I gave my story and to see whether it corresponded with Bruneman's in Long Beach.

Q. They then released you and your wife?

A. Yes.

Q. And you went to Long Beach then?

A. I went to Long Beach that afternoon.

❖　❖　❖

Q. Now, coming back again to Long Beach, you went to Long Beach, now, Monday afternoon, and you saw Mr. Bruneman, in the city jail at Long Beach, in the presence of Mr. Le Barron of the police department?

A. Yes.

Q. At that time you said, "Boy, I got you in a pretty tough spot"?

A. Yes.

On redirect, Mr. Veitch brought out that Caress had paid Bruneman a thousand dollars for his services as an emissary to cash the ransom checks. In recross-examination of Zeke Caress, I was able to establish that my client had not requested compensation for his services—that the payment had been entirely Caress's idea:

Q. He [Bruneman] did not ask you for any money, did he?

A. No, sir.

Q. When you got there, you said, "Here, I want to give you something," and he did not want to accept anything, did he?

A. That is right.

Q. You took it and threw it at him and said, "Here, give it to your wife."

A. Yes.

Q. "If you don't want to accept it, I will give it to your wife"?

A. Yes, that is right.

Q. He did not ask for any more?

A. No.

Despite the testimony of the victim and of the defendant himself, the jury convicted Bruneman of the kidnaping charge.

I appealed his conviction to the District Court of Appeals. I argued that the testimony of an admitted accomplice in the kidnaping, Jimmy Doolen, could not properly be considered in determining whether there was evidence tending to connect Bruneman with the specific crime charged. I pointed out that with the elimination of Doolen's testimony there was nothing in the record to justify the inference that the defendant had had any prior knowledge of the kidnaping of Zeke Caress.

I contended that Bruneman was not on trial for any criminal responsibility in the shooting affray at Long Beach. I emphasized that Long Beach was not the scene of the crime of kidnaping, and that it had always been the law that the mere presence of a defendant, even at the scene of the actual crime and at the time that the crime was committed, was not sufficient in itself to connect the defendant with the commission of the crime.

I argued that the testimony of Mr. Caress, in itself, demonstrated beyond question that the defendant was not even remotely connected with the corrupt intent operating in the minds of the actual kidnapers, but that he was connected only with the innocent intent of the victim. In acting in the capacity of an agent or go-between or contact man, Bruneman's intent was entirely on the side of the victim of the crime, and he did not at any time co-operate with any corrupt intent present on the other side of the picture. This being true, I contended, Bruneman could not be said to be a principal in the crime of kidnaping.

As an additional ground for granting a new trial, I argued that two alternate jurors had been in the jury room while the twelve regular jurors were deliberating, and that, even though they were admonished not to participate in the deliberations, their presence constituted an invasion of Bruneman's right to trial by jury.

At the time of Bruneman's first trial, in 1934, the empaneling of two extra jurors, in addition to the usual twelve, was a new idea in California. The idea was that the extra jurors would listen to the testimony and be instructed by the judge in the same way as the twelve regular jurors were. In that way they could serve as replacements in the event that any of the regular jurors became sick. The trial judge was uncertain about what should be done with the two alternates when the case was given to the jury. He finally decided to send them out of the court with the jury, under instructions only to observe and not to take part in the jury deliberations.

In my appeal I argued that having fourteen people in a jury room negated the age-old right to trial by twelve of a man's fellow citizens, which is the keystone of both our law and the English common law; the fact that I, as Bruneman's counsel, did not object at the time made no difference. The District Court of Appeals agreed, reversed the conviction on this ground and granted Bruneman a new trial. If anybody wants to look it up, the legal point made about the presence of alternate jurors in the jury room being prejudicial error is in the case of People v. Bruneman, 4 Cal., App. 2d 75 (1935).

At his second trial, in October 1935, I got Bruneman off. At the conclusion of the prosecution's evidence I asked the court to dismiss the case on the ground that the crime of kidnaping is completed when a snatch is made and that anything which happens thereafter is not a part of the kidnaping. Judge Fricke, who presided, agreed with me. Since a jury had been empaneled and sworn and testimony had been taken and presented before the court, which dismissed the case, Bruneman couldn't be reindicted and retried, because of the law of double jeopardy.

Not long after that Bruneman was cut down by gangster machine-gun fire in a restaurant on Temple Street called The Roost.

8

The White Flame Case

A MAN named Paul Wright called me early one morning in 1937 from the Glendale city jail. He asked me to come and see him. I went. The police let me in and I had a preliminary talk with him.

He was in a highly nervous state. If I described him as being wild-eyed I would not be exaggerating. Even now I have only to shut my eyes to see his tousled hair, his tenseness, the staring look on his face as he told me his story.

Every veteran lawyer of the criminal courts has a case (even several cases) which fascinates him. This fascination usually stems from a peek given him into the strange jungle of human behavior which springs up when a man or woman loses control of his or her emotions.

Although it is not one of my most recent cases, the Paul Wright case is one of the most dramatic trials I have ever handled. Certainly no story of my life would be complete without a retelling of the incidents which added up to that strange and violent tragedy.

I took Wright's case for a fee much less than my usual charge. Not only did it fascinate me, but I was convinced that I could win it in spite of the fact that before I appeared at the Glendale police station Wright had confessed of his own free will to the police that he had shot and fatally wounded his wife and his closest friend, John Kimmel, when he found them indulging an illicit lust in his home. Moreover, the case was a challenge to my professional pride, of which I have always had my share.

When I talked to Wright at the Glendale police station he was still so emotionally shaken that one theme kept recurring in his statements: "When I saw my wife making love to John, a white flame exploded in my brain. There was a white flame in my head."

I won't repeat the exact words Wright said to me—they are confidential—but since almost everything he confided to me was brought out at some time during his trial and became part of the court record, it is possible to give a résumé of what led up to his ordeal.

Once I was allowed to confer with him, I made sure that he would be less insistent about announcing his guilt than he had been when he telephoned the police and explained hysterically, "I have just murdered my wife and my best friend, John Kimmel. You'll find me waiting for you in my home when you get here."

When a prowl car reached the Wright home, an emotionally shattered Wright was waiting on the sidewalk outside his home. Clutching at the police with frantic hands, he pulled them inside and shouted at them once more the details of the destruction his revolver had sprayed at approximately 4 A.M. on November 9, 1937.

The night before, Wright and some of his friends had been celebrating at the Hollywood Athletic Club at a dinner given by an organization called the Quiet Birdmen, a group of flyers. Afterward he had taken his friend Kimmel home with him for a nightcap.

I didn't get over to Glendale to visit Wright in jail until late the morning of November 9. When I arrived he was being interviewed by the Glendale detectives. A captain of detectives was in charge. At first he wouldn't let anybody interview Wright alone. He changed his mind when I cited that portion of the penal code which describes a man's right to interview his lawyer without outside supervision.

From that moment everybody in my office worked on that case interviewing the possible witnesses. From the ninth of November until the first day of the trial everyone who worked for me put in up to eighteen hours a day.

I remember trying to tell a friend of mine how hard we had worked. "What were you *doing* that could use up so many hours a day?" he asked. "What could you possibly have investigated *that* intensively?"

I explained, "We interview everybody we can think of. We get a lead here, a tip there, then we run them down. We talk to prospective witnesses, measure things, photograph things. In the Wright case we tried to talk to any neighbors who might have heard the shots fired. We talked to the people at the cleaning shop where Kimmel's widow sent his clothes after he died. We had a tip that the prosecution had taken photographs of his body in the morgue, so we got a subpoena *duces tecum*, returnable forthwith. We served it on the morgue employees. They said they had no such pictures."

To put all this into its proper order, the first thing I asked my chief investigator, James Leahan, to do was visit the neighborhood where the Wrights had lived and interview all the possible witnesses there, to find out what they knew. It made no difference whether the potential witnesses were hostile or friendly. I asked Mr. Leahan to interview them anyway. I especially wanted to know whether anyone in the vicinity of Wright's home had heard shots fired and, if so, when they had heard them and exactly how they had been fired. Also, I wanted to know whether anyone who lived nearby had seen any cars arrive, what time those cars left and whether anyone could be identified as leaving or entering the vicinity of the killing.

My investigators (as well as my own inspection of the premises) determined that a fusillade of nine shots had been fired. Some of the bullets had penetrated Mrs. Wright's back. Others had lodged in the front part of Kimmel's body.

Wright's two victims were still breathing when the homicide squad conducted its preliminary research (although both Mrs. Wright and Kimmel expired a few hours after the police received Wright's telephone call). Their bodies lay in a position which made it obvious that they had been seated on a piano bench in the Wright living room. The path the bullets followed indicated that Kimmel and Mrs. Wright had been facing each other before Wright's gun blasted them.

As Glendale Police Officer Harry Reed later testified at the trial, he and Officer Trowbridge were ordered by the desk sergeant early on the morning of November 9 to proceed immediately to the Wright house at 1830 Verdugo Vista Drive. Paul Wright was at the intersection of Verdugo Road and Verdugo Vista waiting for them. He grabbed Reed's right arm and said, "My God, I am a murderer. I killed my wife and my best friend." Quickly he led the police officers to the living room of his house and pointed out his wife and Kimmel.

Reed said he went over to the piano and found Mrs. Wright lying on her right side on the floor, with the upper part of her body underneath the piano bench. Her body was quiet and still. Mrs. Wright was dressed in a black street suit and a black blouse. She wore chiffon hose and black sandals. Her clothes were in their normal position—not disarranged. Reed took her pulse. "It was very slight," he testified later.

Kimmel was lying flat on his back, with his right leg under the piano bench and slightly over Mrs. Wright's body. His left foot was on the keyboard of the piano. His body was moving to some extent. His left arm thrashed the air. He coughed spasmodically, discharging phlegm and blood from his mouth. Reed "heard a terrible groaning sound, as though he was in great pain." The buttons of Kimmel's fly were open except for the top button, and his penis was exposed.

Reed said the Wrights' maid came into the room as the bodies were being removed. Wright told her he had shot his wife—"I caught her cheating on me." Wright sat down at his desk and wrote out a check for the maid. "I have not much money," he told her, "but I will give you seventy dollars. That will take care of you and the baby until I get things straightened out."

Before the officers took Wright to the police station, they permitted him to put in a call to his father in Milwaukee. Reed repeated the conversation as he heard it: "Hello, Father. There has been a terrible tragedy in my home—I have shot Evelyn. I caught her cheating. It is just as you said it would be. You will stick by me, won't you, Father?"

There are, in addition, innumerable facts that the direct and cross-examination of those concerned with this case (as well as the reports of my investigation) brought out. Mrs. Wright was extremely beautiful. Her husband had been very much in love with her. His devotion to her approached fanaticism. Any man who reads what I am about to say will agree that Wright was obsessed with love. Her doctor had told Mrs. Wright that it would be dangerous, perhaps even fatal, for her to have another baby, and Wright's love and devotion were such that he had had an operation performed upon himself to make sure he couldn't father any more children.

While he didn't seem to regret his sacrifice of his powers of procreation, I think subconsciously it worked on his mind. It was easy for me to believe that a man who adored his wife as much as Wright did would be likely to suffer a mental explosion if exposed to the sudden realization that she was being flagrantly unfaithful to him.

I also discovered that he had rented a beautiful house in Glendale although it was over his head financially, so that his wife and their child could have a nice home to live in. As for clothing, his wife had had more clothes in her closets than any man in his circumstances could afford. He himself had only three mail-order suits. Mrs. Wright had wanted a convertible. He had said, "But honey, we can't afford it." She had kept at him until he bought her one. These were some of the human-interest sidelights my investigation developed.

I mention Wright's fanatical devotion to his wife because it helps explain the tragedy which occurred in his home when he unexpectedly found his wife facing his closest friend in a compromising position on a piano bench in his living room.

After the dinner Wright and Kimmel had attended Wright invited Kimmel home with him. Evelyn Wright was still awake. All three of them had a few drinks, but although Wright and Kimmel had already visited a bar, later testimony failed to disclose that either of them was intoxicated upon their arrival at Wright's home.

Around three o'clock in the morning, Wright became tired, excused himself, went into his bedroom to lie down and dozed off. Then something awakened him. The lights were still on, and his wife was not in her bed. Groggy with sleep, he had walked from his bedroom into the hall, looking for her.

Then he heard the sound of a finger tapping piano keys.

Venturing further until he was standing in the living-room door, he saw his friend and his wife sitting on the piano bench engaged in a lustful act. The sight shocked him so much that what occurred immediately afterward happened without conscious thought on his part. Apparently he went back into his bedroom, took his gun out of a drawer, headed back to the living room and fired two or three shots from the doorway, one or two of which had gone wild. I know that because I myself discovered that one of the shots had penetrated a French window.

None of this is based wholly on Wright's testimony. His mind was whirling too wildly for him to describe what had happened in a clear and coherent fashion. On the other hand, it is not based wholly on supposition. It is based on such physical facts as the position of the furniture and of the two people Wright had shot as they lay dying, the location of bullet holes, the evidence of neighbors who heard the shots—all of which was brought out during the trial.

To repeat for a moment, when the police entered the Wright home and found Evelyn Wright and John Kimmel lying on the floor, they found the heel of one of Kimmel's feet still resting on the piano keyboard. The official photographs taken at the scene of the double killing showed that.

That heel caught on the piano caused me an enormous amount of trouble. I spent many bruising hours trying to figure out how he could have fallen the way he had fallen and still have a leg propped up as it was. I use the word "bruising" advisedly, because I practiced falling from a similar bench at home with my wife acting out Evelyn Wright's part. We sat facing each other while I fell time after time.

Finally I had it worked out in my mind just how that fall had occurred, so I was able to demonstrate it successfully before the jury when the case was tried—and with my leg in the position John Kimmel's leg had remained in, I kept right on addressing the jury lying on the floor. I could think of no better way to re-create what had gone on in the Wright home to cause that explosion in Wright's brain. When I pointed out that the presence of the actual piano and the actual bench involved would help show the direction the bullets had taken, the judge granted me permission to move them into the courtroom.

Wright was tried on two counts of murder. The people were represented by Deputy District Attorneys S. Ernest Roll and J. Miller Leavy. They contended that Wright was guilty of first-degree murder, that the shooting and killing of his wife and best friend were willful, deliberate and premeditated. The prosecution asked for the death penalty. The defense I offered was twofold: not guilty and not guilty by reason of insanity.

The prosecution came up with what seemed to me an extremely unlikely theory, and even after the passage of all these years it still seems unlikely. The prosecution's theory seemed to be that Wright purposely lured Kimmel to his house and left his good friend alone with Mrs. Wright in the hope that he would find them later in a compromising position, thereby giving ample justification for killing her.

The D. A.'s office apparently thought that Wright hadn't gone to bed at all, but rather that he had hovered barefooted, gun in hand, behind the door leading into the living room. Then when his wife had begun to make love to Kimmel he had stolen up on the pair and lowered the boom on them with a coolly calculated barrage of nine shots.

If there was one thing which should have been obvious to everyone concerned it was this: There was nothing cool or calculating about that shooting. If retribution was ever dealt out while a husband's gun and brain were both smoking hot, that was such a time. However, since the D. A. took the opposite approach, it was up to me to bring forth the truth.

The truth was that my client had gone to sleep under the impression that Kimmel was on the point of going home; then, after drowsing for a while, he had been aroused by the sound of someone plunking a piano key in his living room. He had gotten up, had gone to the living-room door and had peered in. From that point he could see the why and wherefore behind that piano plunking;

someone was hitting the keys to camouflage the fact that the plunker was otherwise occupied.

When Wright reached this point in his testimony, he sobbed uncontrollably. Weeks after it had happened re-creating that scene still shattered him emotionally. This in itself should have given the jury a clue to what his reactions must have been on the night of the shooting itself. He testified that when he saw what he'd seen his mind became a whirling chaos of nothingness. The next thing he remembered was standing by the piano with his gun in his hand while his wife and Kimmel lay crumpled on the floor groaning.

Wright's inner anguish did not lessen under cross-examination. If anything, it increased. Veins stood out on his forehead until I thought he'd have a stroke. The knuckles of his hands were white as he battled to keep himself under control.

As a commentary on his emotion, Wright's first cousin testified at the trial that many hours after the double killing he had found Paul Wright still terribly shaken by his experience. I shouldn't have thought it necessary to highlight that point, since to me it was eminently clear (it still is clear) that any normal husband who loves his wife and who suddenly, unexpectedly and while still half asleep discovers her engaged in an illicit act with another man in his own living room is bound to suffer an emotional explosion.

Wright's nearest neighbors were two elderly maidens who lived across the street. I had tried my best to find out what evidence they could contribute, but they had refused to talk to me or to my investigators, so I had no inkling of what they knew. They made their appearance on the first day of the trial in the rear of the courtroom among the witnesses for the prosecution. The D. A. kept them there all through the proceedings. He didn't use them until the end. Then he called one of them to the stand and asked her, "Did you hear anything the night Mrs. Wright died?"

"Yes," she replied.

"What did you hear?" he asked.

"I heard a series of shots," she told him.

"Could you tell the court and the jury exactly how those shots were fired?" he asked.

The sequence of those shots was extremely important. Whether they had all been fired in rapid succession or whether they had come in two bursts with an interval between was significant because of what Wright claimed he remembered (albeit fuzzily) about walking out of his bedroom and beginning to blast away.

According to Wright's hysterical story, he had fired first from the living-room doorway; he had then fired the other shots after an interval spent in walking toward the piano bench. The D. A.'s office was trying to show that the shots had been fired in a steady sequence without a break. On the stand Wright told his story once more. He had been wakened from his sleep by a regular tapping on one of the piano keys in the living room. He had gone to the glass door leading into the living room and had seen there what he'd seen. With his brains reeling as if they were popping his skull he had gone back to get a gun—he didn't remember that too well—and had fired several shots, which had gone through a French window. Then he had moved closer to the piano bench, shooting as he moved, until it was clear even to him that he had mortally wounded the couple.

If the prosecution could have shown that there was no spacing between the shots, that they had come in one continuous burst, it would have demonstrated that Wright was lying. On the other hand, it was the contention of the defense that that last fatal fusillade had been fired in a burst of insane but justifiable rage.

Several other questions were involved in the matter of the shots Wright had fired. There was the question of distance—to be more exact, the spot from which Wright had fired his shots. There was the question of timing: whether he had fired immediately upon seeing his wife and Kimmel or whether after he saw his wife with Kimmel he had gone back to his bedroom, had got his gun and had come out, firing as he advanced. As nearly as he could recall it he had fired two shots from the doorway, the two which had gone wild; then he had "whited out." After that he "thought" he had fired the rest of his fusillade in one burst as he stood over the guilty couple.

When the D. A. asked the maiden lady on the stand if there had been any break in the sequence of shots, she denied it. She said that they had all come in rapid succession, without a break. She remembered that five shots had been fired rapidly, one after the other, which left Wright's half-remembered story with a gaping hole in it.

I finished cross-examining her quickly. I had nothing to cross-examine her about. Because of her pre-trial reticence I had been able to find out nothing about her, so I had no inkling of whether she was telling the truth. I was sure of only one thing—from the defense point of view she was a bad witness. The wise thing to do in such a situation is to treat a bad witness as nicely as you can and get him off the stand as quickly as possible.

The D. A. said, "You're excused."

I tried to appear as if her testimony had not affected me, although it had twisted my insides, for that sweet, elderly lady had just given the lie to our theory of how the killing had occurred. Gloating over what he had accomplished, the D. A. went back to his table. Then I saw him whisper to one of his assistants, after which he said, "Your honor, may I delay this lady for one additional question?"

The judge asked me if I objected.

I bowed and said, "No, your honor."

Then the D. A. said to her, "If I hand you a pencil, do you think you can demonstrate to the jury how those shots were fired?"

"Yes," she said, her eyes bright and birdlike.

I naturally expected that her demonstration would follow the sequence to which she had testified: Tap-tap-tap-tap-tap. But she sat there for a while, deep in thought; then she started, and so help me if she didn't do a tap-tap (pause) tap-tap-tap, with an appreciable spacing between the second and the third shots.

I can still see the expression on the D. A.'s face as he realized that he had committed the lawyer's cardinal sin: he had asked one question too many.

"Your honor," I said quietly, "I hope that the record will show—

and I'm sure the district attorney will have no objection if it *does* show—that there was a noticeable interruption between the second and third shots."

The D. A. could only agree to my stipulation. He was stuck with it. After all, the jury had heard and made a mental note of the visual demonstration and the oral testimony. He said weakly, "If you have no objection, I think I'll excuse her now." I had no objection. The expressions on the jury's faces told me that not one tap of the significant difference between her actual demonstration and her previous verbal testimony had been lost on them.

I said nothing to the D. A. then about the one extra question he had asked, but later when I met him one evening at a social affair I asked him, "Why did you recall that woman and have her demonstrate with a pencil how those shots were fired, when you already had the whole thing wrapped up without any demonstration?"

"I'll tell you," he said. "One of my young deputies had taken a course in advanced graphic or visual appreciation or something at U.C.L.A., and he wanted to use a graphic, visual demonstration to nail that woman's testimony firmly in the jury's minds. I did what he suggested, but I should have my rear end kicked all the way from here to San Francisco for listening to him."

When it was my turn to make my argument before the jury, I mentioned, among other things, the deadly nature of the sin of adultery. I called the jury's attention to the fact that adultery committed in the unusual circumstances which had confronted Wright was far more shocking than any common or ordinary brand of infidelity. I directed their minds to the responsibility that should have rested upon a man's best friend left alone with his wife in her own home. I stressed the thought that my client had been more a bolt of lightning in human form loosed by the Almighty to extinguish the offending couple than guilty of the charges in the indictment handed down against him.

If it is true that each major case has a turning point on which it hangs, the Paul Wright case had two such points. The first one was convincing the jury that Wright had seen his wife and Kimmel engaging in an immoral act. I developed that fact in the trial so clearly that there was no question in the jury's mind as to just what had been going on on that piano bench between the guilty couple.

As I've already said, I not only brought into the court the actual piano bench from which Kimmel's body had fallen when he was shot, but I placed myself in Kimmel's place on that bench and demonstrated what had happened to him both before and after the bullets crashed into his body.

If it seems from reading this that I was suggesting that his position on the piano bench had a vital bearing on the outcome of the trial, that is true. I was convinced that it had. I wanted the jury to visualize with its mind's eye what Paul Wright had seen when he looked at Kimmel on that bench and found him with his wife.

Another thing happened in the Wright case which also had an effect on the jury, although it had nothing to do with the facts. To help me deliver my argument, I had brought a Bible into court. I wanted to read the jury portions of the Old Testament, as well as a selection from the chapter of Matthew in the New Testament, concerning adultery. I dwelt upon the point that God thought that grievous sin was punishable by death. If you analyze certain portions of the Old Testament it is surprising how closely it resembles our modern law. In fact, quite a lot of our law has been adapted from Holy Writ. The English common law derives strongly from the Old Testament. When I was through reading that section of Mosaic law to the jury, I laid the Bible down on the counsel table.

In delivering his closing argument the D. A. made still another mistake. He picked up the Bible and said, "Mr. Giesler brought this book into this courtroom and has read sections of it to you to prove that Mr. Wright is innocent. I won't take up any more of your valuable time going into this. Mr. Wright is as innocent as Satan."

Then he threw the Bible onto the table with a scornful gesture. It skidded several inches before coming to a stop.

I know that it was un-Christian of me, but when I saw him do that my heart leaped. He didn't mean it the way it looked, of course, but the result was almost as shocking as spitting on the flag. The thought flashed through my mind, *He'll be sorry he did that.* I was right. I found out afterward from a number of the jurors who had served in that trial that they had been offended at the cavalier treatment he had given the word of God. It was a thing I'm sure the D. A. never thought of afterward; even so, what might seem a trivial incident to some can have an influence on a juror's mind when he comes to render his verdict.

After deliberating less than three hours the jury found Wright guilty on two counts of manslaughter. While it may seem strange of me to say so, that was the very verdict I was hoping for. I was convinced that even if I did my best and everything broke right for me, voluntary manslaughter—killing in the heat of passion induced by jealous rage—was the least the jury would find my client guilty of.

In California the penalty for manslaughter is one to ten years. But because of my double plea of not guilty and not guilty by reason of insanity, Wright had to be declared sane by the same jury which convicted him before he could be sentenced to San Quentin Prison on the two manslaughter convictions, for terms of one to ten years, to run consecutively or concurrently as the court might fix.

The trial resumed Monday morning, February 14, 1938, for determination of the issue of Wright's sanity at the time of the killings. The jury had had only one day's rest since convicting Wright of manslaughter the previous Saturday after a month-long trial, and their faces showed it. I suspected also that for some of them it had not been a peaceful Sunday, as they weighed the rightness of the verdict in their minds. This jury had yet to finally decide my client's fate. A finding by them that Paul Wright was temporarily insane at the time of the shooting—that he was in such a mental state he could not distinguish between right and wrong, or know the nature of his acts or their probable consequences—would mean his freedom, despite the manslaughter conviction. I hoped to focus and pound home the doubt I thought I saw in those faces.

Under California law, the defendant has the burden of proving he was insane at the time he committed the crime. Having the burden of proof, the defense generally puts on its evidence first. Since I had already introduced a wealth of psychiatric testimony

171

at the original trial in an effort to convince the jury that Wright had killed in a "white flame" of rage—which had paid off when the jury declined to return the first-degree-murder verdict asked by the prosecution—I decided to put on no evidence. The defense rested on the stipulation that all evidence submitted on the original trial be deemed admitted in this trial for consideration by the jury on the insanity issue.

The prosecution called four psychiatrists to the stand, three of whom had been appointed by the court at arraignment to examine Wright's sanity at the time of the killings. Their testimony was comparatively brief. All were of the opinion that Paul Wright had awareness of the crime he was committing when he blasted away at his attractive wife and Kimmel as they sat on the piano bench in the Wrights' living room.

The people rested just before the luncheon recess. I was on my feet immediately. I told the judge that since I had the burden of proof, I rather than the prosecution was entitled to open and close the arguments to the jury. So far as I know, this was the first time defense counsel had ever made such a proposal to a California court. The people always had had the opening and closing arguments. My motion threw the courtroom into a turmoil. The deputy district attorneys in charge of the case were so taken aback by my proposal that for a moment they were speechless. Then they were almost violent in pointing out to the court that my motion was unprecedented. The judge adjourned court immediately without ruling on my motion.

At the beginning of the afternoon session, the D. A., his chief assistant and three other assistants went into chambers for a conference with the judge. Then the judge called me in. The prosecution said heatedly that there was no precedent for my motion. They kept saying, "It has never happened before."

I waited until they cooled down a little, then I said, "Your honor, I am upholding the affirmative now, just as the prosecution did during the trial. Whoever has the affirmative is always given both the opening and closing, so why shouldn't I?"

The judge was fair-minded, and the upshot was that he held with me. I had the closing argument. In that argument I reiterated that when Wright had been roused from his sleep and had seen what was taking place on his piano bench, a white flame had flashed in his brain. The press had already gleefully leaped upon that phrase and had labeled Wright's dual killing the White Flame Murders.

Having the final argument, I was able not only to answer all the arguments made by the district attorney but also to come back with some new ones of my own which the prosecution wasn't able to answer because it had no rebuttal.

The case went to the jury at 4:45 P.M. Monday. The jury deliberated the balance of that day, all day Tuesday and into the early afternoon of Wednesday, February 17. At 2:45 P.M. the jury sent word to the judge that they had reached a verdict. A deputy sheriff rushed to the jail to get Wright. The deputy district attorneys and I, with my associates Ward Sullivan and Thornton Rogers, quickly took our places in the courtroom. Spectators and newspapermen hurried in. After Judge Bull had mounted the bench, the jury was brought in.

As the first juror entered the courtroom, he looked directly at Paul Wright and smiled. Those of us who saw that smile were pretty sure what was coming. The formalities of receiving the jury verdict were gone through, and the clerk stood to read from the paper handed him by the jury foreman:

"We, the jury, find the defendant was insane at the time of the commission of the acts charged."

Paul Wright collapsed when the verdict was read. Wright's father, an elderly dentist, put his arm around his son and wept. I put my arms around both of them.

The jury foreman said later that eight ballots had been taken on the insanity issue. The jurors were said to have stood eight to four for insanity until Tuesday afternoon. Tuesday night two of the four changed their votes to insanity. The last two were won over on the final ballot Wednesday afternoon.

As much as anything, my successful motion for the right to the closing jury argument helped win the verdict for Paul Wright.

Working on Wright's behalf was also a law not written in any book—a man is permitted to protect the sanctity of his home and keep it from being destroyed. I'm sure that in Wright's case that unspoken law had something to do with the jury's decision. These things are a part of no legally accepted code, but, no matter how we pooh-pooh them, they do exist in the minds of almost all people.

When the jury found that Paul Wright was insane at the time he committed the double manslaughter, and therefore was not legally responsible for the crime, no prison sentence was indicated. But one obstacle stood in the way to freedom—the issue of his present sanity.

The trial judge ordered Wright committed to the psychopathic ward of the Los Angeles General Hospital for examination by psychiatrists designated by the County Lunacy Commission. Four days later a sanity hearing was held before Superior Court Judge Ben Lindsey, at which the commission's psychiatrists and others expressed practically unanimously the opinion that Wright was now sane.

Judge Lindsey ruled that Wright should remain in custody for another five days, during which period any aggrieved person might file a petition for a jury trial on the issue of whether Wright was now sane or insane. No one did, and Wright walked out a free man.

That case still holds top rank as one of the most sensational cases ever tried in Los Angeles. It was up to me to do my best to defend Wright against the charges that he coldly, calmly, deliberately and with malice aforethought did murder his wife, Evelyn, and his close friend, John Kimmel. After watching me do my utmost to accomplish this, a writer from a Los Angeles newspaper wrote this about me:

> Once years ago I was traveling on a ship, and I had a little money with me. The night before we got into port three fellows got into a poker game with me. How, I don't know. All I know is that I arrived at my destination penniless. I found myself remembering one of the three gamblers on that ship yesterday as I watched Jerry Giesler, the distinguished criminal lawyer, in action. That gambler had the

same rushing-good-humor, torrential way about him Jerry has. He too created a lot of excitement about nothing in particular. Many patent-medicine spielers, auctioneers and politicians have Jerry Giesler's gift of scattering excitement. They wave objects, they walk up and down, they get excited over absolutely nothing and it's infectious. Other people get excited too. That's what they want. They are a combination of hypnotist and sleight-of-hand man. Like exciting movies, they appeal to the nervous system and never to the mind. . . . When yesterday afternoon's session of the Wright trial opened before Judge Ingall W. Bull, in Department 45, the Great Giesler went into action like a voodoo doctor with all the tribal tom-toms beating. . . . You never saw anything as excited as Giesler. He tossed all quietude to the wind.

I did not stand off and watch myself defend Paul Wright. No newsreel cameramen were allowed in that courtroom while the trial was in progress, so I can only say that the Jerry Giesler described so vividly in that Los Angeles newspaper is someone I don't know. I doubt very much if I've ever had anything to do with *that* Jerry Giesler. Granted that no man knows himself, neither the patent-medicine-pitchman Giesler nor the combination hypnotist and sleight-of-hand Giesler is anyone who is known by my wife, my children or those associated with me in the practice of law.

I've seen it printed that the strain and tension under which I had been during the Wright case were so great that when the jury came in I was weeping. That was true. I was not only weeping, I was all in.

My preparation for that case was so trying that I was worn out before I went into court for the first day of the trial, and a doctor had to give me something to lessen my exhaustion. I've never been sure what he gave me—maybe it was massive doses of vitamins— but I'm sure of this: while that case was going on I worked night and day, including Sundays and holidays, for two months.

Not that I'm the only one who gets tuckered out during a trial. I once defended a man against a charge of taking part in the kidnaping of one of the gambling bosses in the Los Angeles area. The

D. A. in the case became so used up physically, mentally and emotionally that when the trial was over he had to go away and rest for three weeks.

Perhaps my excessive loss of sleep during a trial has something to do with the loss of weight I suffer at such times. If I have something chewing at my mind I can't sleep until I get rid of it. I pound out miles of footwork in corridors outside courtrooms while juries are out. I once paced a corridor for three days, waiting for a jury to make up its mind about a client of mine.

Not only do I pace courthouse corridors, I pace up and down in my own house when the jury is locked up for the night. I make sure that I don't go home until they *are* locked up, because sometimes a jury will go out for dinner, then come back to the jury room and deliberate further before being locked up in a hotel. I make it a point to be on hand every second while a jury is deliberating in the jury room.

I know other attorneys—fine, honorable, reputable men—who go back to their offices at such times, leaving their phone numbers, of course, so that they can be back in the courthouse within thirty minutes if the jury reaches a decision. I don't say that's wrong. I do say that I am so constituted nervously and emotionally that I can't operate that way. I've been accused of doing it the hard way. Perhaps I do. The stakes are too big for me to let myself relax: the prosecution is trying to deprive a man of his liberty or his life, the defense is trying to make sure that he walks out of the courtroom free. But no matter how exhausted and drained I am after a trial, it's not long before I begin to itch for another contest. Life would be too tame if I weren't put in the legal pressure cooker often.

9

Lili St. Cyr

W‌HEN I HEARD that Lili St. Cyr had been arrested in Ciro's, the Hollywood night club, for "indecent exposure" while she was doing a strip bathtub act, I wondered why. Among other things she was accused of performing certain movements called bumps and grinds. A bump is a forward and backward snapping of the pelvis. A grind is a rotary movement of the same portion of the body. She had done much the same kind of act for years, and I couldn't imagine why anyone had suddenly decided to take her to task. After all, the D. A.'s office must have been aware that she didn't specialize in giving readings from Shakespeare or in performing interpretive dancing other than the most basic type.

When Miss St. Cyr opened at Ciro's a few ultraconservative matrons were on hand—goodness knows why—and they had become upset by Miss St. Cyr's strip act, so upset that they complained about it to the law.

Miss St. Cyr came out on a small stage fully dressed and wearing a large picture hat and accompanied by thumping rhythmic music. She peeled down to a net bra and G-string and climbed into a bathtub while a maid held a large bath towel between her and the audience. The bathtub was transparent; it was illuminated from the inside and through it Miss St. Cyr's seductive curves and undulations could be glimpsed.

When she had finished pretending to take a bath, her maid held the big towel up once more. The strip-teaser stepped out of the tub, the maid wrapped the towel around her and, as Jimmy Durante says, "that was thata." I'm no authority on strippers (or strip acts), but, in my opinion, compared with the majority of such acts Miss St. Cyr's performance was mild.

Nevertheless, following the complaints registered by the matrons whose modesty had been outraged, a woman sheriff and two deputy sheriffs attended Miss St. Cyr's next performance and decided that her act was lewd and lascivious. They arrested her.

Preparing a case like Miss St. Cyr's involved going to Ciro's to determine what the patrons could see from various points in the room. Obviously, since Miss St. Cyr was accused of exposing more of her person than strippers ordinarily expose, the prosecution's witnesses would have to swear that they had seen such exposure or they would have no case. After visiting Ciro's I questioned whether they could have seen more.

At first I offered to have her put on for the court, at Ciro's, the same show which had stirred up all the ruckus, but the court decided not to accept my offer. Instead, it held the trial in a courthouse on San Vicente Boulevard.

Next I demanded a blue-ribbon jury. That term baffled everyone. People were asking, "What do you suppose Jerry Giesler means by a blue-ribbon jury? What's a blue-ribbon jury, for goodness' sake?"

To some people it meant a jury composed of wealthy and aristocratic people. What I really had in mind was introducing a touch of irony. The ordinary definition of a jury is: "twelve of the accused's peers"—"peer" meaning an equal. As I saw it (perhaps whimsically), in its purest sense if an attorney is charged with a criminal offense and he demands a jury composed of his peers, that jury must be twelve attorneys.

My original idea had been to laugh the prosecution out of court by demanding a jury composed of twelve strippers, but I fought back that puckish notion and subdued it. I decided that that kind of humor would be too broad to be effective, so when I did show up in court I said, "Your honor, my client is accused of indecent exposure. It is our contention that, far from being indecent, the performance for which she was arrested is artistic. We therefore demand a jury made up of people capable of judging such things on their artistic merits."

Of course, I was not given such a jury. I don't think there were any artists, actors or dancers on the jury at all, but as outlandish as it seemed, my request accomplished one point. Everybody began to look at Miss St. Cyr and wonder if he could possibly have made a mistake in thinking of her merely as a stripper who made her living by peeling, when all the time what she was doing might have some vague artistic meaning.

When the trial began, two policemen testified how horrified they had been to see the defendant in a condition of near nudity and to "be forced to look at her indecent bumps and grinds." I pointed out that I suspected that there was a certain amount of hypocrisy on the part of the prosecution's large, burly male witnesses, who had had enough firsthand, close-up experience with non-Sunday-school forms of human behavior not to be "shocked" by Miss St. Cyr's act.

The prosecution next put a deputy sheriff on the stand. This sheriff said, "Miss St. Cyr's show was terrible. I couldn't help noticing that at one point she was in the nude. I was horrified." It was my guess that this testimony was supposed to influence the women on the jury into ganging up on my client, for obviously net bras and G-strings were unheard-of garments in the sturdy, no-nonsense circle in which that deputy sheriff lived.

When I cross-examined the witness, I asked, "You said that Miss St. Cyr did bumps and grinds?" I gave the jury a long, slow, meaningful look (the press described it as a pixy look). Then I turned to the witness again and asked, "Would you call what she did a bump or a bumpity-bump?"

The witness's face turned a cherry red. There was no reply.

The first witness for the defense was Ciro's plump and stocky owner, Herman Hover. I asked Mr. Hover to demonstrate a bump and a grind. He demurred at first, but finally I goaded him into standing up in the witness box and trying a bump. He did his best, but his face was crimson and his breath grew short. His version of that fairly pagan and primitive movement was so ridiculous that titters started in the courtroom—and grew into a roar.

If there was any preconceived notion in the minds of the jury that Miss St. Cyr had committed a serious offense, by the time Mr. Hover finished revolving his body sensuously in the witness box the serious aspects of the affair had evaporated. It is hard to believe a show is lewd when you are laughing about it so hard tears run from your eyes.

Florabel Muir, one of the very best—certainly she is one of the most colorful—reporters who ever worked for a Los Angeles newspaper, was our second witness. She had also been in Ciro's the night Lili was arrested. Mrs. Muir is not the soft, baby-faced, petite type. She is a hearty, sturdy woman. Her hair is flaming red.

When I had her on the witness stand, I asked, "Did you see anything wrong with Miss St. Cyr's performance?"

"No," Mrs. Muir replied.

"Where were you sitting?" I asked.

She said that she had been sitting in a spot where she had an unobstructed view of the proceedings and she had seen nothing wrong with Lili's performance.

The deputy D. A. made a mistake in cross-examining her. He didn't call her Mrs. Muir. He used a sarcastically formal type of address. He asked, "When did you arrive, madam?" "Had you been drinking that evening, madam?" "Where were you sitting, madam?"

This went on for about five minutes, and I could see a slow tide of red start up Mrs. Muir's neck until she couldn't take any more. Leaning her arms along the front edge of the witness stand, she glared at him and said in stentorian tones, "Young man, don't you call me Madam!"

It broke up the whole courtroom.

The young D. A. was thunderstruck. Then he said feebly, "No further questions."

But the biggest help to the defense was that all the witnesses for the prosecution testified that when Miss St. Cyr stepped out of the tub she had been nude, and that, the D. A. insisted, constituted indecent exposure. Some of the prosecution witnesses even said that they could see Miss St. Cyr's nakedness through the towel her maid was holding up. To counteract this testimony the same towel which had been held between Miss St. Cyr and her audience was produced in court. I asked Miss St. Cyr to hold the towel up to herself on the witness stand. There was nothing diaphanous about that length of terry cloth.

To clinch our defense against the nudity charge, I also showed the jury and court the actual net bra and the G-string Miss St. Cyr had worn during her performance, but because I am an old-fashioned kind of man I kept referring to her abbreviated panties and bra as her shorts and her brassière. My lack of familiarity with the modern nomenclature for those trifles seemed to amuse the ladies of the jury (there was even some unworthy talk afterward that I had deliberately *tried* to amuse them).

Anyhow, since both sexes on the jury had been convulsed at the efforts made by Mr. Hover to produce an acceptable bump and grind, I think it is fair to say that I succeeded in having that case laughed into acquittal.

10

Charles Chaplin

No CRUSHING BURDEN of public prejudice rested upon Miss St. Cyr. In fact, as her trial wore on the public howled with delight at some of its aspects. In strong contrast to Miss St. Cyr's tussle with the law, the trial of Charlie Chaplin carried with it the heaviest weight of public loathing for a client I've ever had anything to do with—with the possible exception of the two Alexander Pantages cases and the three times I defended another client, Busby Berkeley, against a charge of killing three people with his automobile.

I am no longer defending Chaplin. That is over and done with, but it is only fair to say that he went through that experience like a man. Prejudice hounded him most of the way through his lawsuit and it was only after we had had an opportunity to cross-examine the chief prosecuting witness, Miss Joan Berry, that that prejudice began to change. I could not only feel it change, I could hear it. Each noon, as we walked down the Federal Building hallway to lunch, a few, then more of those who watched us pass had kind words for Chaplin.

Miss Berry, a curvy, ambitious redhead, had met the immensely wealthy comic genius in the spring of 1941. Neither of them had any inkling of the trouble that meeting would get them into. It is not too much to say that Chaplin's two Berry trials rank high among the reasons why he is spending the last years of his life in Europe instead of California.

Miss Berry had come west from Brooklyn to do what is called

"making good" in Hollywood. Not long after they met, Chaplin had Miss Berry under contract as a "potential leading lady." His interest in her grew. She began taking dramatic lessons, and soon Chaplin announced his intention of putting her in a projected film, *Shadow and Substance.*

She had begun the routine known in Hollywood as "being a protégé." First a protégé is signed to a contract; after that there is talk of giving her dramatic lessons or singing lessons or dancing lessons to help her with her "career." Somewhere along the path the protégé may become her patron's mistress.

According to the testimony of both Chaplin and Joan Berry, their relationship quickly became intimate. As nearly as it could be determined—and once she was on the witness stand Miss Berry was not averse to discussing it—this situation lasted from one to two years.

Then as 1942 blended into 1943 Chaplin's ardor faded. Miss Berry testified that at first her patron delighted in having her visit him five or six times a week, but by midwinter her visits had dropped off to half as many. By the end of the following year Chaplin had decided that she was "not cut out for motion pictures" and had let his contract with her lapse.

Even Miss Berry's sympathizers—and at the beginning of the Chaplin trial they were legion—could not claim that she had been despoiled against her will. Two things were obvious. She suffered from a compulsion to "get a break in pictures" and she found Chaplin fascinating. Which of these two impulses was uppermost in her mind was anybody's guess, but after two final assignations in Chaplin's home in December 1942 she must have realized that her hold on him was almost nonexistent, for at that point she took an overdose of barbiturates.

She was found in time and the Beverly Hills police pumped her out. She was booked on a vagrancy charge and was released on probation with the stipulation that she go back east whence she had come. A representative of Chaplin's saw to it that she was given a hundred dollars and a ticket to New York.

Then suddenly the roof fell in on Chaplin. His protégé announced that she was pregnant and slapped him with a paternity suit.

Chaplin denied the charge. In a later trial than the one with which I was connected, Chaplin was adjudged the father, in spite of the testimony of pathologists who declared that his blood and the mother's blood could not possibly have produced the baby's blood type. But whether he was actually the father of his protégé's daughter or not, he certainly never should have taken up with Miss Berry.

She did a lot of brooding. After a few months of heavy introspection she was back in Beverly Hills creating what the police called "a disturbance" at Chaplin's mansion. When Chaplin complained she was arrested for violating her probation and was put into the county jail.

These matters were called to the attention of a Federal grand jury, and as a result of a trip Joan had made to New York in the fall of 1942 Chaplin was indicted for violating the Mann Act. The grand jury thought it more than a coincidence that he had journeyed to New York at the same time to make a speech at a rally supporting a second front in Europe.

No one claimed that Chaplin traveled with her either way, or even that he paid her hotel bill. The defense went further than that. We contended that going to New York was her own idea.

When Miss Berry went into the details of her trip east, she said that she and Chaplin had somehow become members of the same party at a night spot. Then she got down to earthier facts. Departing from the night spot, she said, they repaired to the Waldorf Towers, where they were intimate. Miss Berry testified that Chaplin also had relations with her in Los Angeles upon their return.

That was where I came in. Chaplin asked me to represent him against that criminal charge.

I do not plan to inflict a verbatim account of my examination and cross-examination in this trial upon those who read this story, but I would like to mention one point I brought out: The Mann Act had been made into a law by Congress to stamp out commercialized vice. None of those who spoke in its behalf thought of it as being aimed at private romance. Nevertheless, it is sometimes—and I think unfairly—used to crack down on an individual who pays a lady's fare from one state to another, even if that fare is only a taxi ride across a bridge spanning a river. Considered in this light, it is an enticement to blackmail or to help a woman "get back" at a man for wrongs either imagined or real.

On March 14, 1944, the Los Angeles *Times* reported the line that Chaplin's defense proposed to take. The *Times* did this with gratifying accuracy, and it might throw light into this corner of my life to give excerpts from the paper's version.

"Ladies and gentlemen of the jury [I was quoted as saying], at this time it is my duty to outline my defendant's case. We hope to establish to your satisfaction that he is innocent of violating the Mann Act as set forth in regard to the young lady, Joan Berry. She came to Los Angeles in 1941, met Chaplin and began to go out socially. We will show that he interested her in pictures, that he believed a screen career was possible for her, and that following up that belief, he arranged a contract for her. Thereafter he provided for her dramatic lessons with Max Reinhardt. He also instructed her himself. We will show that her teeth were fixed at the expense of Chaplin Studios, that he bought a story for her, the purchase price of which was $15,000. Further, she received a bonus of $1,000. In September, 1942, she was irked at the long delay in preparing her story for the screen and told Chaplin that she wanted to go to New York with her mother to live. Chaplin said, 'I have a lot of money invested in you.' She said, 'I am going anyway.' Mr. Chaplin said, 'All right, go. Arrangements will be made for your tickets.' It was all open and above board. The canceled checks which paid for her tickets will be produced.

"We will show that prior to October 1, 1942, she and her mother were occupying the same apartment in Beverly Hills and that she gave up the apartment and went to visit her aunt in New York City. She arrived there on October 5, moved into the Waldorf-Astoria, checking out of there on October 10. Mr. Chaplin did not arrive until October 15. Miss Berry checked in at another New York hotel which was owned by a man she knew and had seen in Mexico. She stayed there from October 10 until October 25. During that time she went out with the person who had checked her in. This person took her to the Stork Club. Mr. Chaplin happened to be there and saw her dancing with another man, but the two parties did not join.

"The sole occasion when she saw Mr. Chaplin in New York was that night at the Stork Club. On that occasion she did accompany him to the Waldorf Hotel but Mr. Chaplin will deny that there was any intimacy. We will show that she was willingly and gratuitously available to him to have relations at any time before her trip to New York, but at no time which involves the Mann Act charge against my client.

"Mr. Chaplin stayed in New York until October 27 and did not see Miss Berry again. He did not pay her bills at her other hotel nor did the Chaplin Studios.

"Briefly, it is the position of this defendant that he did not transport Joan Berry to New York for the purpose of having intimate relations. Nor did he insist upon her returning to Los Angeles for purposes of intimacy."

As evidence began to unfold I sensed the first crack in the iceberg of anti-Chaplinism. During the course of the Chaplin trial, particularly during the session of that trial held on March 28, 1944, I made efforts to find out through questioning Miss Berry whether anyone had made any attempt to blackmail my client or shake him down. Among the other things I asked her was, "Isn't it true that on May seventh, 1943, you telephoned Miss Katherine Hunter, Mr. Chaplin's secretary, and instructed her to tell Mr. Chaplin where you were so that he could have you arrested, and when Miss Hunter said that he didn't want you arrested, you said, 'I'll put his name in headlines anyhow,' whereupon Miss Hunter said, 'You're acting foolishly—that sounds like blackmail'?"

Miss Berry replied, "I did not."

I asked her still another question: "Isn't it a fact that on June first, 1943, in the yard of Mr. Chaplin's home, when you were alone with him, you accused him of being the father of your unborn child, and didn't you tell him that unless he gave your mother sixty-five thousand dollars and placed seventy-five thousand dollars in trust for the baby, you'd make trouble for him—that the press was on your side, and when they got through with him they would blast him out of the country? And didn't he deny the paternity charge and refuse to give you the money?"

Miss Berry announced that that conversation had not taken place.

I still don't believe that Chaplin, who could have enjoyed Miss Berry's favors in Los Angeles for as little as twenty-five cents carfare, would pay her fare to New York, plus her expenses as a guest at the Waldorf Towers, so that she would be there for improper purposes for one occasion only.

The most extraordinary thing was the testimony of Miss Berry herself in that case. She testified that she went to Chaplin's house one night in an effort to see him; that she saw Chaplin enter his house shortly before 1 A.M.; that her rings and knocks had gone unanswered; that she had broken into the house by smashing two windows; that she went to his second-floor bedroom with a loaded gun in her hand; that she held the loaded gun pointed at the comedian for an hour and a half while she talked to him, refusing Chaplin's requests to give it to him; that she put the loaded gun on the bedside table and left it there while she was intimate with him; that afterward she picked up the gun again and went to another bedroom, where she spent the night, and that the next morning she surrendered the gun to Chaplin and his butler after Chaplin agreed to give her money.

It was hard for us in the courtroom to believe our own ears; yet Chaplin himself corroborated what she said. To me, it proved that Chaplin had not transported her to New York for immoral purposes some two months earlier or insisted upon her returning to Los Angeles for such purposes, as the government contended. Miss Berry was readily available in California without his asking.

Chaplin was the best witness I've ever seen in a law court. He was effective even when he wasn't being examined or cross-examined, but was merely sitting there, lonely and forlorn, at a far end of the counsel table. He is so small that only the toes of his shoes touched the floor. He looked helpless, friendless and wistful, as he sat there with the weight of the whole United States Government against him.

Much was made of a trick he did for the newspaper shutterbugs. There was a water cooler in the corner, one of the kind into which someone up-ends a huge jug; then, when a plunger is pushed, bubbles float to the surface while a paper cup fills. There are two versions of what Chaplin did. One was that he placed a conical cup upside down on his head, then swept it off swiftly before the photographers could lens it, chuckling at their frustration at missing such a shot. Another version had him doing an almost impossible juggling act. Supposedly he tossed the paper cup upward end over end with such skill that it landed on its wide end on top of his head and stayed there.

Chaplin's greatest quality on the stand was his outward humility (whether he was inwardly humble or not, I don't know). He wept as he described his relations with Miss Berry and said, "Yes, I was intimate with her. I liked the girl."

During both direct and cross-examination he gave the appearance of utter sincerity. He wasn't arrogant, nor did he duck the verbal blows flung at him. Among other questions, he was asked when he had last been intimate with Miss Berry. He said, quite calmly, that he couldn't remember. He added that sex wasn't that important in his life.

I've heard it said that I did a very clever thing during that trial. I prefer to call it a psychologically sound maneuver. The Chaplin case was tried in our Federal court and a lawyer has far less leeway in the Federal court than in state court. For instance, when selecting a jury he doesn't have the right to question the prospective jurors. The judge does that for him, although the jurist sometimes accepts suggestions for questions.

A Federal judge is touchy about the questions a lawyer may ask during his cross-examination. There were many questions I wanted to ask Miss Berry, but I knew that the judge wasn't about to let me ask them. To cope with this, I adopted a device which, so far as I know, was a departure in forensic tactics. I wrote forty or fifty questions on as many sheets of paper, then took them to the judge and asked, "Which will you allow me to ask?"

He struck out almost all of them, leaving only ten or twelve I could put. But those few questions the judge okayed let the jury in on the fact that Miss Berry was far from being an innocent and unsophisticated young woman, and that Chaplin couldn't be blamed too much legally—although of course his conduct was morally reprehensible—for having been intimate with her.

My next move was to stand as close to the jury box as I could get—in fact, at the very edge of the jury box. It has always been my habit to do that when I am questioning a witness in the courtroom. In our Federal court an attorney is expected to take up his position behind the lectern, but in the Chaplin trial the judge was lenient about where I could stand. In that way I faced the witnesses and the witnesses faced me and the jury too. I held the long sheets of paper on which I had written the questions I had submitted to the judge. I'd ask a question, the jury would hear it, the witness would answer, then I'd say, "That was question number one. Now, your honor, in accordance with your ruling I will skip the other questions you have ruled that I am not permitted to ask and I will go to question number nine." Instinctively the jurors wondered what they had missed in the seven missing questions.

Then, after a while, I'd say, "That was question number thirty-one. Now, since your honor has ruled out the next six questions, I will resume with question number thirty-eight." The questions I did ask were not diabolical or tricky, so the effect of this procedure was to make the jury wonder why anyone could have been afraid of my unasked questions. There was nothing improper in this, and strategically I think it was effective.

All of these things added together had a curious result. The frozen hatred for my client thawed until, at the end of the trial, the audience was more pro-Chaplin than anti-Chaplin.

When the final arguments before Federal Judge J.F.T. O'Connor were made by the U.S. attorney and me, the issue was clear: Did my client have the "intent or purpose of engaging in immoral relations" with Miss Berry in New York when he contributed the money which was spent on a ticket to transport her there?

It was my job to convince the jury that this charge was non-sense, that the government had offered no valid proof that that was Chaplin's purpose. There was no doubt that Chaplin had bought her ticket to New York, but I held that there was nothing cal-culated about that. Unless the twelve people on the jury were con-vinced that Chaplin was incapable of doing anything helpful for anybody, that ticket had been bought in a spirit of helpfulness.

In my final argument to the jury I said, "I wish the government had not said that the defendant is an actor. What difference does it make whether he is a barber, a butcher, a lawyer or an actor? When he came through the door, he came as a human being with all the emotions of a human being. He is to be judged on that basis only. It is likewise immaterial that the defendant is a British sub-ject, although much has been made of that in this room. In this country we like to think that we are fair to foreigners too."

I concluded by saying that I was not there to excuse any mis-take my client might have made or to condemn Miss Berry for anything she might have done. There was only one issue: Was the defendant guilty of violation of the Mann Act within the restric-tions of the indictment? In my opinion, Chaplin had no immoral intent when he gave Joan Berry and her mother railroad tickets to New York. The jury didn't think he had either, for they brought in a verdict of acquittal.

When the not-guilty verdict was handed down, the courtroom au-dience cheered. No one who didn't live through that trial can even begin to comprehend what a switch that was.

After the jury freed him, Chaplin said, "I believe in the American people. I have abiding faith in them. In their sense of fair play and justice, their instincts are correct."

Whether he still believes in those two things is something anyone who has read his statements since he left this country must decide for himself.

II

Ruth Etting and the Colonel

I REMEMBER little Martin Snyder because he is the only male defendant I've ever represented who kissed me in the courtroom. He had two nicknames: "the Gimp," because he walked with a permanent limp, the result of an injury to one of his legs when he was struck down by a Chicago streetcar at the age of five; and "the Colonel," because of the zeal with which he had guarded Miss Ruth Etting's interests in her climb to fame as a star of the stage, screen and radio during the fifteen years he was her husband and manager.

Martin Snyder is still living. The last time I heard of him he was in Chicago, as an employee of that city, but when I first knew him he was still married to the internationally famed singer, whom he adored. According to Snyder, he had first met Miss Etting in 1920 when she was working in a chorus at Chicago's Marigold Gardens at twenty-five dollars a week. Snyder was twenty-six then. She was a year or two younger. He fell madly in love with her. Not only that, he saw her potential for fame. Snyder became Miss Etting's business manager first, then married her in 1922. The short, small-in-frame, crippled Snyder proved himself a devoted husband and a shrewd, hard-driving business manager. Under his guidance, Ruth Etting went to the top. She became a Ziegfeld Follies star and one of the most popular singers of her day.

Everywhere she went, he went; everything she did, he did. There was a close attachment, but, unhappily for Snyder, Miss Etting finally grew weary of it.

Martin Snyder had had powerful connections in Chicago at a

time when it was healthier for you there if your muscles were strong and you had the right connections. It was no secret that Snyder was a bad man to cross, in love as well as in business. Among those who found this out (although it should have come as no surprise to her) was Ruth Etting herself, who, for reasons best known to her, divorced Snyder in 1937.

Myrl Alderman, a young and handsome piano player some twelve years Miss Etting's junior, replaced Snyder in her affections. Ironically, it was Snyder who had hired Alderman as accompanist for the singer some two years earlier.

Miss Etting was noted for her torch singing, but no torch she ever carried blazed as hotly as the one her former husband carried for her. She was the most glamorous, most exciting thing that had ever happened to him. Not even the strong purge dispensed by the divorce court could get her out of his blood. For one thing, he couldn't forget the many services he had performed for her, and there is no doubt that in his own inimitable way he had done much to promote her interests and her earning power as a singer.

His smoldering resentment and his morose brooding focused on Alderman, who had taken his place. Snyder was not one to employ a private eye to do his shadowing for him. He kept his own eyes on his ex-wife and her new suitor. Then, on October 15, 1938, after Miss Etting had moved to Hollywood, he took matters into his own hands.

According to Alderman, Snyder entered Alderman's car as the latter left a parking lot near the broadcasting studio where he was working. Snyder said he wanted to talk "about you and Ruth" because he had heard that Alderman and Miss Etting were married. Alderman denied the marriage and refused to take Snyder to Miss Etting. Shoving a revolver in Alderman's side, Snyder demanded that he be taken to where Miss Etting was or "it'll be the last move you'll ever make."

The singer and Snyder's twenty-two-year-old daughter by a previous marriage (the girl had continued to live with Miss Etting after the divorce) were scheduled to have dinner that evening at

Alderman's house. Alderman drove Snyder there at gunpoint. At least, that was Alderman's story.

When they reached the house, at 3090 Lake Hollywood Drive, Alderman said that Snyder, with gun in hand, marched him from the car to the back door of the house. Ruth, who was preparing dinner in the kitchen, opened the door. Snyder, ordering Alderman to one side, kept the gun on the young piano player and Miss Etting. He told the singer to call his daughter, Edith. Then Snyder marched the three of them to the music room. He was alleged to have said to his own daughter, "You're in this too," and "This is the end of all of you."

In the music room Snyder ordered them to sit down, then said he was going to do all the talking. Miss Etting began to plead with him. When Alderman, who was sitting on the piano bench, tried to say something, Snyder shot twice and Alderman slumped to the floor. As the piano player later demonstrated to the jury at the trial by stripping to the waist, the second bullet entered his abdomen two inches above and to the left of the navel.

Miss Etting said she ran to the bedroom for a small pistol she owned. Snyder followed, and in a wild struggle for the pistol a shot was fired through the floor. Edith said she ran to the bedroom when she heard the shot and threw her arms around her father, pleading with him not to kill the singer, saying, "Ruthie's all I have left." Miss Etting ran from the bedroom, down the hall. Snyder started after her. Edith picked up Ruth's gun from the floor and fired at her father. The bullet crashed into the kitchen wall above his head.

When the police arrived, Snyder was standing on a street corner near the house. The law had come in answer to a call from a neighbor to whom Snyder had reported the shooting. Once he had been taken into custody, Snyder called me.

He branded all the versions of the shooting given out by his former wife, her young lover and his own daughter "utterly incorrect." He denied that he had forced Alderman at gunpoint to drive him to see Miss Etting. He said that Alderman had invited him to get into the car and offered to take him to the singer when Snyder told him that he had come to the broadcasting studio in the hope of seeing her. He claimed that Alderman pulled a gun on him in the music room when the talk got out of hand, and that he had fired in the direction of the piano player in self-defense.

Snyder denied that he had intended to kill Alderman. "Obviously I didn't intend to kill him," he said. "If I had, I certainly had plenty of opportunity to do so."

Fortunately for everyone concerned, the bullet, which tunneled Alderman's abdominal wall, missed all the vital organs in the region, and after hospitalization and a short convalescence he recovered.

Snyder was indicted on three counts of attempted murder: of Myrl Alderman, of Ruth Etting and of his own daughter, Edith Snyder. He was also indicted on two counts of kidnaping: one, the kidnaping of Alderman in forcing him at gunpoint to drive to his house; the other, the kidnaping of Alderman, Miss Snyder and Miss Etting by forcibly directing them from one room to another in Alderman's house just prior to the shooting. A sixth count charged Snyder with violating the California gun laws by obliterating the serial numbers on the revolver he had used in the shooting.

In December 1938, less than two months after this violent session, Snyder's trial got under way. By this time, Alderman had recovered sufficiently to join Miss Etting and Edith Snyder in presenting a united front against Snyder. In testifying for the prosecution, the three corroborated one another on all essential points. Their trial testimony followed, almost to the letter, the three-in-one version they had given to the newspapers immediately after the shooting.

Mr. Snyder's case can be further summed up in the following words taken from his own testimony: He testified that he was forty-four; that he had been born in Chicago; that he had a leg injury which he had received when he was about five years old in a street-car accident; that he had attended school to about the third to fourth grade and was thirteen or fourteen when he left; that he had peddled papers in the Loop district in Chicago until about seventeen; that he then worked for several years for the *Tribune* circulation department in Chicago, after which he'd gone to work in the Sanitary District Department in the city hall. He became Miss Etting's business manager and personal representative and performed those services until 1936. His duties consisted of negotiating contracts and money and seeing that she received all the benefits which were coming to her. She herself handled all the money throughout that entire time. She also paid their common bills.

Snyder further testified that he was in love with her at the time of marriage and that his love continued throughout their entire married life, and that she appeared to be in love with him until 1937. He added that he had never struck her at any time during their married life, nor had he laid a hand upon her.

He said that in 1932 he had entered into a written contract of copartnership with her. The reason for this was that he had opportunities to go into business with other people and she didn't want him to, so the agreement was drawn up, although they had been working under the same arrangement orally even before that time. He volunteered that before their marriage she knew his life history, where he was born, the amount of his education, the work he had been doing. The first time she had said anything to him about divorce was between August 15 and August 20 in 1937. At that time they had been married nearly fifteen years. Miss Etting had stopped working about six or eight months before that, although Snyder had not done anything that he knew of to keep her from working. She had, in fact, opportunities to work in radio, on the stage, in pictures and making records.

According to Snyder, the talk about divorce took place in their home in Los Angeles and (the conversation he reported is given from his standpoint) she told him that she wanted a divorce, that they would divide their common money, that she wanted to take a trip because of her health, *and that there was nobody else in her life*. After that they went to an attorney, Otto Baer, in Chicago, and Snyder signed a statement whereby he was to receive a one-half interest in their Beverly Hills home when it was sold and one half of the rental from it if it was rented. He also signed an agreement that in the event of his death his one-half interest should go to Miss Etting.

He testified that they then went to their safe-deposit box in New York and she gave him fifteen $1,000 bills, $35,000 worth of Liberty Bonds and about $25,000 in securities. Snyder is also the authority for the report that she wrote off $100,000 which she claimed had gone to pay his gambling debts and to take care of his mother and Edith. Snyder said his gambling debts had not amounted to $50,000. He had paid out throughout the time they were together a lot of money to build his wife's career and had told her the money had gone for gambling.

He said that when she gave him the money he told her she had better keep it, that he might go haywire, that she knew how screwy he was with money, but she refused. At that time he did not believe that he had received fifty-fifty of everything. He believed that the total joint accumulation of their married life was between $350,000 and $400,000.

He had stayed in New York after the divorce until he came to California in July 1938. Prior to their separation he had hardly touched a drop of liquor and had sipped a little wine; actually, he said, he detested liquor. Thereafter he had commenced to drink, to help him forget; as a result he drank continually in New York while there and spent his money going to night clubs, race tracks, sporting events and gambling houses, at which he had bet considerable sums.

He had telephoned Miss Etting in January 1938 and had talked with her then and he may have said a lot of things, since he was drunk, but he certainly had no intent to harm her or to kill her. He had come to California in July 1938 because he had been hearing things about Miss Etting and Alderman and he also wanted to go into business there.

The first time he had met Alderman was when he employed him as a pianist. Alderman worked then on the Etting program for thirteen weeks in 1935 but after that time, Snyder said, he never saw him or heard of him until, in New York just before coming to Los Angeles, he had heard radio commentator Jimmy Fidler mention the rumor that "Ruth Etting, who recently divorced Colonel Snyder, will soon marry Myrl Alderman."

The next day—it was in January 1938—he called her on the phone and requested a woman friend to have Miss Etting meet him at her apartment upon his arrival. Describing their meeting, he said that in the course of it, he asked her about the trip she said she was going to take with Edith and asked her if she was sure she had not lied to him about the fact that there was nobody else in her life. He added that he could not understand why Jimmy Fidler had mentioned Alderman, at which point Miss Etting jumped up and left.

He had remained in Los Angeles and had continued to drink and gamble at the race tracks and at night clubs. He admitted that he may have said to someone that he was going to "get Ruth" or something of that sort, but on that occasion he had had quite a few drinks and really had no intention of using physical violence nor did he intend to harm her. What he meant was that he wanted to talk to her and if they couldn't agree on going back together again they'd go to court about the money he thought was rightfully due him. In fact, he had worked as hard as she for that money, if not a little harder. Honestly and in good faith he believed that he had not received 50 per cent of what he had made in their fifteen years together. He said that he had believed her when she said there was nobody else involved; that there was a possibility of reconciliation between them, so he wanted to talk to her; and that if it was true that there was somebody else, he only wanted what was rightfully his due.

He had not told anyone that he was going to shoot Alderman and Miss Etting for revenge. He may have used the word "blast," but if so it was in reference to "blasting" things in the newspapers if they couldn't get together.

Between July 17, when he arrived in Los Angeles, and October 15 he had made efforts to locate Miss Etting to talk to her. As far as he knew, he may have said a lot of things then that he didn't mean because when he was drinking he was moody and melancholy, and everywhere he looked he thought he saw Ruth. He may even have said he was going to commit suicide. He couldn't remember. When he heard the rumor that she had married Alderman, he had inquired several places trying to locate her. Then he had tried to locate her through Alderman. His purpose in wanting to see Miss Etting was that it seemed to him that the best thing to do, now that he thought she was married to Alderman and there was no chance of a reconciliation, was to get what money was rightfully due him, a sum for which they had both worked in partnership.

When Snyder took the stand in his own defense, he told in his volatile way his version of the events leading up to the shooting and the shooting itself. I'll not set out all the details here. I will only touch upon the highlights.

He had gone to the National Broadcasting Company studios on Melrose about seven o'clock the night of October 15th and had met Alderman in the reception room. He said that he had told Alderman he had been trying to talk to Ruth but couldn't locate her. He had thought that she might be there that night, and he very much wanted to discuss things with her before they went to court and threw a lot of mud. He further told Alderman that Ruth had lied to him and tricked him into divorce by saying that there was nobody else in the picture, in spite of the fact that Alderman was in the picture a long while ago and had broken up his home.

He asked Alderman to sit down so that he could tell him about it, but Alderman said that he didn't have time. Snyder also said he would like to talk to Ruth and see if she wouldn't be reasonable. If not, they would end up in court, and he was trying to avoid that.

Snyder continued that Alderman was on his way home, that he had got his car and had opened the door for him and he, Snyder, had got in; that while driving, in answer to Alderman's query as to what he meant about breaking up Snyder's home, Snyder told him that he had discovered that he and Ruth had been running around together for about six weeks in July 1937 while he, Snyder, was in Chicago, and since he had returned to California he had heard tales around the studio about Alderman showing Ruth's picture to people and about how Ruth had been visiting him at his apartment. But Snyder insisted that on the way to the house from the studio he had definitely not drawn a gun and had not forced Alderman to drive him.

Snyder's story was that Miss Etting had been at the door when they got there. According to him she had asked him what he was doing there, and he had said he had come to talk things over. Alderman took her hand and said to her, "He knows what it's all about," and suggested that they go' into his room. Edith was at the stove, and they all walked into the room where Miss Etting was sitting. Alderman sat down on the piano bench. Edith went in directly ahead of Snyder. There was no place for him to sit except on a chair by the door.

Snyder then said he had told Ruth that he understood she and Alderman were married and she said, "No." Snyder insisted that Alderman had told him so. Ruth said she didn't care what Alderman had told him, that they were not married. Then Snyder asked her if she meant to say that they were just living there and that Edith knew about it. Miss Etting said that it was none of his business.

According to Snyder, Alderman also said, "Yes, it is none of your business." Then he looked over at Alderman, and Alderman was trying to stand up with a gun in his hand. Snyder said the lights in the house began to flicker and he had got frightened and had put his hand in his pocket and had shot twice in Alderman's direction. Then the lights really went out.

Snyder said in continuing, "Alderman hollered, 'Ouch,' and there was a noise and Alderman said, 'Honey, get that son of a bitch . . .'" Snyder asked where the telephone was and walked out into the hall. Miss Etting came toward him, calling him a bad name, and asked him what he was trying to do to her baby, and he told her he wasn't trying to do anything, that he couldn't help it. Following which he and Miss Etting struggled down the hall into a room and he grabbed her hand and the gun went off. After that he went down the hall to look for a phone again. When he got to the end of the hall he saw a den or alcove and he dropped his gun to call the police. He said then that he saw Edith and Ruth coming toward him with a gun and they were hollering at him, and he started out the back door and as he was going out he heard a shot.

It was part of his account that he went next door and rang the bell and when a lady answered he told her there had been some trouble next door and would she be kind enough to call the police, since somebody might be hurt. He wanted to make sure that the police arrived, and when they did he told them, "The trouble is in there," pointing to the house. Then he handed the officer his gun and told him to be careful, since Miss Etting had a gun too.

Snyder testified that he had not at any time drawn his gun from his pocket prior to the time he had seen the gun in the hands of Alderman; that he had not used his gun under any circumstances prior to the time he saw Alderman on the piano stool with a gun; that the reason he had drawn it from his pocket then was that he was afraid Alderman would shoot him, and from his manner of expression and the tone of his voice he really thought that Alderman was going to kill him. He absolutely believed it necessary for him to do what he had done under the circumstances. When he fired at Alderman he did not intend to kill him; he did not take aim when he fired, he just shot in Alderman's direction.

He further testified that when he was struggling with Miss Etting for the gun it went off in her hand, and that at that time he had no intent in his heart to kill her either; that he had not gone to the house for any other purpose than to talk to Miss Etting, to come to an understanding of his rights, to avoid scandal-throwing in court. He did not know that night that the numbers had been filed from his gun. The first he knew of that was at the police station when he heard one officer mention it to another. He had not filed the numbers off himself. He had not endeavored to throw his weapon away or dispose of it; he had not tried to get away from the scene before the officers came; instead he had stayed there and had waited for them.

He said he had had that gun about a year. He had gotten it in New York in January or February of 1938. He had obtained it in a gambling place from the doorman there, who had told him he ought to have a gun to protect himself, since he was carrying so much money. He had given the doorman a fifty-dollar bill for it. He had not carried it all the time thereafter, but only when he went out gambling and had large sums of money on him. At other times it was in his bag at the hotel.

When asked when he had put the gun in his pocket (with reference to the affair on October 15) Snyder said that he had done it a couple of days before that, that he was making big bets with bookies and that he had been to certain spots playing the wheel. As a result he had a lot of money about him. He had not put the gun into his pocket to use it on Alderman. In fact, he hadn't gone to see Alderman for any purpose other than in an effort to talk to Miss Etting; that was really all he had in mind when he was seeking Alderman's address from people.

He denied categorically that when he was in the kitchen that night with Alderman he had used his gun to force Miss Etting, Alderman and Edith to go to the music room.

In cross-examining Miss Etting, I was as searching with her as I have ever been with any woman, although even with her I was courteous. However, within these limits, I was very thorough in trying to demonstrate an emotional and sentimental justification for the Colonel's action in taking a shot at Alderman. I drew from the singer that on two occasions following the divorce in December 1937 Snyder had showered presents upon her which were inscribed with sentimental inscriptions, thus evidencing his continuing love for her.

Then I cross-examined Edith Snyder. She had stayed with Miss Etting after her stepmother's divorce from Snyder, and through her I dug into the relationship between Alderman and Miss Etting. But when I cross-examined Alderman on the attempted-murder counts (as with Ruth Etting and Edith Snyder), there wasn't much a defense attorney could do. Only four people knew what had actually gone on in Alderman's house on the night of the shooting, and from direct testimony of the state's three key witnesses it was plain they were presenting a united front against Snyder's contention that he fired at the piano player in self-defense. Nevertheless, as I took Alderman over his direct testimony concerning the drive at gunpoint from the broadcasting station, I pressed hard on the kidnaping charge.

"You were going home anyway, weren't you?" I asked him.

"Yes," he said.

"Then," I went on, "in substance you say that Snyder was forcing you to go where you were going anyway?"

"Well," Alderman said, "I had to drive around a couple of blocks that I didn't intend to."

The gun-laws-violation count was based on the fact that the serial numbers had been filed from the outside of the revolver used by Snyder on the night of the shooting. In California it is a serious offense to carry a gun with obliterated serial numbers. I demolished that charge quickly. When the police ballistics expert was on the stand I had him open the handle of Snyder's gun. The serial number was visible on the *inside* of that weapon. There are two places on a gun, not one, where a serial number appears. Of course, I knew that that second serial number was there—I had unscrewed the gun myself and had looked at it—or I wouldn't have asked the expert to do it.

About halfway through the trial, Alderman and Ruth Etting eloped to Las Vegas and were married. Snyder's daughter made the trip with them. This incident caused quite a stir. It was emotionally hard on Snyder, who was still deeply in love with his ex-wife.

Snyder's story received support from a private detective hired by Alderman's former wife to check on the activities of Alderman and Miss Etting. The detective had been parked near the piano player's house when Snyder and Alderman arrived in Alderman's car. His testimony directly contradicted that of Miss Etting and Alderman, both of whom had testified that Snyder had marched the piano player in at gunpoint.

Before beginning his closing argument to the jury, the district attorney moved to dismiss the count which charged Snyder with the triple kidnaping of Miss Etting, Miss Snyder and Alderman—from one room to another in Alderman's house—just prior to the shooting. This motion was granted.

Ruth Etting and the Colonel

In my closing argument, I told the jury the Colonel was like the Hunchback of Notre Dame. Ruth Etting had used him, I said, just as Esmeralda had used Quasimodo. She had then tossed him into the ash heap when she could no longer find use for him. I said that Snyder had taken her out of the chorus when she was still a kid and had made a star of her. She knew that he was a cripple and that he had come from the streets of Chicago, but she had lived with him for fifteen years anyhow, until she had reached an age where he could take her no further. Her days as the number one song bird of the air waves were almost over, and she was no longer a youthful glamour girl of pictures. It was then that Snyder had suggested they quit work and play together, but she had wanted a younger man and a whole man.

"For her gold she got a younger man," I said. "I sincerely hope her romance will last, but I'm afraid it will not. After all, Alderman is a used article too, for this is his third marriage. I hope Ruth Etting got what she wanted when she got Alderman. But, ladies and gentlemen of the jury, that does not mean that you should give her the conviction of this crippled man who made her what she was for a wedding present."

As in the case of Paul Wright and the "white flame" which had exploded in his head, I laid stress on the overpowering, obsessive love Snyder cherished for his former wife, and the corroding effect of the intense jealousy which had eaten acidlike into his mind.

However, this defense was not as effective as it had been in the Wright case. Perhaps Snyder's Chicago background, reminiscent of a time when an outthrust jaw and narrowed eyes were passports to success, didn't endear him to the jury.

Also, Snyder had not found his wife *in flagrante delicto,* as Wright had. The fact was, the woman with whom he was so inordinately in love was no longer his wife. An outraged *ex*-husband doesn't have as much heart tug with a jury.

After deliberating thirteen hours, the jury of six men and six women returned a verdict on four of the five felony counts against Martin Snyder. They disagreed on the charge that he had kidnaped Alderman. They found him not guilty of attempting to murder Miss Etting, not guilty of attempting to murder his own daughter, and not guilty of violating the state gun laws by obliterating serial numbers on the revolver used in the shooting. But they did convict him of the attempted murder of Myrl Alderman.

I took his case up to a higher court on appeal and I won Snyder a new trial, although he spent a year in jail waiting for the result of my appeal.

In June 1940, when the Supreme Court of California affirmed the order of the District Court of Appeals granting Martin Snyder a new trial, Alderman and Miss Etting were in New York. They told the D. A.'s office that they didn't want to prosecute Snyder further and were unwilling to return to California to testify against him.

Edith Snyder had died in Chicago a year earlier, so in October of 1940 the district attorney informed the court that it would be impossible to present any eyewitnesses to the shooting at a second trial. He therefore moved to dismiss the charge of attempted murder on which Snyder had been convicted nearly two years before. The dismissal was granted.

It was then that Snyder kissed me right in open court. I'll never forget it. He grabbed me around the neck and kissed me on the cheek.

12

Garbo Talks

O NE OF the mental tape recordings from my legal life and times which occasionally plays itself back in my mind is the deposition of Greta Garbo which I took in October of 1936. My client, David Schratter, claimed that he had loaned the glamorous Swedish film star $10,500 when she was launching her screen career in Europe a dozen years before and that she had failed to repay the money. Mr. Schratter, who had been a film producer in Sweden, Turkey, Germany and perhaps other European countries, retained me to file suit against Miss Garbo in order to recover the money he said she owed him. The purpose of the deposition was to determine, in advance of trial, whether Miss Garbo would admit receiving the money from Schratter and what her position was with respect to repayment.

The scene of my deposition-taking was in the star's dressing room in a Culver City studio, and I submit that the following colloquy cannot be billed (except loosely) as GARBO TALKS, the way her first talking picture, *Anna Christie*, was billed.

Miss Garbo, Mr. Schratter and I were seated opposite each other. My examination and her responses were as follows. I offer them for any collector of motion picture memorabilia in Q-and-A form.

Q. Miss Garbo, your true name is Gustafsson?
A. No.
Q. What is your true name?
A. Garbo.

Q. But you are sometimes known by the name Gustafsson?

A. Yes.

Q. Greta is your first name?

A. Yes.

Q. You regard your true name as Greta Garbo?

A. Yes.

Q. Now, Miss Garbo, in 1924 were you residing in Stockholm, or in Sweden?

A. Yes.

Q. Are you acquainted with Mr. Schratter, this gentleman here? I will ask him to stand for a moment. Miss Garbo, this is Mr. Schratter. Are you acquainted with Mr. Schratter?

A. Yes.

Q. Thank you, Mr. Schratter. You may sit down now. You first became acquainted with Mr. Schratter in 1924, did you not, Miss Garbo?

A. Yes.

Q. Do you recall that it was in Stockholm?

A. Yes.

Q. At such time he was introduced to you by Mr. Mauritz Stiller?

A. Yes.

Q. Mr. Stiller was your director, I believe?

A. Yes.

Q. You were employed then by the Svenska Film Company in Sweden?

A. Yes.

Q. Do you recall the first time you met Mr. Schratter? Was it at the Grand Hotel in Stockholm?

A. Yes.

Q. Do you remember meeting his wife then?

A. Yes.

Q. Would your recollection be that it was in May of 1924?

A. I couldn't say for certain.

Q. Was there any discussion at that time between Mr. Stiller and Mr. Schratter as to your ability as an actress, or that you had considerable promise?

A. I don't think so.

Q. Do you recall the discussion with respect to your financial situation then, about the fact that you were not financially affluent?

A. I don't think so. In fact, I'm sure there was none.

Q. Was there any discussion about your supporting your mother and your family?

A. No.

Q. Did you receive any money from Mr. Schratter at the Grand Hotel in Stockholm?

A. No.

Q. You didn't receive five thousand Swedish kronor from him?

A. Not that I know of. In fact, I can say positively no.

Q. When you were first introduced to Schratter, were you not informed that he was president of the Trianon Film Company in Berlin?

A. I don't recollect, except that I was to meet the man to work with. I didn't know in what capacity.

Q. Wasn't there a question about your being engaged by the company as an actress?

A. There must have been.

Q. Didn't you enter into a contract with the Trianon Film Company?

A. I don't think I ever had any contract, or worked for them. [Miss Garbo was gradually becoming more of a blabbermouth.] I came to Berlin. Then I went to Constantinople.

Q. Do you recall that you received payments in Swedish kronor from that company which would be the equivalent of twelve hundred and fifty dollars a month?

A. I don't know.

Q. Do you recall going to a première of a picture which you made for the Svenska Company which was called *Gösta Berling*?

A. Yes.

Q. It was sometime in 1924, wasn't it? And you were in the cast of the picture?

A. Yes.

Q. Do you recall that there was a Mrs. Lars Hansen in the picture?

A. Yes.

Q. And Mona Martenson?

A. Yes.

Q. Gerda Lundquist?

A. Yes.

Q. Were you present at the première of the picture in Berlin?

A. Yes.

Q. Do you recall that after the première you attended a social event at the Hotel Adlon, with Mr. Schratter?

A. With Mr. Schratter and his wife and Mr. Stiller, at the première. But after the première, I don't know. However, I recollect having met Mr. Schratter and his wife and several others at a party.

Q. Did you receive any money for the time you worked for the Trianon Film Company?

A. I did not receive any money as far as I can recollect. Someone paid the fares—who, I don't know. I was merely a young actress working in a picture, and the people in it, like me, were merely put on the train and taken along. How we were paid I don't know. Mr. Stiller was handling all my business affairs.

Q. Do you recall ever visiting Mr. Schratter at his home?

A. If I did, the party I attended must have been at his home.

Q. Do you recall having gone to the home of Mr. Schratter at number twenty-seven on ———— Street?

A. I haven't the slightest idea.

Q. Does your recollection tell you that you were at Mr. Schratter's home twice?

A. I can't remember being there more than at this one party.

Q. Do you recall putting in a long-distance telephone call to Mr. Schratter from Stockholm to Berlin?

A. I never called long distance in those days. Neither do I now, if I can help it.

Q. Do you recall a conversation with Mr. Schratter in the presence of his wife in Berlin when you told him that you had purchased clothes with the money he had given you?

A. No.

Q. Have you received any letters from Mr. Schratter in the last two years?

A. Yes, two or three. I don't know. I never answered them.

Q. You state definitely that you do not owe Mr. Schratter anything?
A. Yes. If I owed any debts I'd be glad to pay them.

This is all that I recall of Miss Garbo's garrulousness. When the case finally came up in Superior Court another attorney (one, I hope, more capable of eliciting streams of conversation than I) represented Mr. Schratter. Perhaps Miss Garbo or Mr. Schratter will remember how it all came out. I don't recall.

I do know this: Miss Garbo answered my questions about her financial dealings with Mr. Schratter in a vocabulary totaling exactly 122 words.

13

Norman ("Kid McCoy") Selby

The TRIAL of Norman Selby ("Kid McCoy") was the one in which I waited ninety-nine hours for the jury to come in. The tension of that waiting was so great (the emotional strain during any major trial is tremendous) that when they finally did come in my head was resting on a supporting frame formed by my two hands.

When that jury found Selby guilty of manslaughter, the verdict was regarded by the press as a victory for the defense. He could just as easily have been found guilty of murder. If it was a victory, Selby and I owed thanks to a maiden lady on that jury who liked his looks. We found out later that it was she who had held out for the more merciful decision until all of the others had come around to her way of thinking. I had picked out another juror as being favorably inclined to him, but I had selected the wrong person. As any lawyer does, I had studied their facial expressions and their general attitudes. I had noticed whether they looked at the defendant or refused to look at him. But these actions of mine were instinctive. I'm not sure that anyone can prejudge a jury.

As Kid McCoy, Selby had once been the welterweight champion of the world. He had acquired that title in 1896 when he defeated Tommy Ryan. Now all that was in the past. He was living in Los Angeles, on West Seventh Street, with a woman he wasn't married to although, in his slap-happy fashion, he adored her. For one thing, he couldn't marry her because she was still legally married to one Albert Mors, an antique dealer, though she was doing her level best to dissolve that marriage.

Selby was a guard at a Los Angeles airplane-manufacturing plant, and so he was permitted to carry a gun. When he came home at night to the apartment where he lived with Mrs. Mors, it was his custom to take off the gun and put it on the table.

One hot August night in 1924 he came home, put his gun down, took off his coat and sat down. He and the woman who shared his bed then shared a number of drinks. When they had had a large quantity to drink, Mrs. Mors got a butcher knife and announced that she was going to commit suicide.

Her gruesome announcement didn't come completely out of the blue. She owned a store on Seventh Street in which she sold *objets d'art* and antiques. Not only was she in the midst of trying to divorce her husband, but she had been questioned by the United States Government about some diamonds which were said to have been brought into the country illegally and which she was supposed to have. There had been talk of her guilty knowledge of smuggling and the customs inspectors had frightened her.

When she told Selby that she was going to kill herself with a butcher knife and thus rid herself of her troubles, he made a grab for the knife. As he grabbed, the knife went through her blouse. This was borne out afterward by the fact that when she was examined there was a minor stab in her breast. She then made a lunge with her left hand at the Kid's gun lying on the table, picked it up and, firing it at her own head, killed herself.

One of the difficulties facing me as Selby's attorney was that Mrs. Mors was not left-handed, although, if she had fired that shot, she had done it with her left hand. To make things even tougher for Selby, she must have pulled the trigger with the thumb of her left hand. I reached those conclusions myself after hours of trying to reproduce the woman's movements as Selby described them.

He said that after she shot herself he had kept on drinking. When he was asked why he hadn't called for help, he said he'd been too drunk. However, he hadn't been too intoxicated to find a photograph of himself which Mrs. Mors had liked and to place it on her breast. Then he had lain down beside her.

In addition to having consumed vast quantities of hooch, Selby was also a little punchy as a result of absorbing countless head blows during his fighting career. He said that he had wanted to die too, so he had kept sucking away at his booze bottle, thinking that if he drank heavily enough he would kill himself. He merely passed out.

When he came to, he got into his car and drove aimlessly around Los Angeles. In the middle of the night he showed up at his sister's house and wakened her by scratching on her sleeping-porch screen with his fingernails. When she let him in, he told her a rambling and incoherent tale about having killed Mrs. Mors. He gave her what valuables he had with him, then he said that he was going to commit suicide too and left.

He was next seen in a little restaurant in downtown Los Angeles, having a cup of coffee. Leaving there, he went back to Mrs. Mors's art-antique shop and waited outside until the janitor, a youngster who opened the place each morning, arrived. Selby followed him in and made the boy sit in one spot while he played music for him on an antique music box.

Selby still had his gun. When customers came in, he made the ones he "liked" sit on one side of the store and those he didn't "like" sit on the other side, and if these were men he forced them to take off their trousers. Then, in a kind of screwball Robin Hood gesture, he took money away from those who had it and gave it to those who didn't.

When one customer came in and saw what was going on, he turned and ran. Selby shot him, although he didn't injure him seriously.

Then, forgetting the customers he had lined up, Selby ran next door to a lingerie shop. The proprietors were a man and wife, and in his confused mental state Selby took a shot at this harmless couple too and hit one of them; then he ran out and jumped on the side of a passing automobile, commandeered the car and told its driver to drive him to the corner of West Seventh Street and Arborata. Once there, he told the driver to turn up Arborata.

Then the police caught up with him, arrested him and took him to his apartment, where they had found Mrs. Mors's body. When he was questioned, Selby insisted that he had shot Mrs. Mors himself.

If he hadn't been so adamant on that point, he probably would never have been convicted of harming her.

To explain this it is necessary to backtrack. Mrs. Mors had had the husband from whom she was seeking a divorce arrested and charged with an attempt to break into her shop and take things which belonged to her. She had afterward filed a criminal complaint against him. Released on bail, he had moved up on the hill above Hollywood and Vine, where he lived alone. On the night of his wife's death, for no apparent reason, he left his home and moved into the Westgate Hotel, near Fifth and Western, registering under an assumed name.

From the room assigned him, he could have gone down the hotel's back stairs, out the back door and into an alley. From there it would have been only a short walk to the apartment where his wife was living with Selby.

In the apartment under the one where Mrs. Mors's body was found lived a woman who worked in the Broadway Department Store. She told police that after hearing a noise overhead she had heard someone come down the back stairs, and, looking out of her window which faced the areaway at the back of her apartment, she had seen a man pass. She identified that man as Mr. Mors.

She absolutely refused to identify the nighttime prowler as Selby. It is apparent therefore that if Selby had not made his impulsive confession, the evidence of this woman and the trouble between Mors and his wife would have made it difficult for Mors himself to avoid a charge of murder.

None of this came out until the trial. By that time I had been retained by Selby to represent him. He had retracted his confession of murder and had told the story of Mrs. Mors's suicide, which I am convinced was the truth. During the course of that trial I did several things. I had Selby tell the jury how she had seized his gun to commit suicide and how it had gone off in her hand with the thumb of her left hand on the trigger. I put Mors on the witness stand and questioned him, but I was unable to get a satisfactory answer to the question of why he had registered on that particular night at the Westgate Hotel under an assumed name.

The Jerry Giesler Story

The result was a crazy, mixed-up one. If Selby hadn't made his earlier confession and if he hadn't done the irrational and violent things he had done that night and the next morning, I might have got him off and Mors would probably have been tried for murder. But added to the murder charge against Selby was a charge of armed robbery (for taking money away from the men he lined up the next morning) and a charge of assault with a deadly weapon (because of the shots he had taken at people that morning). In short, he had done about all a man could do to get himself into deep trouble.

One of the witnesses for the defense was Damon Runyon. He came all the way from New York to testify as a character witness for Selby. I had others, but Runyon was the outstanding one.

After the jury had retired, they came back into the court from time to time to ask questions about the testimony and request further instructions on points of law. The custom was for the foreman of the jury to push a buzzer three times if they had agreed on a verdict. In the meantime, if he wanted something like water or sheets of paper he buzzed the buzzer once. When I heard that buzzer it went through my stomach like a blunt knife, so to get away from it I stayed in the hallway outside the courtroom and paced up and down while the jury was out.

After its interminable ninety-nine hours of deliberation, it brought in a verdict of manslaughter, on December 29, 1924. Selby was then put on trial for the other charges against him. He retained another attorney to defend him against those charges. He was convicted and was sentenced to San Quentin.

When he had been in San Quentin for almost eight years, Henry Ford, Sr., got him out by agreeing to employ him to handle the health and exercise program for his employees in the Ford factory in Detroit. Selby worked for Mr. Ford on parole until he took his own life in a Detroit hotel room in April 1940 with an overdose of sleeping pills. He was sixty-six.

I am still convinced that the shooting for which Selby drew a manslaughter penalty was accidental, that Mrs. Mors shot herself and that Selby confessed because he wanted to die.

14

The Case of

the Fleeced Foreigner

I n spite of the fact that my name is linked in the public's mind with such legal matters as murder and rape, I am not solely a criminal lawyer. The fact is, I usually have a large number of civil clients and I work for them just as conscientiously as I do for my clients in criminal cases.

Civil law has countless facets. Just recently, for example, I have had in my office a condemnation case, a damage case which grew out of a medical malpractice case, and a very interesting libel action pending against the American Humane Society. I have gone to court in many libel cases. I've handled lawsuits to satisfy judgments, motions to vacate judgments and matters pertaining to estates.

However, some civil cases are more stimulating than others. Take the one which involved Fanny Brice's brother, Lew Brice, in April 1938. If Erle Stanley Gardner were writing this, he'd probably call it the Case of the Fleeced Foreigner.

Lew Brice was given to gambling—but not the well-bred games played in gentlemen's clubs. Brice had bigger ideas. The gambling enterprise of Brice's with which I was concerned began on a pier at Long Beach, California, where Brice was killing time with a trio of pals: Tommy Guinan, brother of the famed night-club hostess Texas Guinan of prohibition and "giggle-water" fame, and two

other men, George Lewis and Jack Reynolds. All four had connections in areas which are described as "places with a lot of action."

On this particular day at Long Beach they saw an odd-looking
party approaching. Guinan and Brice had met him before when he
made a previous visit to Los Angeles. On that occasion he had
dropped ten grand to them in a friendly Red Dog game and he had
paid that debt in cash. Neither Guinan nor Brice had ever forgotten
that.

The name of this odd-looking party was Henry Talbot Devers
Clifton. Although he sometimes went around looking as seedy as a
skid-row bum, in reality he was one of England's fast diminishing
supply of millionaires. Among his various properties were five miles
of Lancashire coastline. On that particular parcel of land were five
thousand homesteads, several hundred shops and a score of banks.
He also owned a seaside resort near Blackpool. This real estate
represented only a portion of his holdings.

Socially he was equally well heeled. He could trace his family
back to a hundred years after the Conqueror's landing, and at one
time he had been married to one of the Lowells of Boston.

When Brice, Guinan and company sighted Clifton, they slapped
him gleefully on the shoulder and a motion to adjourn to a neighbor-
ing hotel was quickly moved, seconded and passed. Somehow a
deck of cards made its appearance, and, after a few preliminary
rufflings which gave out the crisp crackle new cards emit when they
are handled by practiced hands, a little game of dealer's choice
began.

Clifton later reported to Buron Fitts, the local D.A., that stud and
draw were favored that session. Clifton also told Fitts with mild
surprise, "At first things went fairly slowly. During the early part of
the game I lost less than a thousand dollars."

Presently the play was restricted to stud, with a limit which kept
on being raised. During this period the bets averaged from ten to
twenty dollars a card. At no time was there any amount of real
cash in sight. I.O.U.s were passed from hand to hand. Matches
were used instead of poker chips.

And then (as always happens sooner or later in such games) the "payoff" hand was dealt. Clifton found himself holding a pair of kings, one up and one down. He was a great believer in riding his luck. Taking counsel with himself, he announced, "I'll bet fifty thousand."

Three of the group—Reynolds, Guinan and Lewis—retired from the competition, but when the third and fourth cards were dealt, Brice and Clifton checked their bets. Two sevens lay face up on the table before Brice. Clifton had two jacks visible. With his two kings, that gave Clifton two pairs. He considered the possibilities for a moment, then said, "I'll bet another hundred thousand."

Brice called him, then showed three sevens, which made Clifton's two pairs of no earthly use. Clifton spent no time in beefing. He gave Brice a certified check on a London bank for $100,000 and wrote out his personal check drawn on a New York bank for $50,000.

The game had been played on a Sunday night. Clifton's checks were no good until Monday morning, when the banks opened and Brice could exchange them for money.

Although Brice didn't know it, there was also another catch. Later that Sunday night Clifton dropped in to see the Reverend Violet Greener, an old friend and the pastor of the Agabeg Occult Temple, one of the edifices which spring up frequently in the Los Angeles landscape to shelter offbeat religions. In the course of their conversation Clifton mentioned the little game he had sat in on and the reverend lady talked him into stopping payment on the checks he had given Brice. She pointed out the likelihood that Brice wouldn't have been able to pay if he had lost, and she explained to Clifton that if this were true it would make his debt to Brice illegal and therefore uncollectible.

Then the Reverend Greener called me. Early Monday morning I appeared—along with Paul Schreibman, who was associated with me in the case—before Superior Judge Emmett Wilson, to ask for a restraining order stopping payment on the two checks. It was granted.

At the same time Brice, who had risen with the birds, was dashing into a Hollywood bank and shoving his checks across the counter. He was told that there would be a delay while they wired Clifton's banking connections in New York for confirmation of the validity of the draft and the check. Brice gnawed his fingernails until word came back that Clifton was good for those large sums.

At that point a teller prepared a bundle of bills totaling $150,000, but before Brice could pocket it I arrived with my restraining order and that $150,000 went back into the safe.

Brice screamed like a wounded stoat, contending that he had won the money fairly in a legal game and that therefore he had a legal right to collect it. I countered that contention with one of my own. I was familiar with a California law passed in the early 1890s which stated that, while some varieties of poker were legal in the state—along with fantan, craps and roulette—stud poker was specifically singled out as being illegal. Not only were any debts arising out of stud games legally uncollectible, but I also pointed out what the Reverend Greener had suggested to me: that the courts had established the fact that gambling debts are collectible only if the winner can prove his ability to pay if he had lost.

That did it, for Mr. Brice was unwilling or unable to demonstrate that he could have written a valid check for $150,000.

15

The Perjured Witness

I ALWAYS THINK of the Dazey case as the Case of the Perjured Witness, although actually there may have been two forsworn witnesses involved.

Dr. George Dazey was a prominent Santa Monica physician. He lived in a nice home and was married to an exceptionally beautiful woman. Occasionally they had spats, but nothing really serious; certainly not serious enough to prevent her from having a baby by him. Its delivery was difficult, and when she came home from the hospital she was still very ill. The truth is she had been ill before that, for her lungs showed traces of tuberculosis, and perhaps she shouldn't have had the baby.

Shortly after her return from the hospital, Mrs. Dazey was found dead. Her body was lying on the floor of the garage, near the car, the motor of which was running. The coroner's autopsy report showed that her death was the result of carbon-monoxide poisoning.

Later it would be said that Dr. Dazey had killed his wife. It would be claimed that he had been seen carrying her body, conscious or unconscious, to the garage, and that he had then left it on the garage floor and switched on his auto motor to make her death seem to be suicide. It would be implied that his motive for murdering her was that they had difficulty in getting along. To me that was no motive at all. If every man killed his wife because he occasionally had trouble getting along with her, the countryside would be littered with corpses.

At the time, however, there was only a mild flurry of investigation into the circumstances surrounding her death. Then she was officially pronounced a suicide.

Dr. Dazey turned his newborn child over to his wife's mother and father to raise. They kept the child for nearly three years and grew to love it as their own. Then Dr. Dazey met another woman and fell in love with her, and they were married. Once he was remarried, he wanted his child back, but his dead wife's parents didn't want to give it up. The maternal grandmother applied for the guardianship of the Dazey son, and, as a result of the wrangling over her application, the circumstances surrounding Mrs. Dazey's death were re-examined.

Although three years had passed since his first wife's death and no charges had been brought against Dr. Dazey before, family relationships being what they are and the love of a child being what it is, his former in-laws now convinced themselves that they suspected him of taking their daughter's life. Evidence was dug up and taken to the D.A.'s office. On the strength of that evidence, Dr. Dazey was indicted for murder and held for trial. I was asked to defend him.

What had put Mrs. Dazey's death back on the front pages was the fact that two key prosecution witnesses had appeared out of the blue. As Dr. Dazey's attorney I knew about one of them, a man who swore that he had seen Dr. Dazey carrying his wife's limp body through his back yard toward the garage, but in spite of all the preparation I had done I didn't know about the second surprise witness until the trial began.

I worked very hard on that case, but apparently I had overlooked something, for I had never seen or heard of the maid-housekeeper witness the prosecution produced who swore that she had worked for Dr. and Mrs. Dazey prior to Mrs. Dazey's death. She said that on the day Mrs. Dazey died she had been in good spirits, that she had made calls to friends and had laughed and joked with them, all of which tended to show that she was not in a suicidal state of mind.

In a further burst of remembering, the housekeeper-maid swore that Dr. and Mrs. Dazey had fought constantly, that Dr. Dazey was a "wife beater" and that he had called Mrs. Dazey a "bitch" and their baby an "s.o.b." The witness didn't seem to realize it, but if what she testified to was true, that gave Mrs. Dazey a possible motive for suicide.

The sudden appearance of this housekeeper-maid was such a shock to me that I could scarcely believe I was listening to her. Turning to Dr. Dazey, I asked, "Why didn't you tell me about her?"

The doctor whispered to me, "There's something queer going on. She wasn't with us before my wife died."

"Are you sure?" I asked.

"As sure as I'm sitting here," he said.

"Yet she testified that certain things occurred," I said.

"I can't help it," Dr. Dazey insisted. "They didn't occur."

I've schooled myself not to show surprise. If something happens which slugs me in the pit of my stomach, I busy myself examining papers and documents, studying copies of the transcripts or making notations. My whole attitude proclaims that having the keystone fall out of my legal archway onto my head hasn't bothered me at all.

Once I've decided that a client is honest, I take his word for statements like the one Dr. Dazey had just made to me; so I told the court that I would like a little time to make an investigation before I cross-examined the witness.

The court let the maid step down, and the prosecution called other witnesses. I turned to my investigator, James Leahan, and told him, "Mr. Leahan, that woman on the stand is lying. Find out why and how."

Mr. Leahan traced the witness back to her home in Arkansas. He not only found out the exact date when she had bought her tickets to California, he even found her redeemed baggage tickets in the railroad's baggage department files. Through a friend of his who worked for the Santa Fé railroad, we were able to check the maid's baggage from the time it left her home in Arkansas until it reached Los Angeles. A witness from the Santa Fé testified that those baggage checks were an accurate record of the maid's arrival. That was important, since she had testified she had never been out of her home state before she came to the Pacific Coast.

The baggage checks which had been issued to her showed that she hadn't reached Los Angeles until a year after Mrs. Dazey's death, so she couldn't have worked for Mrs. Dazey; yet there was the maid testifying that she had been in the Dazey home and had witnessed unpleasant scenes between Dr. Dazey and his wife. I don't know who had taken that maid through the Dazey house and told her how every room had looked and what furnishings had been in them during Mrs. Dazey's lifetime, but she must have been thoroughly coached, because she described those things convincingly enough.

As a result of Mr. Leahan's discoveries I was able to call the witness back for further questioning and confront her with the inconsistencies between her sworn testimony and the facts. I made no point of supposing that her testimony had been suggested to her (or by whom), but it was obvious that someone had persuaded her to testify to untruths.

The other key witness had served the Dazey neighborhood as a private patrolman. He had been in Hawaii for some time when "someone" sent him money to return to the mainland to testify about Mrs. Dazey's death. When he returned, he was taken to the D.A. It was then that he made his statement to the grand jury that he had passed Dr. Dazey's house at the time of Mrs. Dazey's death, that there was a wall bordering the Dazey place low enough for him to see over, and that he had seen a man come out of the house bearing a shape on his shoulder (it was obvious that by "shape" he meant body) and carry it into the garage.

His testimony would have been tough to controvert except for one thing he didn't know. He didn't know that after careful investigation of the house as it had been when Dr. and Mrs. Dazey had lived there, I had discovered that between the Dazey yard and the sidewalk there had been a hedge so thick no one could see through it over the top of the wall.

At first I had only the word of the neighbors for this, because there was no longer any hedge there—it had been cut down by the new owner—but I asked my investigator, Mr. Leahan, to see if he could locate a photograph of the hedge as it had been during the doctor's ownership.

Fortunately such a picture was in existence and it showed clearly that the hedge had been impenetrable to the human eye. I had an enlargement of that photo made. It was three or four feet high and five feet long. During the cross-examination of the private patrolman I showed him the enlargement and asked him, "Do you recognize this hedge?"

He said that he didn't. Then I proved that it had been there when he had seen Dr. Dazey engaging in his alleged incriminating actions.

In the testimony he had given the grand jury, the ex-watchman testified that he had been on the sidewalk when he saw what he described. But once he learned by grapevine that we had a picture of the hedge he tried to make it seem that he had been in another spot when he saw the doctor carrying the body—on the inner side of the wall, inside Dr. Dazey's yard (of all places). I don't know what he hoped to gain by this switch, for his own previous testimony gave him the lie, but by this time he was so enmeshed in contradictions that his testimony did the prosecution more harm than good.

I can remember no trial in which preparation was as vital as it was in that one. Dogged, intensive investigation that brought out the fact that both the maid's and the former patrolman's testimony was—well, let us say peculiar.

Toward the end of the trial, I recalled the maid to the stand and confronted her with the letter of recommendation given her by a former Santa Monica employer which had been previously introduced by the prosecution to bolster the testimony of the maid that she worked in California prior to the date on the Santa Fé railroad baggage checks. I pointed out that the date on the note, purporting to be March 2, 1936, appeared to have been altered. I asked her if she had changed the date from 1937 to 1936. The maid denied tampering with the date.

I said nothing more about the altered date, but when I made my final argument before the jury I did two things: I set the enlarged photograph of the thick hedge before the jury and kept it there, and I handed that letter with the altered date to the jury with my magnifying glass and told them to study it.

If you have a point to make, it is sometimes more effective to allow the jury to think they have discovered it themselves than to shove it down their throats. I let the jury study the date on that note and discover for themselves that it had been altered.

I'll say this much for the D.A.: he had that maid arrested and prosecuted for perjury. She admitted she had forged the letter of recommendation to the extent of changing its date and that she had lied on the stand. She was convicted and was sentenced to a term in the county jail for giving false evidence.

Nothing happened to the private patrolman with the X-ray eyes. It seemed clear to me that he had been promised immunity by somebody if he got into trouble as a result of his testimony.

Although the truth had been kicked around savagely one woman on the jury held out for conviction. The only reason Dr. Dazey didn't get a hung jury was that that woman finally became so nervous and upset with the other eleven members hammering away at her that she asked the court to excuse her and substitute an alternate. She told the judge she was ill and could no longer serve.

Five minutes later I had a not-guilty verdict. It was a verdict of thoroughness in preparation and of care in following all leads.

Incidentally, I am still convinced that Mrs. Dazey's death was suicide.

16

The Tokyo Club

IT WILL COME as no news to anyone who knows me that not all of my clients have been Hollywood celebrities by any means. To me, one of the most interesting of my non-Hollywood cases was the Tokyo Club Case. The Tokyo Club was a gambling hall on Jackson Street. It was patronized largely by Japanese Angelinos who came to try their luck at fantan or other, more Occidental games of chance.

The head man of the Tokyo Club was a hard-nosed gentleman named Hideichi Yamatoda. There was rivalry among the other local Japanese gambling-circle wheels over who should succeed Yamatoda as head of the Tokyo Club when he had made his pile and had retired to more placid pastures.

There had always been a custom with the Tokyo Club that management was supposed to succeed management, but Yamatoda was greedy; he was reluctant to call it a day, to let someone else have a go at the loot. This embroiled him in hot water with his associates whose feelings were hurt by his cupidity.

The water really began to boil when Yamatoda was indicted on a charge of killing a countryman of his named Namba by means of caving in his skull with a blunt instrument. The blunt instrument in the case was said to have been a billiard cue.

Namba came from the vegetable-growing country up around Lodi. He was a small farmer who had saved his money so that he could go on a gambling binge. The trouble was that while he was on his binge he didn't lose gracefully, and when he beefed loudly that he had been bilked somebody slugged him on the head.

There was evidence that thereafter the unconscious Namba had been carried out of doors, but his body was never found. Nevertheless, in spite of the fact that they had no corpse to display, the D.A.'s office indicted Yamatoda for murder for having had a hand in Namba's demise. A confederate of Yamatoda's, Kinowaki, was said to have hit Namba with the billiard cue, after which Yamatoda was supposed to have carried Namba's body across the back yard of his gambling joint.

The police department hauled and pushed manfully on the case, because they were engaged in a drive to stamp out local gambling. Their thought seemed to be that if they could get Yamatoda on a murder rap, not only could they wipe out the gambling fraternity of which he was the head man, but it also would be fine publicity for the police department.

Yamatoda, Kinowaki and a few other Japanese whose names I don't recall were convicted of manslaughter. Because I had represented Yamatoda in his trial, I filed an appellant's brief in an attempt to get his conviction reversed on appeal. In Yamatoda's trial there had been testimony to the effect that he had been seen lugging a body resembling Namba's across his back yard, which apparently convinced the jury that they had no choice but to give Yamatoda the works, without further corroboration.

To me, the case of Yamatoda was not so much a matter of whether Namba's body was ever found or not, but the far more important issue of whether he had ever actually died. I obtained a reversal in Yamatoda's case by making an issue of that question.

There was clearly a reasonable doubt of Namba's demise. I don't know whether that would have been enough to obtain a reversal in itself or not, but it was never put to the test because, in the original trial, in two of the instructions which the court had given the jury the judge had referred to Namba as "the deceased."

Because he had disappeared completely, the police assumed that Namba was dead. That wasn't enough for me. I didn't insist that anyone produce Namba's body, but I did insist that somebody prove that that body was dead before it disappeared.

Understandably, the jury was immediately persuaded that the judge believed Namba was dead or he wouldn't have used the word "deceased." In the brief which I prepared arguing for a reversal of Yamatoda's conviction, I said that the fact of Namba's death had been an issue for the jury to determine, not the judge, and that by assuming out loud in court that a missing man was dead the judge had committed judicial error. It proved a judicial error big enough to set Yamatoda free, for the higher court agreed with me.

Yamatoda was not retried. World War II stepped in and scattered all of the people involved in his first trial like chaff. Yamatoda himself went back to Japan and was killed there during the war.

Sometimes, but not often, when a man has been convicted of murder and condemned to death I have carried the case as high as the governor of the state in an effort to save his life. I have in mind the case of Wesley Robert Wells, who was condemned to the gas chamber for hurling a cuspidor at a prison guard. Wells was a life-term prisoner and the law books said that striking a prison guard was punishable by death, although the way the statute on the California State books in 1954 really read was "the death penalty shall be mandatory for a life termer convicted for assault with a deadly weapon." Wells was convicted and sentenced to die in the gas chamber pursuant to this statute. If he had died he would have been the first person put to death in California when no life had been lost.

In my appeal I went back to the beginning of Wells's case, the trial which had landed him in prison in the first place. I brought out the fact that Wells had shot a man because the said man was running around with Wells's wife. I further brought out the fact that the way he had fired showed he had merely wanted to wound, because he had fired so low. Also, after he had shot, his gun still contained unused bullets. If he had wanted to finish the job fatally he would have emptied the chamber of his gun. It was my contention that he had merely wanted to scare the man he had shot in order to end his finagling. As I recall, the legal phraseology I used was: "The fact that the defendant had unused bullets with equal opportunity to fire proved that, after a moment of emotional and mental instability, he was restored to full competency and normalcy."

Governor Goodwin Knight agreed with me and he spared my client's life.

While I am on the subject of my non-Hollywood activities, perhaps it will not be out of order, although it has no law court background, to go into the time when the Governor of California appointed me chairman of the State Athletic Commission (I served without salary). I didn't have to be a "brain" to know that there were flaws in the way the sports I enjoyed as a spectator were being run. It was equally obvious that most of those faults could be eradicated if the various sports in question were operated by commissioners who had no financial stake in the sport they administered, and no ties, personal nor financial, with any sports promoter.

The first sport I tried to launder was the so-called sport of wrestling. I mean that "so-called" literally. When I was a boy in Iowa, champions like Frank Gotch had made the sport enthralling, although it was minus the grunts and groans, the twisted faces, the grimaces of pain, the fists flailing the canvas in agony, which are a part of "wrestling" today.

I was proud when *Turf and Sports* in its issue for January 1941 printed a story called "The Case of the Curious Commissioner." In it I was given credit for sending certain citizens—known in the wrestling arenas as Chief Dew on the Puss, the Mohican Mauler, Pete the Ponderous Pachyderm, Chew Chin Chow Sub Gum, the Cantonese Crusher—back to their jobs as soap-and-towel attendants in Turkish baths.

Turf and Sports said:

> The corner of Vine Street and Hollywood Boulevard is fantastic enough ordinarily, but all at once it is peopled with a race of bearded giants, blubbery behemoths, muscle-bound mammoths and

The Tokyo Club

tattooed titans. These are the wrestlers Giesler has ordered to grapple instead of grimace. Along with the wrestlers went the promoters and the vicious camp-followers. It seemed impossible that one man could have cleaned up such a long untouched stable full of muck in such a short time.

I am proud of the fact that I was able to purge California's grunt-and-groan racket—at least for a time. While I was in charge, the wrestlers who entered California's rings were not merely examples of pituitary glands run riot. They were physically equipped to give and take punishment the way Lewis, Stecher and Zybysko once did, without phony dramatic trimmings.

I was also given California's toughest job, chairman of the California Horse Racing Board. I held that job without benefit of salary too. That board had been the subject of innumerable legislative investigations. There had been a celebrated case in which a trainer for a wealthy owner had been barred because a horse in his care was said to have been doped. Shortly thereafter the board reversed its original ruling. There were charges of a Santa Anita monopoly. There had been a bitter Hollywood Park–Santa Anita fight. It had lasted for years before it was settled. There was the charge that northern-California tracks were being discriminated against. When I entered the picture, the Golden Gate Turf Club in Albany, just outside Oakland, was building a track and was spending hundreds of thousands of dollars on their plant, with no assurance that they would even be given a racing license.

However, my first concern was not with such matters, but with a number of small experiments in social welfare. I insisted that the tracks carry insurance on all jockeys, and by "carry" I meant pay for it. When I affixed my signature to that ruling, I was paid a great compliment. It was said of me that I had done in two minutes what the jockey guild and the dozens of other organizations had tried to do for years.

I saw to it that the burden of paying for Social Security for the jockeys and exercise boys was taken off the backs of the horsemen and shifted to the track owners themselves. I listened to ideas and

229

complaints from all kinds and conditions of people. I found out that although the mutuel clerks were supposed to be making a minimum of six dollars a day, their workdays were staggered so that some of them worked only three days a week. That meant that they earned the sweatshop salary of eighteen dollars every seven days. This was done to make it possible for the tracks to take care of job moochers recommended to them by petty politicians. I straightened that out, and to protect the public I demanded that track clerks be bonded, photographed and fingerprinted.

The beginning of World War II marked the end of such sports as horse racing for the duration. When that happened, I went back to defending people who had run afoul of the law. Not that I had ever really left it. The work I had done in trying to clean up sports was a part-time job.

I'd like to let Damon Runyon take over this story for a few moments. In 1941 Runyon said this about me in his column, "The Brighter Side":

> Jerry Giesler, noted Los Angeles attorney, is mentioned among his hometown folks as the "double-breasted" sports commissioner in the United States. He is Chairman of the California Racing Commission and Chairman of the California Boxing Commission.
>
> Giesler is more of a complete sports czar even than the redoubtable Kenesaw Mountain Landis, overlord of baseball, but with a slight difference: the judge gets a chubby salary for his work while Giesler's two jobs have probably cost him a fortune in time taken out of his own business and money from his own pocket. Obviously, it is a labor of love for him. Between the two sports he seems to have no special fancy, though probably racing with its classier following and its spectacular presentation appeals to him more than the manly art of scrambling ears. He was appointed to head the Boxing Commission by Governor Olsen two years ago and did so well that the Governor insisted that he accept the chairmanship of the Racing Commission.
>
> There is seldom anything wrong with any sport that a firm hand and fair-mindedness will not cure. Even his severest critics concede

that Jerry Giesler is not afraid of belting the biggies when he thinks they need it, which is a novelty. It has been our observation that most sports administrators deal for the important guys first.

Moreover, he is always trying to do something practical for the little fellows. The hard-bitten pugilistic mob, which always views government with a great skepticism, says Giesler is all right. This is a high tribute from that gang, and he is sponsoring a movement to provide a retreat for old and sick turfmen. . . ."

If Runyon meant that I wanted to see that everybody connected with California's racing got an even break, he was right. I raised the jockey fees. I exposed the gamblers who were fixing races with bribed jockeys, by turning information about them over to the grand jury; that in turn led to indictments. I helped put through laws which secured more pay for the cashiers and ticket sellers at the tracks, and I saw to it that officials and judges took eye tests because it was important that they have perfect vision. Among other things, I brought pressure upon turf clubs to pay a share of their receipts into the state treasury and I even tried to do something for the horses themselves. I put up a fight to keep them from being exploited after their racing days were done. I disapproved a proposed match race between a fourteen-year-old race horse and an automobile. I enlisted the help of the A.S.P.C.A. They saw to it that this cruel match was canceled.

17

The Missing Stomach

Another case which proved to me the value of preparation (that, of course, includes investigation) involved three elements: a man in California whose wife said he had accidentally stabbed himself while cutting a piece of ham; neighbors who said that the ham was a figment of the imagination, that there hadn't been any ham for him to cut; and the incredible payoff.

I call it the Case of the Missing Stomach.

The punctured man was an Army officer. The stomach sticking occurred several months before the United States entered World War II. The Army officer was stationed at an Army installation in southern California. He lived off the post with his family. He was stabbed in his own home with a butcher knife. The knife penetrated between his fifth and sixth ribs, piercing his stomach. He was rushed to the Army hospital at the post where he was stationed, for emergency surgery. When his condition did not improve, the officer was flown to an Army general hospital in northern California, where he died. His widow insisted that the stabbing had been accidental. Before the officer died he insisted she was right.

So much for the facts.

After making its own investigation the Army was satisfied that the officer's death was accidental, precisely as his wife said it was.

Several weeks after his death a woman who had lived nearby volunteered the information that she had overheard a quarrel in the dead man's house on the night he was killed.

As I have indicated, the story told by the Army officer's wife (and the officer himself, for that matter) was that her husband had been cutting a ham when the knife slipped in his hands and then penetrated his abdomen. The former neighbor now said that she had been the first one in the officer's house after the fatal stabbing and that there had been no ham in the house that night. Other neighbors who had gone to the officer's house that night to help out confirmed this. The officer and his wife had been to a cocktail party earlier in the evening, and there was evidence that the drinking had continued after they came home. As a result the widow was indicted for stabbing her husband. She was thereafter charged with murder, and I was retained as her attorney.

After the officer died at the Army general hospital, his body was returned to Southern California for burial. Now that the neighbor had told her story about the quarrel she overheard and had volunteered information about seeing no ham in the house, an exhumation and an autopsy of the officer's body was ordered.

The local D.A.'s investigators were on hand at the morgue where the coroner's autopsy was performed. They took photographs of such things as the chest bone, the butcher knife with which the stabbing had been done, and the sutures which had been used in sewing up the outer abdominal wall. Then the body was reburied. Among other things in the autopsy report was a complete report of the condition of the officer's stomach.

Being a great believer in checking and double checking other people's findings, I sent my chief investigator, James Leahan, up to the Army hospital in northern California to talk to the surgeon there. Mr. Leahan was armed with the transcript of the testimony before the grand jury and the coroner's report plus the photographs taken at the time of the autopsy.

What I didn't know, and neither did he, was that before the officer's body had been returned for burial his stomach had been removed at that hospital and had been kept there in alcohol.

In the course of Mr. Leahan's conversation with the Army autopsy surgeon on the case, he told the surgeon about the autopsy after exhumation and about how the autopsy in southern California had involved the dead officer's stomach.

With that the Army surgeon said, "But they don't have the stomach down there. I have the stomach right here in the morgue laboratory. It is routine for us to keep such things to ship to the Army Medical College in Washington, D. C., in case the Surgeon General wants to look at it."

Mr. Leahan was flabbergasted. "Are you kidding?" he asked, and the Army surgeon said, "Certainly not."

Mr. Leahan said, "May I see it?"

The Army surgeon took him down to the laboratory, and there, in a large glass container, was the officer's stomach with the suture still in it, just the way he had been sewn up several days prior to his death. There was also a nick in the rear part of the stomach. It was obvious that the knife had gone through that far, although there was no mention of that nick in the coroner's report which Mr. Leahan had with him.

Whoever had written that autopsy report had never seen that stomach.

My investigator called me long distance and said, "Mr. Giesler, I'm mighty happy about what I've found out. The stomach is still here."

"Mr. Leahan, have you been drinking?" I asked, although as far as I know he doesn't drink.

"No," Mr. Leahan said, "I haven't. I've seen it. It's tagged with the dead man's name. It has the date on it and everything."

"Mr. Leahan," I said firmly, "there must be something wrong with you. Go back to that hospital morgue laboratory again and have another look."

I imagine Mr. Leahan felt foolish, going back and talking to the Army surgeon again, but he did what I told him to do. Once more he called me, and this time he convinced me that what he had told me before was true. I told him that I'd get a subpoena to him quickly to hold that stomach there because we'd need it in our case, which had been set for trial on December 8, 1941.

Pearl Harbor was bombed on Sunday, December 7. When the case was called for trial the next morning most of the witnesses, both prosecution and defense, were unavailable. The court was informed that Army officers who were to have testified both for and against the widow were unable to leave their posts or had been transferred. The judge marked the case off the calendar, to be reset on thirty days' notice, and permitted the widow to remain at liberty under the $5,000 bail previously posted.

My client never was tried. In 1947 the court dismissed the murder charge against the widow for lack of evidence.

In one way it is too bad that that trial never occurred. It's not every day that a defense attorney gets a chance to toss such a high-explosive bomb into an unsuspecting courtroom, and Mr. Leahan's discovery would have been a blockbuster. Finding that stomach in the Army hospital would in my opinion have destroyed the case against my client.

When that case vanished into the clouds of war, there were one or two sneering remarks to the effect that "Jerry Giesler will do anything to foil the prosecution; he'll even start a war."

18

Benjamin "Bugsy" Siegel

and Murder, Inc.

I NEVER CALLED HIM Bugsy Siegel. For one thing, he hated his nickname frantically. If anyone used it, it sent him into one of the fits of psychopathic rage from which the sobriquet derived; for the moment he went "bugs." As a result I still find myself thinking of him as Mr. Siegel or, more informally, as Benny—using the diminutive form of his first name.

At the time I was asked to defend Siegel, the New York authorities had named him one of the "six most dangerous gangsters in the United States." It was up to me to "free" him from a charge of complicity in the fatal gunning of a New York mobster, Harry (Big Greenie) Greenberg, whose alias was George H. Schachter and who was a former member of Murder, Inc. When he was killed, in November of 1939, he was trying to sink out of sight in California.

A murder charge was also brought against the New York and Seattle fight manager Frankie Carbo. He was said to be equally culpable with Siegel. The prosecution contended that they had both been seen outside Greenberg's home on the night he was shot.

The motive for the murder was supposed to be a fear that Greenberg, harking back to his gaudy past, might "sing" to the law about the nefarious activities of himself and others—including the chairman of the board of Murder, Inc., Louis Lepke Buchalter. If he did, it might land a number of nervous gentlemen in jail. If he had any such intentions, he wouldn't have been able to hide in Siberia, much less in the neighborhood of Hollywood and Vine in Los Angeles.

Greenberg was believed to have demanded money from "the organization" in exchange for not singing.

He tried to hide from his onetime associates by living unobtrusively in rented rooms, but the mob fingered him anyway. As a result, at a moment when he least expected it, three bullets found their target—his head.

For a while the Los Angeles County authorities made investigative motions. Then they called it a day. Greenberg would have been rubbed out mentally as well as physically if, nine months later, in August 1940, Allie Tannenbaum, also a member of Murder, Inc., hadn't started singing his own tune to a Brooklyn grand jury and to William O'Dwyer, who was then the D.A. of Kings County, New York. Tannenbaum's confession was born of the fear that he himself had been scheduled as a victim by the ring. His only hope lay in having the law throw a protective cordon around him.

When Siegel and Carbo were named by Tannenbaum as having taken part in the killing of Greenberg, Siegel was arrested by the Los Angeles police. Carbo was supposed to have been the trigger man. I was employed to represent Siegel.

Another reason given for arresting Siegel was that when the law called upon him to question him, in his beautiful home set in the rising ground behind the city of Beverly Hills, he ran like a startled fawn and hid in his attic. According to the D.A., this flight was highly suspicious, if not an outright admission of guilt. He described Siegel's action elegantly, if ponderously, as "trying to evade interrogation and arrest."

After a preliminary hearing Siegel was indicted and sent to jail to await trial, which was set for November 1940. However, when that time came the indictment was dismissed because of insufficient evidence to convict before the trial began.

Nevertheless, he wasn't out of the woods yet. In January 1942 back in New York, William O'Dwyer was showing signs of peevishness about the way the Los Angeles County enforcement officers had let the strings they had been given to the Hollywood chapter of Murder, Inc., slip through their fingers. As a result of certain heated conversations between O'Dwyer and the Los Angeles police, Frankie Carbo and Siegel were arrested and reindicted on the original charges.

Meanwhile back in New York the law had been keeping Tannenbaum on ice in a fancy hotel suite, ready to turn state's evidence against Murder, Inc., but they generously lent him to the Los Angeles D.A.'s office. He waded ankle-deep through the thick red carpet provided for him by the law upon his arrival in Los Angeles.

On January 19, 1942, Siegel and Carbo went on trial for the 1939 murder of Greenberg. To me it was a fascinating legal foray fought out against an unusual background. It was a pleasure for me to cross-examine Allie Tannenbaum, the prosecution's big-wheel witness from the East, because he had been a very bad boy. I had peered into his past and had found out why his name had appeared on so many police blotters.

I began by asking him how he liked his quarters in the hotel where he was staying, as opposed to staying in jail. Then I questioned him gently and courteously as to whether or not he was known as a gunman. I hoped to cast doubt upon his character by persuading him to admit that he had been a hood who had used his gun on behalf of Murder, Inc.

For a few moments I questioned him about things far removed from violence. Then pleasantly, and with no perceptible change of inflection, I asked him—in a way I imagine one member of a skeet club asks another—"Do you shoot with your right hand or your left hand?"

With almost contemptuous scorn for my unfamiliarity with his skill, he said, "I shoot with either hand."

After that it was clear that nothing the witness said could be regarded as the remark of a scrupulously upright citizen. And this helped, especially when I got around to questioning his testimony concerning the use of a "crash car." I had never heard the term before, but, listening to him, I gathered that a crash car is a second car which accompanies the car which transports the actual killers. In that way, if the police show up either ahead of or behind the killers' car, the gun-toting delegation will have a car handy (which seemingly is not connected with them) which can crash into the police car as if by accident and put it out of business.

It was then Mr. Tannenbaum made a mistake that damaged the prosecution's case even more than his own reputation. He swore that Benjamin Siegel's Buick had been the crash car. Not only that but he insisted that it had been registered in Siegel's name.

That was obviously untrue. No one, not even a punch-drunk moron—and Benjamin Siegel was certainly not that—would use his own car, registered in his own name, as a crash car, which would tie him up with the murder as surely as if he left his personal card of condolence propped against the body.

Nevertheless, Tannenbaum stuck to that story, although in my argument I submitted that it was probably the biggest, most barefaced lie in legal history.

On Siegel's side was the law which says that the testimony of a self-confessed participant in a crime is not sufficient corroboration of the participation of another person accused of participating. The law of California (Section 1111 of the penal code) requires that an accomplice must be corroborated by independent evidence which of itself tends to connect the defendant or defendants with the commission of a crime, and in the Carbo and Siegel case the catch for the prosecution was that it couldn't come up with any satisfactory independent corroborative testimony.

It was on this point of law that Superior Judge A. A. Scott on February 5, 1942, granted my plea for a dismissal of the charges against Siegel, and once more the people's case against him was thrown out of court on the grounds that there was insufficient evidence to connect him with the crime.

Sometimes, pondering my past cases, I find myself idly thinking, Maybe if I hadn't sprung Benjamin Siegel, he might be alive today.

There is no doubt that he would have been far safer in a penitentiary than running around doing as he pleased. He was definitely not safe in the house on Linden Drive occupied by his girl friend, Virginia Hill. The *Facts on File Yearbook* for 1947 put what happened to him there tersely and pithily:

> June 20, murder—Benjamin (Bugsy) Siegel, 42, reputed No. 1 gangster, shot to death through window of the house of a friend, Virginia Hill, 30, in Beverly Hills, California. He was indicted in 1942 as West Coast chief of "Murder, Inc.," but not convicted.

To get back to Frankie Carbo, he remained on trial because Judge Scott felt that the prosecution had produced enough corroborating testimony to justify the jury's consideration of his case. I was asked to stay in the case and assist Carbo's lawyer, Willard Burgess, with the defense.

The principal witness against Carbo was a woman who claimed that on the evening of Greenberg's death she had been taking a walk along the opposite side of the street from where the killing occurred, and that under a street light she could see the car in which the deceased had been sitting. She swore—in good faith, I'm sure—that she had seen a man, wearing a brown hat pulled down over his face, in the area near the actual shooting, immediately after the killing, and that the man was Carbo.

Part of the prosecution's story was that still another Murder, Inc., gunman, Whitey Krakower, had been in Los Angeles when Greenberg died. The D.A. made the claim that there was every reason to think that he had been flown in and flown out to help Carbo get Greenberg.

Listening to that woman's testimony, I had an idea. The question of identification by a prosecution witness is always worthy of testing by the defense. Sometimes such identification is one part wishful thinking, one part a desire to please the D.A. and one part self-delusion.

In an effort to demonstrate whether the woman identifier could distinguish Carbo, at that distance and under the conditions she described, from anyone else who even vaguely resembled him, I had a display constructed and I used it as an exhibit in the courtroom. It consisted of two enlargements of photographs of Carbo and Krakower taken from the police files. I had them super-imposed on black blotting paper, then mounted on a sheet of gray paper. Then I had two brown-paper cutout hats made to fit the heads in the photographs. Each was attached to the photograph be-neath it by a thumbtack so that it could be adjusted up or down.

I had the two photographs held up in court for the jury to see. Once I had pulled the two brown-paper hats down over the photo-graphed eyes it was difficult to say which photograph resembled which man. I defied the jury to make a positive identification of either man under those circumstances.

The woman witness's testimony was so much more positive than the facts justified, I told the jury, that it reminded me of the story of Chicken-Little, which I proceeded to tell in detail: how the little hen was struck on the head by a falling acorn and became convinced—and convinced everyone she met—that the sky was falling in. I said that Chicken-Little had exaggerated everything. I claimed that the woman witness had done the same thing.

An even more powerful lever working in behalf of the defense was the fact that when I sent my chief investigator, James Leahan, to Seattle he was able to prove that during the time when Green-berg was being killed Carbo had been registered at a hotel there. Not only did the records of the hotel show that Carbo was there, but we had testimony from the maids and the manager definitely placing Carbo in Seattle at the time of Greenberg's slaying.

The jury stayed out fifty-three hours. They failed to agree and were discharged.

Afterward a reporter friend of mine asked one of the jurors who had voted for Carbo's acquittal, "Why did you vote the way you did?"

I'm not sure that it speaks too highly for the mental caliber of that particular juror, but he replied, "Any man who loves chickens the way Mr. Giesler told us Carbo does couldn't be guilty of killing anything."

The flabbergasted newspaperman asked groggily, "What do you mean, 'loves chickens'?"

The juror drew himself up indignantly and said, "I heard what Mr. Giesler said about Chicken-Little and I know that this man Carbo is a chicken lover. That's why I voted not guilty."

In the story he filed about this exchange of remarks, the news-paperman said that the only time Carbo had ever seen a chicken was on his plate—or on his knee.

The district attorney, John F. Dockweiler, a good friend of mine, didn't prosecute Carbo a second time, possibly because it would have been too expensive to bring the well-kept witness Allie Tannenbaum west again with all the foo-fa-raw, whoop-de-doo and deference which had accompanied his first visit. I also seem to recall a reluctance on the part of William O'Dwyer to let his valuable witness out of his jurisdiction. The case was closed.

19

Edward G. Robinson, Jr.,

and Robert Mitchum

SOMETIMES when I think back on Eunice Pringle's change of clothing in the Alexander Pantages case and the effect it had on the jury
it makes me recall the time when the rapid changing of a pair of
shoes kept a jury from acquiring a feeling of antagonism toward
another client of mine, Edward G. Robinson, Jr. The case of young
Robinson, who was charged with armed robbery, proved once more
a fact which has been demonstrated in many other courtrooms: the
nonexistence of such a thing as a positive identification.

Young Robinson was identified by two taxi drivers, both of whom
claimed that he had held up their cabs and had robbed them at gunpoint. Robinson denied it.

In both cases he was accused of getting into a cab and shortly
afterward holding up the cabbie. In one case he was accused of
putting a gun at a cabbie's ear; in the second one, the cabbie said
he had threatened to pound him over the head with a long flash-
light. In each case the principal evidence identifying the man as
Edward G. Robinson, Jr., was the fact that he had put a foot shod
in a black-tasseled moccasin over the back of the front seat. Why the
stick-up man was supposed to have such odd foot-parking habits,
I don't know, but that's how the taxi drivers told it.

They said that young Robinson resembled the stick-up man

physically, but it had been dark and they had caught only fleeting glimpses of him. Hence the importance of the black moccasins with the black tassels.

All of this didn't happen right away. About two months after the robberies were said to have occurred, the police picked up young Robinson one night in front of his apartment as he was returning from a round of the bars. He was picked up for suspicion of armed robbery on the complaint of the two cab drivers, who claimed that they recognized him from pictures of him appearing in the newspapers at the time of his reconciliation with his wife, Nancy.

His wife heard the ruckus outside and saw the police carrying him off. She called one of my young associates, Rex Eagan, but we soon discovered that the police had their prisoner on "the bicycle." This means that they took him to a police station; then, when they learned that I was on my way, they took him from that station to another station, and from that station to still another station. They kept him on the bicycle all night.

There were advantages to the police in keeping such a prisoner away from his attorney. He might not have enough strength of character to stick to the story he had told them. If they "reasoned" with him hard enough, they might even get him to accept their version of his story.

They knew that once I got to him he'd talk to no one about anything, for the first thing I tell a client is, "Say nothing to anybody. I'm your lawyer. I'll do the talking."

I finally caught up with young Robinson in jail, at six o'clock in the morning, and I got him out.

Just before he was put on trial in the courthouse at Santa Monica, I was waiting in the corridor outside the courtroom with Rexford Eagan. The jury panel was roaming up and down the corridor too. When Edward G. Robinson, Jr., showed up, I took one look at him and, to my horror, saw that he was wearing black moccasins with black tassels. The preliminary hearing had already been held, so I knew how important those shoes would be as evidence.

To me the fact that he would wear such shoes to his trial was a sure indication of his innocence. If he had been guilty, those moc-

244

casins would have been the last kind of footgear he would have worn, but I was afraid a jury might not think about this point so logically. Mr. Eagan acted quickly. He switched shoes with Robinson, although Eagan was wearing a brown suit and black moccasins looked odd with the rest of his outfit. Also, Mr. Eagan's feet are a size or two larger than Robinson's, but he bore up bravely under the ordeal.

The keynote of our defense in the Robinson case was: Why should a youngster who had a father so well heeled turn to robbery to get money? It was easy to prove that young Robinson had all the money he needed. There was, therefore, no motive for him to engage in stick-ups.

Then there was young Robinson's alibi. His wife and the woman who had been his nurse when he was a child, and who had been with the family ever since, both testified that on the night he was supposed to have committed the two crimes they had been with him all the time. That weakened the identification evidence against him considerably.

Both drivers had also testified that there had been no ring on the fingers of the youngster who had staged the stick-up—and both admitted they had had a good look at the bandit's hands. Young Robinson had been given a *bar mitzvah* ring when he was thirteen. He had never taken that ring off. In fact, over the years it had become too tight to get off, no matter how hard he tried.

When young Eddie showed up in court wearing his *bar mitzvah* ring, his father, who was in the courtroom too, took him from the witness stand, walked with him before the jury and said, "This is the ring I gave him on his *bar mitzvah*. He's never taken it off." Then the senior Robinson pulled at that ring, but it wouldn't move a fraction of an inch. That etched an indelible impression on the minds of at least some of the jurors.

They hung, but reportedly stood eleven to one for acquittal. Later young Robinson was spared a second trial when the court dismissed the charges on motion of the district attorney.

I was satisfied then that he couldn't have been involved in those holdups and that the charges were based on mistaken identity. I'm still satisfied. Nor did it ever occur to me that anybody was "out to get" young Eddie Robinson because he bore the same name as the motion picture celebrity.

There was no doubt in my mind, though, that when actor Robert Mitchum found himself in trouble, his tribulation was the result of a deliberate design on the part of someone who wished him ill. He had even received warnings, "Watch your step or something will happen to you."

His trouble began one night when his wife was away. Being a presentable male temporarily on the loose, he was invited to drop in on a party in Laurel Canyon, and he accepted.

As soon as Mitchum stepped into the room where the party was going on, the scent of burning marijuana smote his nostrils. The smell was unmistakable to him because in his teens he had hoboed his way along the highways and through the backwaters of America where reefer smoking was not unknown.

One of the people lolling in the Laurel Canyon cottage handed him a reefer. A split second later the door crashed open. Mitchum and some of the others at the party were caught with lighted marijuana cigarettes they had just put down.

That wasn't all. The place had been bugged; a microphone had been planted on the wall. But the most peculiar thing about the whole affair was that the press had the story before the cops crashed in. To put it mildly, I call that having a super nose for news.

Mitchum and his employers were miserable at the thought of losing his huge teen-age following. Their first move was to get in touch with me.

There are two ways in which an individual can be brought to trial in California: by information or by indictment. In the first, a district attorney initiates a prosecution by having his office swear out a complaint. After that the accused is given a preliminary hearing before a municipal-court judge and, if the facts warrant it, he is bound over to the Superior Court for trial. Then the district attorney files an information. An indictment, on the other hand, is an accusation returned by a grand jury after it conducts its own hearing.

Edward G. Robinson, Jr., and Robert Mitchum

Ninety per cent of all cases are prosecuted as a result of an information originated by a D.A. The grand jury can't possibly conduct
hearings for all the cases which occur in a big city.

Preliminary hearings are a very important part of criminal law,
although most people don't recognize them as such. To me it is just
as important to have my facts and my law prepared for the
preliminary hearing as for the trial itself. The real importance of
the preliminary is this: Through cross-examining witnesses carefully, I can find out what they know. This is vital, because if I
don't cross-examine a witness thoroughly at the hearing, and that
witness dies or leaves the state before the case finally comes to trial,
my only chance to ask further questions is gone. The prosecutor,
on the other hand, isn't worried; he has his testimony and he can
read it to a jury.

Unlike the bulk of the narcotics cases in Los Angeles County,
Mitchum's case went before the grand jury, which indicted him on
two counts, possession of marijuana and conspiracy to possess marijuana. On my advice he did not accept the district attorney's invitation to appear and testify. The accused cannot be represented
by his lawyer at a grand-jury hearing, and there is no opportunity
to question the prosecution's witnesses, as at a preliminary hearing
before a municipal judge.

It was my idea not to enter a plea for Mitchum. A plea of not
guilty would lead to a jury trial, with the D.A. grilling everyone
concerned and digging for dirt. Instead I proposed simply to ask
the court to decide his innocence or guilt on the conspiracy-to-
possess-marijuana count on the basis only of the transcript of the
testimony before the grand jury.

Perhaps it has been forgotten, but Mitchum never did plead
guilty.

My plan met with violent opposition, not from Mitchum but
from those with a financial stake in him as a motion picture actor.
Mitchum himself thought I was right.

My reasoning was this: To many moviegoers, Mitchum was a
hero, and a long, nasty trial might damage him beyond hope of
rehabilitation. I told him that if he wanted me to I would do my best

247

to bring out the possibility that his arrest was the result of a frame-up—an idea which the district attorney's office itself investigated some months later—but he preferred my plan.

Among other considerations which influenced my move were letters flooding in from all over the country pointing out that it would be a bad example to the youth of the nation if Mitchum were let off too easily. That factor was a consideration I couldn't ignore. So I decided to do what in effect was to "throw him on the mercy of the court."

When I faced the courtroom packed with people avid for scandal, there were representatives of the press from all over the United States, as well as from other countries. They were slavering for scandal in raw, juicy chunks. I hadn't said a word about what I was going to do, and when I announced that I would waive a jury trial on the conspiracy-to-possess-marijuana charge and submit the case solely on the transcript of earlier testimony before the grand jury their disappointment and frustration were pitiful. After the judge studied the transcript of the grand-jury testimony, he found Mitchum guilty on the conspiracy-to-possess-marijuana charge.

The court announced that his sentence would be two years, then reduced it to sixty days, the remainder to be a suspended sentence. Mitchum served his time without complaining. By taking his medicine like a man, he gained rather than lost public sympathy. Instead of boycotting his films afterward, people flocked to see him in greater numbers than before.

For those who have, in the past, called me a publicity hound, I might point out that if I had been interested in publicity, all I had to do was allow the Mitchum trial to proceed and I would have been buried in an avalanche of headlines. The way I handled the case saved the motion-picture industry much grief, but they didn't appreciate it then. They don't appreciate it now. It has always been the industry's weakness that it can see only an inch in front of its nose.

20

Busby Berkeley

THE CASE of Busby Berkeley, a motion-picture executive, was a much harder one to try. For one thing, I tried it three times; for another, it had aspects which lifted it out of the ordinary. Its key phrase, "the cancerous tire," still intrigues me.

In Berkeley's case I am convinced that the prosecution made a mistake in charging him with second-degree murder instead of manslaughter. It is much harder to persuade a jury to convict a man of murder than of manslaughter if the killing he has done results from an automobile accident.

In this case the accident occurred on September 8, 1935, on Alternate Highway 101, between Santa Monica and Malibu. Berkeley had been attending a party in the hills near Los Angeles. He was on his way home in his roadster. It was alleged that he had had too many drinks at the party. Several actors were present, including Pat O'Brien. I used them afterward as witnesses to testify that Berkeley was not intoxicated when he left the party.

The road Berkeley followed was narrow and twisting. The evening was pleasant and the traffic was heavy. Suddenly there was a crash as Berkeley's car collided with two cars traveling in the opposite direction—one carrying five people and the other the driver and a passenger. When the police unscrambled the debris, all of the five persons in the small sedan which suffered the most serious damage were badly injured, three critically. Berkeley, who was driving alone, received head and leg injuries.

Two of the critically injured women passengers in the sedan died the following day. The driver died six weeks later.

At a preliminary hearing following the deaths of the two women, Berkeley, who was taken into court on a wheeled stretcher, was held on two counts of manslaughter. After the hearing, the Municipal Judge ordered the charges changed to second-degree murder. When the driver of the sedan succumbed, a third count of second-degree murder was added on a complaint issued by the district attorney.

Since the public takes it for granted that anyone who has anything to do with motion pictures is automatically very wealthy and very powerful, the popular view of Berkeley was that he was extraordinarily well heeled and influential.

Berkeley's prosecutor, David Coleman, who is now a superior court judge, was then a member of the D.A.'s staff. The first Berkeley trial was held in December 1935.

On Berkeley's side all I had was my conviction that it wasn't his fault—that the accident occurred because his left front tire had blown out, thus causing his car to swerve into the wrong lane. The D.A. thought he had me there, since he was able to prove that my client had bought a complete set of new tires not long before the accident. He said that the tire blew out because of the impact of the accident, rather than before the collision.

But I brought tire experts into the courtroom to testify that his blown tire could have had a "cancerous" spot. Because of its horrifying aspects, cancer wasn't a word people used lightly at that time any more than they do now. However, it was one way of describing a tire which has a chemically (or structurally) weak spot which could give way at any moment, thereby causing the loss of human life.

The court pounced on Berkeley when he took the stand in his own defense. Berkeley testified on direct examination that his left front tire went flat just before the accident; that he fought as hard as he could to bring his car under control to keep it from veering into the oncoming traffic lane; and that as he did so the crash came. Then Judge Burnell went after him:

Q. The tires on your car, they were of the most expensive make, weren't
   they?
A. I couldn't say as to that. They were four or five months old.
Q. They were in good shape then?
A. I didn't notice particularly.

Actually there was little need for any cross-examination by
the District Attorney. Judge Burnell seemed to have taken over
for the prosecution.

I also produced as witnesses several guests who had been at the
cocktail party with Berkeley, including movie actors Frank Mc-
Hugh, Guy Kibbee and actress Glenda Farrell, movie directors
Mervyn Leroy and Bobby Connolly, and the host's brother, Ben
Koenig. Their testimony was intended to rebut the State's contention that Berkeley was intoxicated when he left the Hollywood
party shortly after 10 P.M. All of the guests testified that Berkeley
was "sober when he departed"; that "he was absolutely sober at the
party"; that he had no more than two drinks at the most.

When Actor Frank McHugh said on the stand that he did not see
anyone in particular drinking at the party, Judge Burnell could not
contain himself. By the tone of his voice, as much as by his words,
the judge let the jury know that he did not believe the witness:

> "This cocktail bar must have been like an altar, because no one
> got near it. Here were 200 people at a cocktail party and all they
> had to drink was milk. Was that it?"

Dance director Bobby Connolly testified that Berkeley was absolutely sober when he saw Berkeley at the party, and that Connolly himself had had only two drinks. On cross-examination, Deputy District Attorney Coleman asked Connolly:

Q. Was everybody drinking?
A. I couldn't see everybody.

Connolly's flip, and for us rather unhelpful, answer set the court
off again. Judge Burnell asked sharply:

The Jerry Giesler Story

Q. It wasn't a cocktail party given by the W.C.T.U.?
A. No.

Through the testimony of Ben Koenig, I brought out that Berkeley had circulated among the guests and that consequently many of them had had the opportunity to observe his condition on numerous occasions throughout the evening. In his testimony Koenig mentioned that Berkeley had been sitting at a table in the patio with Pat O'Brien, Guy Kibbee and others, but that he had left the table to join two other guests in a song at the piano. Again Judge Burnell appeared to be at pains to make it clear to the jury that he viewed with suspicion the defense's contention that Berkeley had been sober when he left the party:

"What were they singing—'Sweet Adeline'?" the court asked.

Based on the reaction of the trial judge to the testimony of the many party guests I called to the stand, it seemed highly probable the jury might conclude that Berkeley was in no shape to be driving when he left the party. Our only real hope was to convince the jury that Berkeley's left front tire had blown out before the crash. Under the law, a blown-out tire would break the immediate chain of events which would otherwise link his driving to the accident.

Let me put it this way: you are driving a car while sodden with drink; another car comes along and runs into you, thereby ramming you into still another car. If that happens, there is no legal connection between your drinking and your final accident.

As another example I offer a case I tried in Ventura, California. My client was riding a motorcycle while drunk. An auto driving too close to him sliced off one of his legs. He sued for damages and won. Why did he win? Because the tire marks on the street showed that, drunk as he was, my client was on the side of the street where he was supposed to be and the car which crashed into him was on the wrong side. The fact that he was plastered had nothing to do with the accident.

That suit was for civil damages. But the same rule applies in criminal law. However, my motorcycle client's drinking did enter into the decision in this way: the law decided that his leg was

252

worth only $12,500. I am sure that he would have received a lot more for it if he hadn't been drunk.

At the time of the Busby Berkeley accident, Berkeley was working at Warner Brothers Studio and that studio employed me to defend him. I labored hard preparing his case. To help me in my defense Warner Brothers had its miniature department make a model of the coastal highway on which the accident had occurred. It was so perfect it even had small telephone poles and it showed the marks of tire skids.

I also had small models made of the cars involved. My model of Berkeley's green convertible was fashioned in such a way that I could demonstrate what had happened to it when its left front sidewall exploded while the car was in motion. I even had a special axle put in the model so that its left front wheel swung out during my demonstration.

That little model is still on my desk. I still find myself reaching out and touching it from time to time.

After giving the elaborate scale model of the highway much thought, I decided not to use it. I was afraid that it might create the impression that too much money was being poured into Berkeley's defense. So instead I used an aerial photograph of the highway. It was almost as long and as wide as the model, but it didn't smell so strongly of Berkeley defense money.

I used that aerial photograph to show the road's windings and its hairpin curves and to demonstrate that it was extremely unlikely that a person who was as drunk as Berkeley was said to have been could have negotiated them. Before I was through I made it clear that it was quite a feat for even a sober person to drive that roller coaster of a highway.

At the end of the first Berkeley trial the jury was hopelessly deadlocked.

Although I didn't admit it, that was a better result than I had hoped for. In addition to my aerial photograph of the road and the tire experts, I attribute that first hung jury to the fact that the judge rode Berkeley and our other witnesses unmercifully all through that trial. That may seem to make it tough for a defendant at the time, but in reality it enlists the sympathy of the jurors in his behalf.

I have represented clients in cases in which the public was with the defendant from the start, as is usually the case with injured husbands. With Berkeley the opposite was true. The public made up its collective mind that he was a dipso-playboy whose drunken carelessness had butchered innocent people. That Hollywood party before the accident stuck in the public's craw. People said, "You know how wild those Hollywood parties are."

Although the hostile atmosphere which surrounded Berkeley's first trial made his defense difficult, it was as nothing compared with the handicaps which confronted me during his second trial, which began in April 1936. Not only did the prosecution know in advance what I would say; I didn't even have the stimulation of gearing myself up to the pitch I'd reached the first time around.

I try to be up on my toes every minute in the courtroom, but you know what's coming in a retrial and it's hard not to let down. You know what the witnesses are going to say, you've read the testimony they gave before and, although you're primed for them, you can ask only just so many questions.

Any power of initiative and surprise you had is gone. It's like running a film you've seen before, the only difference being you hope someone has tacked on a happy ending since the last time you saw it.

In Berkeley's case I went through all that not twice, but three times. It was more than sheer drudgery, it was unmitigated hell. I liked Berkeley personally. I still do, but that wasn't the reason I went step by step with him through those three bitterly fought trials. I don't drop a case just because I've scored the temporary victory of a hung jury in a trial which the public and the papers have decided I can't win.

Some attorneys who make legal bricks out of straw, as I did in that first Berkeley trial, might say, "O.K., Buz, get yourself another attorney. I don't want your second trial. I've done all I can for you." I don't play it that way.

The second trial ended in a seven-to-five vote for acquittal. Although the D.A.'s office moved to dismiss the three counts of second-degree murder against Busby Berkeley and I joined in the motion, a third trial was ordered. The third time around fell in September 1936, and I got him off.

Why was Berkeley acquitted the third time and not the first two times? In what way did the third trial differ from the other two? As much as anything else, the difference was psychological. The fact that the jury in the third trial knew that there had been a majority in favor of acquittal in the second trial weighed the scales in Berkeley's favor.

21

My First Murder Case

THE FIRST MURDER CLIENT I ever represented was a sixteen-year-old boy. His father habitually beat his wife in his son's presence. One day, after knocking the boy's mother around, the father went into the back yard. The boy grabbed a .22 rifle, went to the door and, sobbing hysterically, fired a shot in the general direction of the figure disappearing in the distance. The bullet went between the turning spokes of two wagon wheels and killed his father.

The boy was arrested and charged with murder. I defended him. It was not long after the Harry Thaw trial, in which a new defense, *dementia Americana,* was offered. *Dementia Americana* meant the effects of the pressures, tensions and abrasions of American life as it is lived in the twentieth century. Although nobody had ever heard of it before, it worked. It got Thaw into an insane asylum instead of into an electric chair, and eventually he was set free. In my case, I offered as my defense something I called *"dementia matri amo"*—insanity induced by passionate mother love. Not only did *dementia matri amo* seem just as valid as *dementia Americana* to me, but it worked for me, too, and the jury found my client not guilty.

I also told that jury that I regarded that small .22 bullet as God's avenging thunderbolt rather than a piece of lead.

Another client of mine was a Negro whom I defended against a bootlegging charge. He lived in the little California town of Watts, and I went there to represent him. The D.A. didn't show up, but the judge announced, "We'll proceed anyhow."

256

"Your honor," I objected, "there's no district attorney."

He looked at me coldly and said, "I'll handle the prosecution myself."

I was stupefied with astonishment, but the judge called the witnesses, examined them, then said, "Now, Mr. Giesler, you may cross-examine."

I kept telling myself, *This can't be happening*, but the judge was doing it. Not only that, he cross-examined my witnesses, too. When we got around to the arguments, he said, "You open for the defense and I'll close for the people."

He made an argument for the prosecution, then turned himself back into a judge and gave the jury its instructions. I didn't know (and no one told me at the time) that he had never been a lawyer. He had been a shoemaker and before becoming a judge his only legal experience had been as a justice of the peace.

The unbelievable pay-off was the fact that in spite of the insurmountable odds I confronted—and what could be more insurmountable than the judge being the D.A. too?—the jury disagreed.

All in all, as the song says, it was a most unusual day. The next time, I succeeded in having the trial held in a more orthodox manner and I got an acquittal.

22

Divorce Cases I Have Handled

Ｉ N CONTRAST to the life-and-death tension of a murder trial, some of the civil cases I have handled seem lighter and less wearing. Even so, they can be pretty interesting.

In one of my civil cases for a change I represented the husband instead of the wife. The couple had got into a battle, and had separated, and *she* had sued *him* for divorce. While she was at it, she employed several of the best-known psychiatric experts in Los Angeles to prove that her spouse was mentally incompetent. By the time I was brought into the case she had had him committed to an asylum. It was legally possible to bring action to have him declared competent again. I brought such an action. It involved a jury trial.

I should have been flattered because the defense summoned a horde of psychiatric experts to make sure that I lost. Each of them went on the stand and testified that my client was not only incompetent but was suffering from general paresis, a disease which causes mental degeneration and which would surely kill him within a year.

I called no experts. Instead, I summoned my client's neighbors, the people who knew him best. They testified that in their opinion he was not insane, that his only trouble was that his domestic affairs had upset him emotionally and nervously.

The jury held with me and restored him to competency.

I mention this because it offers a clue to the value of some expert testimony. All those experts had said that my client would be dead within a year. Yet about five years later I walked into the Hall of Justice one day to try a case and there he was, on the jury panel, healthy, hale, happy and with all his buttons buttoned, and his incurable disease had been cured.

I also represented Zsa Zsa Gabor when she and her husband, George Sanders, agreed upon an uncontested divorce. Shortly after filing a cross complaint on behalf of Zsa Zsa in Santa Monica Superior Court, I announced the agreement. My cross filing denied Sanders' original complaint that Zsa Zsa had ignored and humiliated him. Zsa Zsa's cross complaint accused Sanders of mental cruelty, but it did not cite specific instances, so I was able to tell the court that Sanders had agreed to step aside and allow the actress to secure a decree by default. I also announced that a property settlement had been reached. I did not reveal its terms other than to report that Zsa Zsa had retained an $85,000 home she had bought with her own money.

While all this was going on, Zsa Zsa was appearing with her sisters in a Las Vegas night spot and was telling the press that she was thinking of filing a million-dollar damage suit against Porfirio Rubirosa for blackening one of her eyes. This lawsuit was never pressed. My personal opinion of Zsa Zsa Gabor is that she is as smart as a whip but that she has been spoiled by her own beauty. One side of her nature, a side which seldom draws any publicity, is that she has a daughter upon whom she dotes and whom she cares for devotedly.

But pinwheels, Roman candles and skyrockets shot off during those proceedings were as the fizzing of damp firecrackers compared to the fireworks which crackled between Shelley Winters and her husband, Vittorio Gassman, when they flung themselves angrily from each other's bed and board.

After their separation Shelley retained me to file suit for separate maintenance against Gassman, but the glare of verbal fireworks still lighted up the countryside near Milan, Italy, where Mr. Gassman was maintaining his own rocket-firing site. As relayed by the press, the unrehearsed dialogue went like this:

Vittorio: "I am far more interested in art than in finance."

Shelley: "I already have two Academy Award nominations*; now I'm interested in finance rather than art."

Vittorio: "I will never drop my rights as a good father to my ten-month-old daughter."

Shelley: "As a good father he should know that she is eleven months old."

Vittorio: "I asked for a divorce after a long series of quarrels."

Shelley: "We were never together long enough for a long series of anything. He only stayed at my house when he made a movie. Probably he did that to save rent."

Vittorio: "I was unable to be in America when our baby was born because I was in a play in Rome."

Shelley: "He asked me to stay out of Italy because he didn't want a pregnant woman hanging around while he was costarring in a Shakespearean comedy. As soon as he had a picture offer he dropped his play and hustled out to Hollywood."

Vittorio: "From now on my main interest is in the theater, not the movies."

Shelley: "Translated, that means Hollywood didn't take up his option."

I helped Miss Winters win the suit and also the custody of her child, and although it was not easy, I persuaded both parties to the litigation to stop issuing statements to the press.

I have long been aware of the fact that "Get me Giesler" has become a gag used by a husband when he is in the doghouse for some minor domestic offense which has riled his wife. I suppose that an attorney can't take part in as many trials of national interest as I've been involved in without becoming a household word, but this fact really hit me for the first time when Ingrid Bergman's divorce from Dr. Lindstrom was racing the stork.

Close friends of hers had talked to her by overseas phone in Italy and had suggested to her that she retain me to represent her. Apparently those friends thought she had agreed to this, for one

* Since then, of course, Miss Winters has won an Academy Award for her supporting role in *The Diary of Anne Frank*.

Monday morning as I came out of the Hall of Justice I saw a headline which said, "GET ME GIESLER!"

Those three words hit me like a ton of granite tumbling down a mountainside. I had had no word of warning, yet there they were screaming at me. Nothing came of the story that Miss Bergman might want me to represent her, but I'll never forget the peculiar feeling it gave me when that headline leaped at me.

I was connected with another divorce case which began when Mrs. Betty Hickman Healy, the young second wife of comedian Ted Healy, could stand her mate's stooges no longer, although they had helped make him successful and wealthy.

The Hollywood roller coaster which zooms a personality up to the topmost peak has a way of dropping him into the pit of public forgetfulness. That roller coaster now has its TV equivalent. TV's late, late movies, or films shown in the afternoon for the kiddies to see, have zoomed several personalities back to the peaks again. When I first began to tell this story, I wondered whether anyone would remember either Ted Healy or his stooges, but in the short time since I began this tale his Three Stooges have had a second birth of show-business life. Once more they demand big money as entertainers.

A rip appeared in the silken fabric of the Healy marriage when Mrs. Healy, a bride of four months, announced, "I guess our romance is over. It would have been a beautiful thing just to be married to Ted, but to be married to his stooges too, that was awful. Every room in the house seemed filled with his relatives or his stooges or his managers or someone, and they all stared at me as if I were an outsider. Then they'd do their unfunny little dances and their unfunny little comedy routines, and it was more than I could bear. In the middle of dinner one of the stooges would hop from his place at the table and do a buck and wing which was supposed to be side-splitting. The trouble was, when I didn't laugh they glared at me as if they thought something was wrong with me. The fifteen thousandth time this happened, I got sick and tired of them all and threw them out of the house."

261

Mrs. Healy made these statements to the press while confined to a Santa Monica hospital by influenza. She showed some temper when Healy said she had "run home to Mother."

"I didn't run home to Mother," she declared. "I'm not going home to Mother. Ted tells me that he has hired Jerry Giesler to protect his interests. Well, I've engaged a good lawyer too, Mr. W. I. Gilbert."

Mr. Gilbert and I had no trouble working out an arrangement suitable to husband and wife—and Mrs. Healy was free of the stooges.

Several months after Mrs. Healy obtained her interlocutory decree of divorce, she and Ted were reconciled. They had the divorce action dismissed in June 1937, six months before Healy died following a mysterious beating administered to him outside a Hollywood night club. The reason for that beating has never been discovered.

When a couple is considering a divorce action, I always try first to exercise a conciliatory effect upon both parties, no matter how rancorous their hatred may be. I make it a point to get them together, and if I can't effect a reconciliation I usually try to make them understand that the best interests of everybody will be served if they stop their name-calling outside the courtroom and dispense with a trial which will leave bitterness on both sides.

I am willing to sit for days with people who are determined not to "give in," explaining the reasons why one party should give a little here and the other party a little there. Of course, the opposing lawyer is there too, listening while I do this, but most lawyers are happy to see a warring couple settle their differences with a measure of reasonableness.

However, a few lawyers hide their clients or won't bring them in and as a result I have no chance to talk with them. Such lawyers are either fee-greedy or litigious, which is the same thing as being knife-happy if you are a surgeon. So far, I am proud of the record I have established of keeping many messy private brawlings out of the public domain.

23

A Boy from Iowa

Y OWN UPBRINGING was just about as remote from Hollywood's glitter and tinsel as it is possible to be. I was born in November of 1886 in the little town of Wilton Junction, Iowa, a community of three hundred souls. My father was a moderately prosperous cashier at the local bank. I was christened Harold Lee but I prefer the nickname Jerry and have used it professionally for many years. Nothing very unusual happened to me as a child. It is perhaps for this reason that the small, human, unimportant things stand out in my memory. For instance, in accordance with the custom of the times, my mother dressed me in a Lord Fauntleroy suit, and I was afflicted with the long, uncut curls that went with it. When I was sent downtown to one of the local stores to bring home packages, I was so ashamed of my attire and coiffure that I sneaked down back alleys instead of walking down the main street.

I remember that I did one thing which had a Tom Sawyerish flavor. When my small brother was born—he arrived nine years after I did—I let my school friends carry firewood into our house as payment for allowing them to look in our bedroom window to look at the baby. For some reason they thought it ample recompense for their labor, and I was not above taking advantage of their soft-headedness.

When I was in the first grade my mother washed out my mouth for swearing. The soap she used must have been caustic, for I never swore again. I don't swear to this day. I don't say it with any holier-than-thou attitude, but I don't smoke either and I can't remember ever having told a dirty story. It is my conviction that a dirty story is the kind of story a gentleman not merely refrains from telling a lady but also refrains from telling to another gentleman.

And while I'm at it, in this story of mine you will have noticed that I don't often call people by their nicknames. I am not even given to a one hundred per cent use of their first names. I was brought up to call people Mr., Mrs. or Miss, as a matter of courtesy, and it comes naturally to me to address people that way, especially those I work with. I even find myself referring to my wife as Mrs. Giesler.

One winter I went to school in the town of Oakley in the western part of Kansas. An uncle of mine lived there. He and his wife had no children, and they wanted me with them. One incident which happened there still haunts me. When I was fourteen, the Masonic lodge in Oakley had a function. My Uncle Henry belonged and I was asked to recite Mark Twain's "Toast to the Babies." I studied it until I had learned it by heart. The place was jammed. When my turn came to recite, I couldn't say a word; I just stood there, hoping to die. Panic-stricken, I ran out on the back porch. No sooner was I there, of course, than Twain's toast came back to me. It was the only time I've been at a loss for words and it taught me a lesson. Since that day I have never tried to learn anything by heart. When I present an argument to a jury, I do it extemporaneously. A courtroom has no back porch.

As a boy I read avidly. I joined three churches so that I could draw books from three Sunday school libraries. Since my mother and father were affiliated with the Presbyterian church, I read all of the books in the Presbyterian Sunday school library first—books like James Otis's Blue and Gray Series and the Frank series by Frank Castleman. Then I joined the Congregational church and read all the books in that library too. Next I joined the Episcopal church. I think it was not long after that that someone—probably the rector —suggested I join the public library as well.

After my mother died, when I was fifteen or sixteen, I was sent to an academy in Morgan Park, near Chicago, where I stayed for almost three years. The episode that sticks in my mind about that school was the great prune strike. We decided that we were being fed too many prunes, so we refused to eat in the mess hall. Our belligerence made the front pages of the Chicago papers. I was one of those who bravely kept away from the mess hall and ate instead at lunch counters and soda fountains until the academy gave in. My attitude during this episode will probably not surprise some of the district attorneys I have faced in California courtrooms.

I was never much of an athlete, although I passionately wanted to be. In one of my scrapbooks are carefully pasted some pages from the *Tip-Top Weekly,* "the Largest Weekly Circulation in America, an Ideal Publication for the American Youth." The lead story in that issue was "Frank Merriwell on Carson's Ranch, or, The King of the Cattle Thieves." But the important thing to me in that issue was a letter I addressed to a Professor Fourman (whoever he was):

I am a constant reader of your splendid weekly [I wrote]. I have not missed a number for a year and a half. There are a few questions which I take the liberty to ask. One: I am sixteen years old, weight 105 pounds, and am five feet nine inches in height. I desire to know how my weight may be increased. Two: Is cigarette smoking harmful if I limit myself to two a day? Three: Kindly give me the address of a firm that publishes a book on physical training. Four: I expect to be a candidate for the track team next year. Knowing, as you do, what my present weight and measurements are, what distance would you advise me to run? I have a record of fifteen seconds for the hundred yards. Is that good for one my age?

> Yours truly,
> HAROLD L. GIESLER,
> Morgan Park Academy,
> Morgan Park, Illinois.

Professor Fourman's answer to me was:

One: Your weight may be increased by drinking plenty of water, hot or cold, and by indulging in out-of-door exercise. Everyone who gets out in the open air and plays or works in such a way as to arouse the system and create circulation is in a fair way to gain weight and add to their strength. Anything, football, baseball, handball, tennis, rowing, skating, walking, running, punching the bag, wrestling, horseback riding, bicycling, all serve the same purpose. You need not do more than one at a time, but you should do something. Two: Yes, two a day is bad. You should not smoke cigarettes at all. Three: Frank Merriwell's Book of Physical Development is an excellent treatise of this kind. You can secure it of us by sending ten cents to cover the cost of the book and four cents for mailing. Four: That would be very hard to say. Your record of a hundred yards in fifteen seconds seems to indicate that it is the best length for you at present. It is very good.

My best length today is five feet eleven, stretched out in bed looking at television.

Omnivorous reading weakened my eyes while I was at the Morgan Park Academy but I had made up my mind to go to college. I had even selected my future alma mater, the University of Michigan, because the football star Willie Heston had played there. But after I completed a summer school make-up session in mathematics in 1905, my eyes gave out. By this time my father had switched to the lumber business. He had moved to Eau Claire, Wisconsin, and I went there for the rest of the summer. A specialist advised me to give my eyes a year's rest, and I decided to do it in California. I had been corresponding with Alex Ogilvie, a boy I had known in Iowa when he and his family lived near us. They had moved to Los Angeles and when they heard that I had to stop school they asked if I would come west and stay with them. My father consented.

When I reached Los Angeles, I found the Ogilvies in an apartment perched on Angel's Flight Hill, in downtown Los Angeles. It is called Angel's Flight because it has a cogged railway which climbs its steep sides. The Ogilvies had arranged for me to stay in a little room in the basement of their apartment house. That room was pretty sad. To reach it I had to grope my way through an alley full of garbage pails.

My father had made it clear that he expected me to earn my own living in Los Angeles, so once I had settled down I went to a nearby park—it was known as Central Park, but today it's Pershing Square—picked up newspapers which people had left on the benches and searched the want-ad sections. Finally I located a job driving a lumber wagon. Back in the Midwest I had worked in lumber mills, carrying slabs away from the slab saws and stacking boards, so I felt competent to fill any job connected with lumber.

My new job was with the Builders' Supply Company. My wages were two dollars a day. I drove a big gray mare. I saw to it that she was curried and fed and that her stable was kept clean. Every day, after greasing the wheels of my lumber wagon, I hitched up my gray mare and made deliveries all over town. I say "town" because Los Angeles wasn't really big then. It numbered only 125,-000 people.

Some of the window frames I hauled in that wagon are still in use. Occasionally, when I'm downtown, I go out of my way to have a look at houses containing them. My interest in the buildings to which I delivered lumber grows every year. It may be that subconsciously I think of them as pieces of my youth, still remaining unchanged.

Sunset Boulevard wasn't paved then, and adobe was pounded into the ground to form a roadbed. That pounding helped keep down the dust, but when it rained the adobe changed to a gluey substance in which a big gray mare pulling a lumber wagon could get stuck. I adopted the habit of driving with my wagon wheels on the flanges of the streetcar tracks. Sometimes a streetcar would come along behind and give my wagon a helpful push. Some motormen were human beings in those days.

I hauled lumber all that winter. I got up at four o'clock every morning and walked down to a little eating shack at Fifth and Spring, where the Security Bank now stands. I paid ten cents for my breakfast and another ten cents for a carry-out.

I worked through the spring of 1906. Then I stopped because I got homesick. There was too much sameness about the southern-California weather. There was too little rain; there was no snow. I wanted to go back to Iowa. I resisted the impulse for a while until the fire hit San Francisco. I went to San Francisco to see the results of that catastrophe and, having seen them, I kept on going until I reached Iowa. Soon after, I entered the law school of the University of Iowa.

The ambition to become a lawyer had taken hold of me when I was in grade school. We had a current-events class. Each of us had to stand up and talk about what we had learned from reading the big daily papers from Chicago. Bloody labor wars were tearing the country apart then. One casualty was Governor Steunenberg of Idaho. He had been assassinated by dynamite, which seems to me a particularly repugnant way of killing a fellow man.

Since it was easy for workmen, especially miners, to lay hand to explosives, quite a lot of dynamite killings were going on. Several men, two of them members of the I.W.W., were being tried for blowing up Governor Steunenberg. A lawyer named Clarence Darrow was defending them. It was the first time I had ever heard of him, but as I read about him and his handling of that case excitement mounted inside me. I contracted a case of hero worship for Clarence Darrow then from which I have never recovered.

The prosecutor in the case, the district attorney of Boise, Idaho, was a talented young man named William E. Borah, who later became a famous United States senator. Even so, the upshot was that Mr. Darrow won an acquittal, although to do so he had to scratch and claw his way through hedgerows thick with thorny public prejudice.

His victory filled me with a desire to practice criminal law. The battling and tension which Mr. Darrow faced appealed to me. They still do. I've been asked what I admired about Mr. Darrow most, his tactics, his strategy or his courage. I couldn't slice it that thin. I admired the whole man.

24

Earl Rogers and the Bar

Examination

I HAD LEARNED to admire another famous advocate while I was driving a lumber wagon in Los Angeles. His name was Earl Rogers. One case in particular made me intensely Rogers-conscious. One of the reigning oil kings of the time was a man named Doheny. He had a partner named Canfield. Morrison Buck, a former coachman employed by the Canfields, shot and killed Canfield's wife. Buck had dropped in on Mrs. Canfield one day and put the arm on her for working capital with which to start a bakery business. When Mrs. Canfield said no, Buck pulled a pistol out of his pocket and shot a bullet through her heart.

In those days it was possible for any citizen to hire a private prosecutor to assist the state's attorney. Canfield was a wealthy man; he wanted Earl Rogers, and he was willing to pay for his services "even if it takes millions."

In his long and spectacular career Earl Rogers was employed as a prosecutor only twice. This was one of the two times. The most important battle in the warfare between Rogers and the defense occurred when Rogers took on a raft of defense medical experts and demonstrated that his knowledge of pathology was so good that he could shoot their testimony full of holes. The jury found Buck guilty and he was hanged.

I drove my lumber wagon by day, but by night I read the papers, following the news of this legal chess master with bated breath— until I fell victim of the grippe. I can't recall now how virulent my grippe was; perhaps my fever was mostly a consuming desire to be in the courtroom watching Rogers at work. I do know that day after day I failed to drive my lumber wagon and instead wedged my way into that courtroom and watched the trial. Once I was in and saw Mr. Rogers in action, fingers of excitement felt their way up and down my spine.

I've been asked, "What is your first memory of Earl Rogers?" I always answer, "My first impression of him was that he was nattily dressed. He wore a swallow-tailed coat, a stand-up collar, a tie in which a diamond stickpin glittered. He was very handsome. He had an air which made it possible for him to carry off his dressiness without seeming foppish. He was dynamic, impressive and dominant."

He fascinated me. When I was in the same courtroom with him, I couldn't pull my eyes away. I watched him the way small boys in Urbana, Illinois, were to watch another man, Red Grange, drift through a broken field in the 1920s. So in addition to my earlier hero worship of Clarence Darrow, I now had a newer one. Even so, in spite of my dual inspiration, I was no ball of fire as a student at the Iowa Law School. In one subject, contracts, I was given a condition instead of a passing grade.

I had wanted to go home to Iowa to see snow float down between me and the street lights, but that winter I spent at law school was an unusually severe one and I began to think of the balmy California weather. I had only to shut my eyes to be drenched in southern-California sunshine and to feel the softness of the Los Angeles air. I finished out the school year. Then I hurried back to southern California. I've never left it since except on business trips and for one short stay in Las Vegas, to recuperate from an operation, and an even shorter vacation in Palm Springs.

When I returned to Los Angeles I enrolled in the U.S.C. Law School. In those days, a student didn't have to take prelaw; he just enrolled. I was still living on Angel's Flight Hill, although not with the Ogilvies. I had taken a really cheap apartment up there. I'd got used to the hill and I liked going up and down on the little incline railway which lifted me to its top.

At U.S.C. the law school classes began each morning at eight. They ran for one hour and then recessed, to reconvene each evening from five to six. There was a dinner break of an hour, then afterward classes continued from seven to eight. There were no classes in the middle of the day. That made it possible for a student to work his way through. Most of us did.

I felt I had grown beyond lumber hauling—my law school hours and my wagon-driving hours would have conflicted anyhow. In addition, I wanted work which I thought would more or less tie in with my law studies. So with two other boys, John Richardson and Edward Allen, who were also taking law at U.S.C., I formed a partnership to go into the bill-collecting business.

We called our firm Allen, Giesler and Richardson. After a while we decided that that name didn't have enough tone, and we changed it to the Prospect Law and Collection Agency. We used no great variety of stratagems in collecting bills. We just kept ever-lastingly after the no-payers and the deadbeats until even the most confirmed bill-dodger grew so weary of the sight of us that he dug into his pocket and gave us the money.

The opening of our business coincided with an election year. One of the law professors at U.S.C., Professor Williss, was running for a judgeship on the Republican ticket. The Democratic candidate for judge was Albert Lee Stephens, who is now a judge for the Circuit Court of Appeals for the Ninth Circuit in San Francisco.

Before it began its career as a collection agency, the firm of Allen, Giesler and Richardson visited Judge Williss. We told him we wanted to help him win the election. I'm afraid that was not wholly true. What we really wanted to do was make enough money to pay the rental on an office so that we could have a headquarters we could work out of. After some eager talk on our part, we persuaded him to put up enough loot for us to lease a tiny room at Third and Main for three months.

Then we went to Judge Stephens, who was then a J.P., and told him that we wanted to work for him. We were too young to vote, but we could go to the convention hall and make noise, exude enthusiasm and cheer like mad when his name was mentioned. The fee Mr. Stephens paid us took care of furnishing our office.

One day when I reached the office first, I found in the mail a letter from a lawbook publishing company. It contained a long-overdue bill owed by Earl Rogers. I stuffed it into my pocket and said nothing about it. I wanted to take that bill to Mr. Rogers personally. I hoped to meet him rather than to collect anything.

It was a good thing I was in that frame of mind, since, as it turned out, Mr. Rogers was collector-proof. His office staff was trained to smell bill collectors the way bird dogs smell bobwhites, and once they had scented me they wouldn't let me near him. So I went into the courthouse—anybody was allowed there—and waited outside his courtroom for him when he was trying a case. I knew that sooner or later he would come out. Smoking wasn't allowed inside the courtroom and he was an inveterate smoker. When he needed a smoke, he asked one of his associates to stay in the courtroom while he took a stroll outside, puffed a cigarette and walked up and down. He rolled his own, sprinkling tobacco from a sack onto a brownish cigarette paper. He made a symmetrical tube, then licked the edges of the paper and closed the tube.

When I first approached him I said, "Mr. Rogers, my name is Giesler. I have a bill here from—"

That's as far as I got. He brushed me off like a mosquito. But I kept after him, accosting him whenever I could. Finally one day I told him that my real ambition was to be his office boy.

"But I have no opening," he said.

"I'll keep trying," I said. "You will someday."

Eventually one of his office boys did leave and there was an opening. "Mr. Giesler," he said (he had learned my name by that time and he made a fetish of courtesy and politeness, even if he wouldn't pay his bills), "go to my office and tell them I said to put you to work."

I never did collect that bill. I think it was between one and two hundred dollars. He owed the money to a law publishing company which put out the old *American Encyclopedia of Evidence*. If that company were still in business, I'd be happy to pay them what Mr. Rogers owed them, plus interest, for bringing us together.

When I reported for work with Mr. Rogers I left the collection agency, and I never went back. But I kept right on going to law school. I was supposed to be paid twenty-five dollars a month. I seldom got it. I was paid a little something now and then, but it was spasmodic. I lived precariously, often borrowing from relatives and friends.

I was a clerk. I carried books. I cleaned up the office. I put papers away or stacked them up in Mr. Rogers' office. When a case was finished, all the papers connected with it were folded and put into a heavy paper wrapper. Then Mr. Rogers tossed the bundle into a corner. The pile grew until it became a paper Matterhorn. If anyone needed a certain document, I was the one called upon to burrow into that paper mountain and find it. I also accompanied Mr. Rogers and his associates to court, giving a good imitation of a small, sweating pack mule loaded down with stacks of lawbooks.

In addition I was expected to do a little light detective work—investigating murder cases and interviewing witnesses and the like. Mr. Rogers was a great one for finding out as much as possible about the lives of the venire he might face. In a day when the courts drew their juries from one venire of jurors and the number of those on it was small enough so that each venireman could be investigated individually, such information was invaluable.

Even if I had been paid regularly, the most valuable part of my pay still would have been sitting in court watching Mr. Rogers try cases. I learned more from him than I learned in the law schools and the lawbooks.

Scores of young lawyers have asked me about the things I learned from Mr. Rogers. I can only answer that I watched him prepare his cases for trial, I watched him cope with questions of law, I saw how he approached them, I heard his arguments to the jury, but most important of all was the chance to study the art of cross-examination as he practiced it. That was his forte.

Other lawyers did one or two things well. Some of them may

273

have done three or four things well. Mr. Rogers differed from all the rest in that he could do almost everything well. Instinctively he possessed legal talent other people didn't have.

I had been with him only a few months when he asked me to drop out of law school temporarily and come with him to San Francisco to run errands and do odd jobs during the graft trials which were going on there. Some of the city fathers had been accused of larding their bank accounts with boodle for seeing to it that the "right people" controlled the city transit system. The principal defendant was Patrick Calhoun, the president of San Francisco's street railway system. He had been indicted for alleged crookedness. One of his ancestors had been John C. Calhoun of South Carolina, and although his enemies said that his ethics were as convoluted as a conch shell, he was aristocratic, distinguished and upright-looking.

When I got to San Francisco Mr. Rogers said, "I want you to stay with me throughout the trial. I need somebody I can depend on to carry papers, documents and books back and forth between the United Railroads office on Market Street and the courthouse."

That courthouse had figured in an attempted killing in the trial which had immediately preceded the Calhoun case. The man being tried then was Abraham Ruef, the political boss of San Francisco, whose conviction in an earlier trial had been set aside on appeal. He was now being prosecuted for bribery. The prosecutor in his trial was Francis J. Heney, who had been loaned to San Francisco by the United States Government as a special prosecutor, after having done outstanding work for the United States Department of Justice.

The prosecution also had William J. Burns, later the head of the U.S. Justice Department's Bureau of Investigation, as its chief of investigators. When not on loan to such causes as the preservation of San Francisco's municipal purity, Burns was the J. Edgar Hoover of his day. It didn't take me long to see that I was carrying papers and documents back and forth in a big-time legal battle.

Not only was Heney a ruthless courtroom fighter, but, aided and abetted by Burns, his investigation of prospective jurors achieved startling results. In the first Ruef trial, he had exposed a prospective juror, Morris Haas, as an ex-convict. When Haas was dismissed as a juryman, it preyed on his mind to such an extent that before the second Ruef trial was over he aimed a pistol at Heney, who was seated at the counsel table, and shot him.

Mr. Heney wasn't killed, but his convalescence was a long and doubtful one. By a quirk of fate, the bullet of that would-be assassin also catapulted a young San Francisco lawyer named Hiram Johnson into national prominence. When Heney was wounded, somebody had to take his place, and young Johnson was pressed into service as prosecutor. As a result of the work he did in that trial, he was elected Governor of California. From there he went on to become Senator. He could have been President of the United States if he had accepted the Vice-Presidency when it was offered to him before it was offered to Calvin Coolidge.

By the time the Calhoun trial got under way, Heney had recovered and was prosecuting the case, but because of what had happened in the preceding trial the atmosphere was so tense in the courtroom I could feel the air around me vibrate like a plucked cello string. Mounted police rode up and down outside and policemen stationed at the door searched those who entered for weapons. Two armed guards sat immediately behind Heney, facing the courtroom. Two other guards faced toward the rear, watching everyone who was seated behind Heney. It was not a time, a place and a situation easy for a youngster to forget, and I never have forgotten.

When I reached San Francisco, Mr. Rogers told me that I'd be more useful if I lived in the St. Francis Hotel with him. To me that was like being suddenly elected President. The St. Francis was a luxurious place, and I was still pretty much a green kid from the farm belt. Also, I was paid regularly. The reason for that was that I was being paid by the United Railroads instead of Mr. Rogers. Every week I received thirty dollars in gold. I had seen little hard cash up to that time, and being paid in money I could feel and spend was bliss.

When I wasn't carrying papers between the courthouse and the United Railroads office on Market Street, I sat in the courtroom directly behind Mr. Calhoun. Mr. Calhoun not only had Mr. Rogers as his lawyer, he had the two principal attorneys for the Southern Pacific Railroad defending him, as well as the former district attorney of San Francisco. In his corner was also Alexander King of Georgia, who later became the Solicitor General of the United States under Woodrow Wilson. Only Francis J. Heney and his assistant, a young man named O'Gara from the district attorney's office, occupied the front-line trenches for the state. However, Mr. Heney was easily the equal of two ordinary lawyers.

One day I was sitting in the courtroom when I saw Mr. Heney and O'Gara look my way, then talk to each other, and I wondered what was going on. At that moment Mr. Rogers was cross-examining the head of the Board of Supervisors. He had succeeded in getting him muddled and mixed, and, looking back on it, it seems clear that Mr. Heney hoped to interrupt the proceedings with a diversionary tactic.

Standing up, he said, "Your honor, I'd like to call attention to the young man sitting behind Mr. Calhoun. When anything favorable to the prosecution is brought out, he frowns at the jury. When anything favorable to the defense occurs, he smiles at the jury. It is the opinion of the prosecution that his behavior is improper, reprehensible and is designed to influence the jurors."

Such a remark may seem childish, but childish or not, it accomplished what Mr. Heney hoped it would accomplish. It interrupted Mr. Rogers' cross-examination and gave the head of the Board of Supervisors a chance to unscramble his brains and reassemble them. Up jumped a defense lawyer to light into Mr. Heney for interrupting the trial with such a triviality. It was, he said heatedly, a barefaced attempt to prejudice the jury, since the young man in question (meaning me) was innocent of anything except pulling for his side to win, and that was certainly normal.

Finally, Mr. Calhoun himself stood up. It was the only time during the trial that he said anything. He was six feet four. He was very dignified. He drew himself up to his full height and said, "Your honor, in reality it is my life which is at stake here, because these proceedings involve my reputation, which is more valuable to me than my life, and for Mr. Heney to interrupt the proceedings upon which a man's precious reputation hangs with such foolishness is unseemly."

He looked at me and said, "This young man has been sitting near me throughout this trial and I have never seen him do anything which would be described as reprehensible. But apparently Mr. Heney is willing to try any trick, no matter how cheap or tawdry, to create a momentary interruption."

Realizing that he had got into deeper waters than he had intended, Mr. Heney backed out. He admitted that perhaps he had been mistaken, and the judge let the matter drop.

It didn't drop for me. The next morning the incident was described on the front pages of the San Francisco papers. My name appeared in print for the first time and my chest expanded several inches. It was still expanded when, while I was stationed by the "defense" automobile parked out in front, to see that nothing was removed from it, the jurors in the trial called out to me in mock seriousness as they passed by, "Don't you flirt with us."

That trial lasted nearly six months and in spite of all the expenditure in time, money and effort it involved, it ended in disagreement. The jury was ten to two for acquittal. Mr. Calhoun was never tried again.

As for me, I had begun to pick up the rudiments of how to conduct an effective cross-examination. But the lesson that stood out in my mind was the discovery that, with few exceptions, really big lawyers handled themselves with dignity and decorum. That lesson of courteousness sank into my soul at an impressionable age. It has stayed there since. I believe that it is the greatest asset a lawyer can have in his relations with both the judge and the jury. It is even more so today than it was then. because women sit on juries now.

After the Calhoun trial I went back to Los Angeles with Mr. Rogers. Because I had missed six months of law school I decided to cram for my bar examinations and take them as soon as possible instead of waiting until I completed my university course. That was 1907 and students didn't have to wait until they had finished law school to take the bar exam. They could take it any time they felt qualified.

Once I'd made up my mind, I really studied. The apartment house in which I lived on Angel's Flight Hill had no porch or balcony, so when it was unseasonably warm (and whenever it's too warm in Los Angeles it *is* unseasonable) I sat on the fire escape on the third floor and read Robinson's *Elementary Law*.

As the time drew nearer for my session with the bar examiners I was as nervous as a cat. The examinations were held in the Supreme Court room in the old International Bank Building. They were conducted by three judges of the District Court of Appeals. Those judges sat on a rostrum. Beginning with the candidates in the front row, they asked those who offered themselves as candidates a series of oral questions.

When my day came, I reached the old International Bank Building a little late, and there was no place for me except on the last row of seats. This turned out to be very fortunate for me, for the first people examined were given the longest and hardest questions. As the session continued the questions grew shorter. Not only did the examiners became weary, but time was running out and they were running out of questions. By the time they reached the last row, I was asked only three questions: my name, where I lived, what I had studied. I mentioned Robinson's *Elementary Law* and a few other books. That was all.

I couldn't believe it, and instead of being hilariously happy at being let off so easily, I was horribly worried. I thought of all of the dire reasons why they had skimped in questioning me. It was no trick at all to decide that in three questions they had found me a meathead unsuited for the California bar.

The names of those who had passed were posted in a hallway the next day. I was sure that I had flunked, but like a murderer who is said to be drawn irresistibly to the scene of his crime (I have never found this to be true) I came back the next day to study the list of names anyhow. I was so nervous I could hardly read. I saw no name which resembled mine.

One of the other candidates said encouragingly, "Look again, Jerry, and take your time!" I did and my name was there.

Suddenly I was a human skyrocket. I was Daniel Webster and Rufus Choate. I was standing at the threshold of wonderfully exciting things. When I walked down Broadway, I felt I was floating over the sidewalk at an elevation of twenty feet. I passed the courthouse, in front of which stood a statue of Stephen M. White, a former United States senator from California who had been one of the community's great lawyers. I looked at him and I thought the wildly soaring thoughts kids think at such times. Someday, I thought, I may be as big as Senator White.

Then I began to worry about what to call myself. Attorney? No. Lawyer? No. Barrister? That sounded better. Solicitor? That sounded even better, although a little British.

When I reached Mr. Rogers' office, he cocked an eye at me and asked, "Well?" and I said, "I'm a lawyer." He congratulated me and said, "Put your name on one of our windows."

That was an exceedingly important invitation. The geographical location of Mr. Rogers' offices at First and Broadway was a good place psychologically for law offices to be. Mr. Rogers' offices were down the street from the Central Jail and people who were brought there invariably looked upward to catch a glimpse of blue sky before they entered its dismal confines. As they did, there on the windows of the second-floor offices across the way they could see Mr. Rogers' name and the names of his associates. If those persons looking upward were interested in obtaining legal assistance, succor was one story up. Such was Mr. Rogers' fame that just seeing his name there on his windows recalled the many sensational victories he had won.

In my case the catch was to persuade Mr. Rogers to install a new window, because all of the window space available was filled with the names of his associates and even the names of those who had left him to branch out on their own. He saw no reason to remove the names of those departed ones, since they did his practice no harm.

Eventually one of those windows got broken, and when it was

replaced my name was on it. I'm sure that everyone who reads this will nod knowingly and decide that he knows exactly how it was broken. Knowing looks or no knowing looks, I had nothing to do with it, but I'll confess there was real joy in my heart when it happened.

25

My Early Cases

WHEN THAT BROKEN WINDOW in Earl Rogers' office was replaced and my name was on it, it was more a theoretical advantage than a real one. Any clients who got down to my level never had any money. Mr. Rogers took the well-heeled ones. Those who were less well fixed went to the next senior member in the office, and so on down the line. By the time they got to me, if I held my clients upside down and shook them I would have heard only the small change dropping to the floor. Nevertheless, if I have developed long, sharp legal teeth (and I have been accused of it) it is because I cut them then on a gritty fare of cases no one else wanted.

I remember one client who filtered down to me. He had no money but he had a case, and I was so eager that that in itself was a sufficient inducement. In a preliminary examination he had been charged with grand theft. As a result, he was coming up for trial. I read the transcripts of his preliminary investigation. Then I looked up the law as it applied to his offense and I found a decision from the Appellate Court of California which seemed on all fours with his. The case I looked up had been thrown out by the District Court of Appeals on the ground that it wasn't a legal offense and therefore wasn't a crime. I told my client that I would not only take his case but would get him off. It's the first and only time I've ever told anyone that.

Finally the day of the trial came and we went into court. I had the book in which I had found the decision which had given me such overwhelming confidence. I was keeping it in my briefcase to spring on the prosecution.

The trial began and the opposing attorney presented his evidence. When he was done I stood up, pulled out my book and told the court that since the District Court of Appeals had held my client's offense was no crime, there was no case.

My client was reaching for his hat when, to my horror, the district attorney said, "Your honor, what Mr. Giesler says is true, but he has forgotten to mention one small fact. After the District Court of Appeals handed down the decision to which he refers, the Supreme Court reversed the District Court's decision."

That courtroom was right over the county jail, and if the boards under me had opened and had let me down into it I would have been happy. That judge, bless his wise, kind heart, was a decent fellow. "We will adjourn," he said, "and I'd like to talk to you in chambers, Mr. Giesler."

In his chambers he said, "I know you must feel very small and very ashamed, and I suggest you regard this as a useful lesson rather than a humiliating experience. Your lesson is: Always Shepardize your case."

I didn't know what Shepardize meant, but I soon found out. It meant not only following through on your cases to see what happened to them when they were appealed to a higher court, but following them even further, to find out whether those decisions had been sustained or reversed by subsequent decisions. Shepard is the name of a company which prepares and publishes compilations of all court decisions. From that day on I have Shepardized every case I have handled. I keep two complete sets of Shepard—one in my office and one in my home. Unhappily, they did me no good then. My client didn't get off. The jury found him guilty and he was sentenced to prison.

I climbed slowly until, in two cases, I was actively associated with Mr. Rogers himself. Each of them involved contributing to the delinquency of a minor. Both of those trials were famous in their day, since they were based on charges against two prominent citizens who were running for office in Los Angeles. The first one involved

Los Angeles' chief of police, Charles Sebastian, who was then a candidate for mayor. The charge against him was that he had contributed to the delinquency of an eighteen-year-old girl who claimed that Sebastian had been keeping company with her older sister and that he had made passes at her while her older sister was in the same room. The older sister was charged with contributing to the delinquency of her young sister.

Mr. Sebastian employed Earl Rogers to defend him, and I was invited to associate myself with Mr. Rogers in the trial, which lasted eight weeks. In the middle of the legal hassle Mr. Sebastian was nominated as a mayoralty candidate. He was found not guilty after he was nominated. Following his acquittal he won the election.

When such charges are made against such a man during a red-hot political campaign, it seems likely to me that they are merely attempts at political filth-throwing, and Mr. Sebastian's victory in the primary election while his trial was still in progress showed that the public thought the charges against him were a frame-up.

The other city official we defended on the same sort of charge was Los Angeles' city prosecutor, Guy Eddy. Once more an election was imminent. Mr. Eddy was about to run for district attorney of Los Angeles County. He seemed sure to be elected, for he was extremely prominent in the local Republican Party organization which was then in power.

"Contributing to the delinquency of a minor" was a popular brickbat to throw then, because it was a new offense. The statute making anyone under twenty-one a juvenile had gone into effect only a short time before. Mr. Eddy's troubles began when a woman who legally was still a girl (she wasn't scheduled to reach her twenty-first birthday for two days) dropped into his office on a pretext of complaining about something; then, after having made what was vulgarly called "a pass" at him, she left. A couple of days later she came back to take up where she had left off.

When Mr. Rogers and I were retained to combat this poison-gas attack, we immediately claimed that Mr. Eddy's political rivals had hired the girl to lay a trap for him.

Before she came back the second time, certain members of the police department had bored a hole in the door of Eddy's office and had plugged the hole with putty. They testified that on the day of her second visit they had pushed the putty out and, watching through the peephole, had seen her sitting on Eddy's lap while he committed acts which were calculated to contribute to her delinquency. They further testified that they had then broken the door down, arrested him and charged him with "contributing."

Mr. Eddy's trial lasted more than two months. Because of the political issues involved, everybody wanted to get into the act, and this led to a multitude of witnesses. It didn't require a first-class brain to realize that drilling a hole in that door, then putting putty in it, preparatory to the young woman's deliberately going in there (even she didn't claim she was forced to go) was a plot to kill off our client politically. Mr. Eddy was acquitted, but as phony as those charges were, they killed him politically, and he withdrew from the D.A. race.

It was because of those rotten and stinking political cases which I was associated with as a youngster that I've never taken part in politics, although I've had my chances. I learned very early how dirty it could make a man.

26

Defending Darrow

THERE ARE MOMENTS when I feel I have lived through more emotional high points than most men. But I am not complaining, because one of them was helping to defend Clarence Darrow. Mr. Darrow was in Los Angeles defending the McNamara brothers, who were standing trial for dynamiting the Los Angeles *Times* Building, a tragedy in which many people had been killed and maimed. That crime was part of a brutal war between union and management.

Realizing the impossibility of winning for the McNamara brothers, Mr. Darrow finally hit upon the hope of saving Joseph J. McNamara from a long prison term and settling for a life sentence for his young brother, James B., by entering into an agreement with the state to accept a plea of guilty for J.B. with a life sentence; and in a separate case, a plea for J.J. with a ten-year sentence. The judge crossed up all concerned by insisting upon giving J.J. a fifteen-year stretch instead of the one agreed to by the state.

But as it turned out, the McNamara brothers were not the only ones charged with committing crime. Mr. Darrow was accused of attempting to bribe two of the jurors, at Third and Main streets. Lured there by a ruse, he had foolishly shown up there alone. Consequently it was possible for his enemies to say he was in the neighborhood when two potential jurors in the trial (they were on the panel but hadn't been selected) were given money to favor the defense. It was then that Mr. Darrow himself needed a lawyer.

Mr. Rogers was in Hanford, a small town in central California, trying a contested will case. I was with him, carrying his books and papers and looking up points of law. One morning Mr. Darrow turned up in the little Hanford courtroom with his wife, Ruby. For three days they sat there watching Mr. Rogers. They had been told that he was a great lawyer, but they knew nothing of him at first hand. Mr. Darrow liked what he saw. He employed Mr. Rogers as his attorney.

We came back to Los Angeles and went to work for Mr. Darrow. I helped as best I could. Although I had passed the bar and I could call myself a lawyer, I was still a callow youth who was looking up the law for my betters.

Mr. Darrow became aware of me after he and Mr. Rogers asked me to look up a point of law for them. Before I finished I had prepared a brief forty pages long. The day before the trial began I gave copies of my brief to Mr. Rogers and Mr. Darrow. They read it, they liked it, and they said, "Jerry, we are going to let you sit in on the trial. You will be an attorney of record in this case."

I have already described how I felt when I discovered that I had passed the state bar examination, but never, not even then, have I had another thrill to equal what I felt on being allowed to be a member of such a team. There I was, just a kid, and the two men I idolized most were treating me as an equal. My eyes smarted. I couldn't talk. I couldn't even thank them.

The two charges of attempted bribery lodged against Mr. Darrow were tried separately. There were so many witnesses, examinations, cross-examinations and arguments, and so much legal tanglefoot, that the first case took three months to try. Lincoln Steffens sat there in the courtroom throughout the entire three months and covered the case as the country's leading liberal writer. He was a great friend of Mr. Darrow. All of the country's labor leaders were on hand too, for, rightly or wrongly, the case was regarded as capital versus labor instead of the state of California versus Clarence Darrow.

Once more William J. Burns handled the investigation for the prosecution. Mr. Darrow himself did some of the cross-examining for the defense, but Mr. Rogers did most of it. Such was the force of Mr. Rogers' cross-examination that once, when he had Burns on the witness stand and pulled a lorgnette out of his pocket, snapped it open and glared at Burns through it, Burns turned and frantically demanded protection of the judge.

The Darrow bribery case hinged on Darrow's own argument to the jury. He insisted on making it on his own behalf. I have a copy of that argument open before me now, and as I reread it I can see why so many of those in that courtroom wept unashamed.

The jury was out only a short time before it brought in a verdict of not guilty.

A group picture hangs on my office wall. It shows the defense team in that Darrow trial waiting for the verdict to come in. I am proud of that picture for two reasons: because I was so young to be in such important company and because I had a glorious mop of hair, which somehow, in all the years of pacing corridors outside courtrooms and waiting for verdicts to come in, has grown scantier.

One of the things I wish I could forget about that first trial was the consternation I felt at seeing my boyhood hero, Darrow, so discouraged that Earl Rogers had to give him fight talks to keep him from giving up the battle.

Although it was basically a repetition of his first trial, Mr. Darrow's second trial was not dismissed as it might have been, because of its capital-versus-labor aspects. When that second trial began, there were only Mr. Rogers, myself and one other man, a former judge named Powers, on Darrow's legal team. On the first day Mr. Rogers fell ill and his doctor ordered him to take an ocean trip.

In the second Darrow trial, although I was one of the attorneys for the defense, Mr. Darrow really defended himself. My part lay in looking up the law and making suggestions. I did examine and cross-examine some of the witnesses, but not the important ones. That second trial lasted six weeks and ended in a disagreement. The district attorney decided not to try it again, and the case was dismissed.

After the trial I was walking down Broadway with Mr. Darrow when he said, "Come in here, Jerry," and led me into a tailor shop and bought me an overcoat. That's the only fee I received for working in his two trials, but the photograph I have of myself standing between Mr. Darrow and Mr. Rogers is worth far more to me than any fee.

Mr. Darrow was deeply embittered by the treatment he had received in Los Angeles. When he left town, he shook my hand and said, "Jerry, I'll never come back here again," and he never did.

I saw Mr. Darrow once more before he died. He had asked me to come to Chicago to talk about coming into his office with him. I stayed in Chicago for a week while he introduced me to his friends. Although I said no to him, I've always considered it the greatest possible honor that he offered me a place in his office. If I had joined him, I could have told my grandchildren that I had, in my time, worked in the offices of two of America's greatest criminal lawyers.

27

Observations on the Law

O<small>VER THE YEARS</small> I have formed a few convictions about criminal trials and cases. I offer them here for what they're worth.

Rape cases are the hardest to defend. The victim can testify. Moreover, since she is usually a young girl, she is automatically a witness to whom a jury is sympathetic.

Murder cases are the easiest to defend. They are usually based upon circumstances rather than direct testimony. There is seldom an eyewitness to a murder. That absence sometimes provides a chance for the defendant to plead self-defense.

I'll make it even stronger: If you have a halfway believable case of self-defense, you're almost certain to win—even if your client's case is based upon his having defended someone else.

I have my own ideas about the reasons for murder. Aside from gang war slayings, murder is usually committed by someone who has never committed a crime before and who won't do it again. It is my opinion that murder is a product of the moment. It usually happens on impulse. It probably would never have occurred at any other time in the life of the person who commits it, if he could have got past that particular moment without violence.

Since I believe so deeply in this theory of momentary impulse, I am unalterably opposed to keeping a gun in the house. An immense amount of grief—including a number of impulsive suicides —would be avoided if everyone else felt the same.

Another intense conviction I have about criminal trials is this. (I have already mentioned it, but I'd like to expand upon it a little.) The preparation of the law and the facts is so vital that a lawyer should know the other fellow's case as well as he knows his own. It should be possible for a defense lawyer to study the prosecution's case so thoroughly that he can conduct a better case for the prosecution than the D.A.

In preparing a case, I usually ask one of the younger men associated with me in my office to take the prosecution's side. I say to him, "O.K., you're the prosecution. What would you do?"

He usually has fun pretending to take the part of the prosecution, for the state's side of a criminal case is always the easiest. For one thing, the prosecution always has more evidence. If you are a defense lawyer, your client wouldn't be in court at all if the prosecution didn't have something up its sleeve, such as a dead body, the gun used by the killer, telltale fingerprints, expert medical testimony—something of that nature. Also working on behalf of the prosecution is the feeling the average witness has that any decent, law-abiding citizen should automatically line up on the side of law and order, which of course means on the side of the police and the D.A.

I think I've mentioned my next point too, but it's so much a part of me that it seems hard for me to overemphasize it. During a trial I stay home Saturdays and Sundays and work on the transcripts of the previous week's testimony. I have inserted hundreds of yellow-paper markers in those transcripts. In that way I know where every bit of pertinent testimony is. Each one of those little slips of yellow paper bears a notation in my own indecipherable handwriting to help me find what I need so that there won't be any long, boring delays for the jury.

When I'm on an especially long case, I ask the court to order a daily transcript for me, and my secretary, Mrs. Fitzpatrick, digests those transcripts. She picks out the lean, meaty material, separating it from the fat, and types it. She may reduce a hundred pages to six or seven typed pages. As a part of her digesting she also types out the page number and the line number in the transcript where she found that particular morsel.

This seems a sensible process, yet, as far as I know, I'm the only lawyer who does it. Perhaps most attorneys don't do it because it adds so much to the expense of trying a case. Some of my clients have paid substantial fees, and by averaging my expenses I can do a thorough job even on cases for which I am skimpily paid.

Now and then I am asked whether I have any special knack as a cross-examiner. If I do—and I suppose I must be gifted in that way, for the figures in my legal won-and-lost column indicate I am—how can I describe it? For a starter, I can say that many lawyers automatically become pugnacious when cross-examining. Perhaps they think it is expected of them. I have made a lifetime habit of being courteous and gentlemanly to those I face on the witness stand. Subjected to this mannerly forensic approach, even the most antagonistic witness will lose some of his prickliness. Sometimes he even seems to want to help me because I've been so nice to him.

Many lawyers feel that they must cross-examine all witnesses. They may have no idea what they're hoping to reveal, but they suffer an irresistible compulsion to cross-examine anyhow. Because they can't resist this urge they sometimes stick their toes into the fire and get burned. There's no sense in using cross-examination as a fishing expedition. The lawyer who does that is liable to be swallowed by his fish. Unless a cross-examination seems to prove something, it's best to say, "Your honor, I excuse the witness."

Modern cross-examination is subtle compared to the hectoring and bullying which once was the accepted way. I once saw Earl Rogers deliberately bait a witness with word and gesture until the witness, a burly law enforcement officer, turned to the judge and begged, "Make that man stand further away from me. He's trying to intimidate me."

Among the subtleties involved in the art of modern cross-examination is the knowledge that you are bound to be cross-examining someone who has been primed against you by the police, the detectives and the D.A.'s office. As a result, when they get on the stand their mental fists are up. So another facet of the art is the calming of the fears that the police have injected into a witness's mind and to make him realize that you're not out to trick him into committing perjury. If you do a good job, you'll be able to convince him that you are merely out to get the truth and at the same time convince the jury that the truth is all you need on your client's behalf. Once you've sold that idea to a witness, he will relax. If he relaxes enough, he'll go out of his way to help you—in spite of the fact that he is a witness for the other side.

To me it's only common sense not to cross-examine a witness unless I know I'll develop something which will help my case. I may know that a certain witness has committed perjury on direct examination. For instance, a witness may have made statements to people outside the courtroom, when he was not under oath, inconsistent with the statements he's made in court. He may have testified before the grand jury or at a preliminary hearing and his testimony on those occasions may differ from that which he is giving on the witness stand when the case is actually tried. If that is true, I'll lead that witness into reasserting his perjured testimony during my cross-examination. Then I confront him with evidence that he's not telling the truth, but I save this as the climax after the witness has perjured himself once more.

I have searched my memory to see if there is anything else I have learned in a long life spent at the bar which will be of service to youthful lawyers in court, and it occurs to me that there is a right way and a wrong way to impeach a witness's testimony. I see lawyers all the time who ask a witness questions while the witness is in the witness chair and the lawyer is sitting at the counsel table. To me that is wrong. When a witness is on the witness stand, I am not only up on my feet, I almost have one foot in the jury box. I am as close to the jury as I can get.

When the witness's testimony is inconsistent with that which he has given to the grand jury or at the preliminary hearing or at a former trial, I hold up the transcript of his previous testimony so that the jury can see it and I say, "Mr. Smith, you remember testifying on January sixteenth, 1952, do you not?" Mr. Smith will say Yes, and I'll say, "I direct your attention to the testimony you gave then and particularly to the testimony on page one hundred, line sixteen to line twenty. I'd like to have you read it to yourself. Don't bother to read it out loud."

I hand the witness that transcript and let him read it. When I get it back, I ask him, "You've read it?" he says Yes. Then I ask, "When you were asked the following questions at that time didn't you give the following answers?" And I read both questions and answers so that the whole court can hear.

No one can make me believe that this does not have more effect on a jury than doing the same thing standing in the back of the courtroom or sitting at the counsel table removed from the jury box and just holding the transcript in my hand.

When I get around to "Isn't it true that you told the grand jury so and so and so and so?" the witness has already read his previous testimony to himself and the jury knows he has read it. Not only does this give the cross-examining lawyer a psychological edge, but sometimes a witness who realizes that he has contradicted himself is visibly flustered as he reads. So when I put the question, "You testified as follows before the grand jury, did you not?" and he replies Yes, and I further ask, "Did you tell the grand jury the truth or are you telling us the truth now?" the effect is striking.

He will try to come up with a swift explanation which will account for the difference between the contradictory things he has testified to. Not only does the jury have a shrewd hunch that those thoughts are whirling rapidly in his mind, but no matter how hard he tries he usually can't think fast enough to produce a logical explanation for the difference between his two testimonies. He almost invariably falls back on ridiculous reasoning. Sometimes a wriggling, squirming witness will blurt out, "I didn't understand that question when it was put to me before the grand jury."

"Let me read you that question once more," I say. Then I read it and ask, "What is there about that question you didn't understand?" Since this usually leaves him floundering even more, it has a further effect on a jury.

I am not one who argues vehemently over a court's ruling. If an objection is made to one of my questions and that objection is sustained, I never repeat the question. That objection is part of the record. If the court is wrong I can always take up that point in my appeal—if I make one.

I've always believed that there are certain elements in my final argument to a jury which are of great importance. I do not believe that an attorney should make his argument unless he can inject tremendous sincerity and conviction into it. Aside from giving the jury a clear picture of the case, if his summation is strong, if he is obviously sincere in his belief in his client's position, he transfers to each member of the jury a part of his conviction and the jury carries that conviction into the jury room with them. Sometimes a jury-man himself subconsciously becomes an advocate for a client and uses the defense attorney's conviction on other jurors.

If, on the other hand, a defense attorney is weak, if the jury feels that he is not sincere or that he does not honestly believe in his cause, even those who started by being predisposed toward the defense may end up by becoming advocates for the other side.

I hope very much that the ability to deliver a sincere and convincing summation is one of my assets. I am not one of those who believe that because of the prevalence of other forms of communication such as radio, television and motion pictures the day is over when an effective talk to a jury means anything. In words spoken person to person people are the same today as they were fifty years ago. There are, however, some lawyers who have adopted the idea that summations no longer mean much, who think in fact that they're as old-fashioned as the pep talks given by the football coach of the 1920s.

I don't agree. I don't believe that people today differ fundamentally in their emotions, their thinking and their reactions. Before the present glut of electronic speechmaking to audiences numbered in the millions, people didn't hear many speeches. Today they can hear great orators in action by merely turning a knob or pushing a button. But if you're one of twelve human beings in a jury box, with the responsibility of life and death in your hands, you're pretty much the same human being a juror was half a century ago and no one can convince me that you're not.

I have never been called an orator, nor do I think of myself as one. I try to make up for my oratorical shortcomings by thorough preparation, detailed analysis of the evidence and a sincere advocacy of my cause. I don't say that oratorical ability is undesirable. A little of it is all right, but if you have that and only that, you have nothing.

In my opinion, a thoughtful and forceful summation is even more important in our American courtroom today, when our minds are torn in so many different directions, than it was when I was younger. A juror goes home at night and looks at TV or listens to radio (when he is not reading the newspapers), so no juror can remember clearly all that has been said during the course of a long trial. A detailed summation is required to bring it all back to him.

I have a theory which has proved out for me: Juries will not convict on a molestation or sex charge if the veracity of the woman complainant can be impeached. I try to find out from her neighbors if she has a reputation for lying or if she is known for her sexual promiscuity. You will never lose a case if you can produce a witness who, in answer to your questions "What is Miss So-and-so's reputation for truthfulness where she lives? Is it good or bad?" replies, "It's terrible."

In the matter of fees I have made up my mind not to mention figures in any discussion of the sums I have received, but it would surprise those who read this if I revealed the names of some of my famous clients who have welched on paying me what they promised to pay when they were in trouble. If you are a defense lawyer, my advice to you is to be sure to collect your fee while the tears are still falling and your client is still fearful of the jailhouse. When the client of the criminal lawyer in the best-selling book, *Anatomy of a Murder,* by Robert Traver, ran out on his attorney without paying him, it was not a fictional device to me.

A young criminal lawyer should face up to the fact that his clients will promise him the world until he gets them off, but once they are acquitted they often forget him. Some of them even turn against him after deciding with a weird and unfathomable twist of the mind that if it hadn't been for him somehow they would have got into less trouble.

I have known a few exceptions to this rule. Once a songwriter employed me to represent his son when the boy was in trouble. Not only did he pay me what I asked, but when I got his boy off he gave me a bonus.

A subject on which I have firm convictions is one that I once debated before the Lawyers' Guild of Los Angeles against the veteran attorney Frank Doherty. Our subject was, "Are there too many women on our juries?"

My opponent bravely delivered himself of the following sentiments: "Our juries are from two-thirds to three-fourths women. I say to you that such predominance weakens the jury system, because women, for all their fine qualities, do not have the breadth of experience men have. Women's lives are too sheltered."

Mr. Doherty also declared, "Women are too partisan. If they're for you, they're for you. If they're against you, they're against you. A jury must be flexible enough to change its mind if the evidence warrants it. You don't get a flexible jury if it has eight or ten women on it."

I didn't agree. There can't be too many women on a jury for me. I've tried most of my cases before juries with feminine majorities and I like it that way. For one thing, women are more attentive than men. For another, they are tougher-minded than men. They not only bring womanly intuition into play, they also base their findings on the facts. I have only one minor criticism of women as jurors: they have a tendency to be rougher than male jurors on women defendants. If my woman defendant also happens to be pretty, give me an all-male jury.

Otherwise male jurors leave a lot to be desired. The number one idea which possesses their minds is to get excused from doing their duty as citizens. They keep telling themselves that they can't afford it and they worry about what will happen to their businesses while they're away.

The admission of women to jury duty has had a clearly discernible effect on courtroom behavior. In the days when the juries were a hundred per cent male, many of them chewed tobacco. Spittoons were placed in front of the jury box, and not only the jury but the lawyers and the judges used them. The D.A. and the defense attorney vied with each other to see how far they could stand from the spittoon and still hit it. Any D.A. who could score a fifteen-foot bull's-eye impressed the jury. Of course, there was nothing to prevent a defense attorney from planting himself near the D.A.'s chair and having a shot himself. If he could score a bull's-eye both sides were even again. The result was trial by expectoration.

Another firm policy of mine is this: If I don't feel that a man who has asked me to defend him is telling me the truth, I say to him, "If you don't level with me, I don't want you or your case." I warn him that if he doesn't tell me the truth about the weaknesses of his case, so that I can shore those weak spots up, he is leaving open avenues of attack through which the prosecution can bulldoze holes big enough to drive teams of horses. Most of the cases I accept are so serious in nature that I can't afford to let the defendant fool me. A lawyer who goes into court half cocked is likely to come out wholly cooked.

I also have a few convictions about civil cases. There's my old friend the Lawsuit Cow. I have a clipping of a cartoon drawn by Winsor McCay which I cut from a newspaper in 1923. I show it to clients who are hard to satisfy—who are greedy and grasping. It features an animal labeled "The Lawsuit." McCay depicted one person pulling at the cow's head, another at her tail. Between them a lawyer is busy milking her. The milk foaming into the bucket beneath her udder represents money. The only mistake McCay made was in not showing another lawyer on the other side of the cow milking her, too.

I have found it useful to show this to people who are hard-nosed about settling a case. With its help I sometimes convince them that it is foolish and wasteful to take a long time to settle a lawsuit.

The best illustration of this I've ever heard is a suit, tried in the South, about a borrowed buggy whip. When the whip was returned, the lender found that seven inches had been worn from the lash. High words ensued which led to a quarrel. The quarrel was carried into a court, and from that court into another court. What with the accompanying delays, matters dragged on until the cost to the aggrieved party amounted to $70,000—or $10,000 for each inch of worn lash.

28

Advice to Young Lawyers

THIS MAY BE AS GOOD a time as any to disabuse the public mind of a misconception which is deeply imbedded in it. The misconception is this: that no one can ever be successfully prosecuted for murder unless a corpus delicti is produced.

The public takes it for granted that the word "corpus" means a corpse. Actually, it means a body, and "delicti" means an offense. "Corpus delicti" therefore means "the body of the crime." There can be a corpus delicti in a civil case as well as in a criminal case. A personal-injury suit would contain one.

There is a public delusion that if a murdered body is never discovered the killer is automatically free of all danger of conviction, but I know of at least three cases in California in which circumstantial evidence was so strong that the accused person was convicted of murder in the absence of any dead body. In one case a man was sentenced to death for the murder of his wife, although no trace of her has ever been found, because of evidence that the accused showed up with her forged signature and rummaged through her safe-deposit box after she was last seen alive.

Once in a preliminary hearing at which I defended a client accused of murder I was able to disprove a corpus delicti in such a way that the D.A. was defeated. The accused man's wife was found gasping her life out in their cleaning establishment after having swallowed a quantity of a caustic fluid. The husband and wife lived in the rear of the cleaning place, and he was the only one, other than the dead woman herself, who could have had access to the fluid she drank.

The fluid ate away part of the lining of her throat and damaged her digestive tract. The husband, who was horribly distressed, took her to the hospital, but she died before she arrived. On the theory that he had placed the fatal fluid in a cup so that she would think it water, he was charged with murder.

I sat with him at the preliminary hearing, and to me it was clear that her death was a suicide. I still don't know why the D.A. thought it was murder. An only son testified that his parents had had trouble getting along together and that he had heard his mother threaten to kill herself many times. Specifically he had heard her say that she was going to drink poison. There was evidence that the husband was asleep at the time his wife gulped the lethal dose and also that his wife had what was charitably known as a "mental problem." I won that case at the preliminary hearing without even going to trial, because the prosecutor was unable to establish a corpus delicti.

I won a case for the Irish actor Barry Fitzgerald on the same grounds. His case, which should never have been brought up, involved a charge of "killing with automobile." The accident occurred on Hollywood Boulevard, near the Gotham Hotel. Fitzgerald was out driving one evening when two women stepped from a curb and started across the street. They were wearing dark clothes. He saw neither of them, and the right front part of his car struck them. One was injured. The other was killed.

Fitzgerald was not going fast. He had not been drinking. He stopped, rendered what aid he could, then summoned medical help and the police. Nevertheless, the D.A. held a preliminary hearing and the judge held Fitzgerald for trial. I carried that issue to the Superior Court under Section 995 of the penal code, which provides for a motion attacking the corpus delicti. My motion was granted, and the charge against Fitzgerald was quashed. For there to have been a corpus delicti in Fitzgerald's case it was necessary to show not only that the victim was killed by manslaughter but also that the defendant was guilty of negligence and that negligence was a proximate cause of death.

The death of a person is not a corpus delicti in itself. Let us assume for a moment that you issue a check on your bank account and that you are arrested for issuing a check without enough funds on deposit to make it good. The check is there, the lack of funds is established, but a third element must be established too. If there is no knowledge on your part that your account was overdrawn there's no body of the crime.

Or suppose somebody takes John Jones's auto from a parking lot where Jones has left it. The police find a man in North Hollywood driving Jones's car. Is it a stolen car? If Jones gave his consent to the man's driving his car or even if there is reasonable doubt whether Jones did or didn't consent, there is no corpus delicti.

There is one subject I haven't yet touched upon. It's my ideas about selecting a jury.

In a criminal case in California, the defense is allowed ten peremptory challenges without cause; in a murder case, twenty. All the defense attorney has to say is, "Excuse Juror So-and-So," and he's dismissed. When I am involved in the important matter of deciding whom to challenge and whom not to challenge, I usually wander over and sit down in a chair beside the jury panel. As I question each prospective juror, I try to learn something about his occupation and background.

Generally speaking, it is my feeling that people who are in sales work or the entertainment field, or who are successful in business, or who are nice-looking and, therefore, have had a better chance of having life smile on them than others, or who not only are married but are apparently happily married, are apt to make good jurors from the defense point of view.

On the other hand, I am inclined to challenge people who are grouchy; those who are in professions which demand meticulous care and finicky attention to detail, such as handling figures; science professors; and those who have encountered hard luck or bitterness in their lives.

In a criminal case I am shy of military men who have been in positions of command. I'm wary of people who have led narrow existences as opposed to broader lives. An unmarried woman, for instance, may not be a good juror for the defense in a sex case. If a case involves child-molesting, I've always taken the position (and I've been proved right) that from the defense point of view a schoolteacher is a good juror. Teachers know that their pupils often lie merely for the sake of being dramatic or to be the center of attention.

When questioning a panel of jurors, it is important not to offend a juror. In one case I was about to try, I brought out that one of the women on the panel had a husband who worked in the city's sanitation department. I felt that there was no need to pursue that line of questioning further, but when the prosecution took over, the D.A. insisted that the woman state exactly what kind of work her husband did in the sanitation department.

She backed and filled and said, "He handles the general duties of that department."

The prosecution persisted with "Well, what does he do? Does he work in an office?"

Reluctantly she said, "No."

Growing irritable then, the D.A. asked, "Why can't you tell us what your husband does?"

Cornered at last, she said—and with a noticeable dislike for the D.A. in her voice—"He is a garbage man."

As bubbleheaded as that D.A. was, he could now see that he had an offended woman on his hands, a woman whose pride had been hurt, so he challenged her. But there was a further danger he couldn't cope with; how many women on that jury were her friends? How many had come to know her and like her while serving on the panel?

There was no way he could find out.

I never ask a woman, "Do you have a husband?" or even, "What does your husband do?" Instead I say, "Is there a Mr. Jones?" If she is a widow, she will say, "I am a widow." If she does, I say, "I'm very

301

sorry," and pass on to something else. If she's a divorcée, my question gives her a chance to answer in whatever way will make her happiest.

The selection of a jury is, of course, a very important part of a case. It's the one time before I get around to presenting my argument that I really have a chance to talk with and get to know the people who are there to decide my client's fate. Then, when I make my final argument, I say, "When we talked together at the beginning of this trial, you told me that you'd play the game fairly and listen to the whole case until it was finally submitted to you." They nod their agreement when I say that. In that very simple way I tie my original talk with them to my final argument. It is like saying to a friend, "Remember when we first met . . . ?" And from a human and psychological point of view, I think it is a useful thing to do.

I always tell young lawyers, "If you take a criminal case, be the lawyer yourself. Don't let your client be the lawyer. If you let him be the lawyer, he is liable to have learned more in the county jail from the jail lawyers while he's waiting trial than you've ever learned in law school." By jail lawyers I mean the inmates of prisons. They are like sea lawyers who have learned their maritime law in bull sessions before the mast. It would be better to follow the legal precepts learned in a law correspondence course than it would be to be guided by such kangaroo notions of jurisprudence.

I cannot impress enough upon young law students the danger of taking a civil case on a contingency basis, although some of them do it anyhow. From time to time I've been asked, "What's wrong with that?" My answer is, If you take a case on that basis, you are subconsciously (or even consciously) likely to try to gouge the opposition financially far more than is equitable, the reason being that the more you take from them the larger your share will be. The pecuniary temptation may be so great that an attorney with a weak moral fiber may even stoop to trickery and chicanery to gain his ends.

There should be no contingency fee in a divorce suit. Divorce interferes with the sacred state of marriage, and any ethical lawyer's first consideration must be to try to reconcile the couple rather than collect a fee for driving a wedge between them. To put it bluntly —no marriage should be disturbed solely on the basis of money.

It may be that I go in too strongly for ordering my life by rules and suggesting that others follow them. I remember that when I addressed a group of new admittees to the Los Angeles County Bar Association I outlined several points a young attorney should keep in mind. The first was a constant awareness of the ethics of his profession. To be respected in his community, an attorney must be more honest than most people about everything. He must deposit in a separate account any funds his client gives to him to hold in trust, and if he wants to avoid trouble he must never mix these funds with his own. Also, an attorney should make no promises to a client. Laws change from day to day, and he has no right to guess the outcome of any case in which he is involved.

Still another suggestion I made was that a young lawyer must take out insurance against negligence. It is difficult to know the difference between negligence today and what will be considered negligence tomorrow.

I have two more suggestions before I let up. In a divorce which involves a property settlement I never make a settlement without first consulting a tax attorney. Years later the fact that you, as the attorney involved, were not tax-wise at the time of the property settlement may boomerang against you.

In law hard work is essential, but in the final analysis the facts are everything. Know where to find the point of law you need to put your hand to. It is easy to start a lawsuit, but it is not always the best thing to do. A settlement is usually far better.

Rummaging through my files for ideas to help me tell this story, I ran across a set of notes for still another speech I made. I called it "Surprises at the Trial." These notes are almost a form of shorthand, and I offer them capsulized just as they are, although, for all I know, I may have touched on them before. I must have planned to expand upon them once I got to my feet:

You must investigate not only the big aspects of litigation but the trifles as well. It is a small bit of evidence which has not been discovered because you've been too busy to prepare your case thoroughly which can change the entire atmosphere of a trial. Bigger and better settlements result from proper preparation. You must not rely on your skill and experience to carry you through. You must take complete and thorough notes and keep your ear open to your client, while reserving the right to form your own conclusions. You must be patient with him. If you aren't, you may upset him and make him so nervous that his memory will not work properly. You must strive to gain and retain his confidence.

Talk to all essential witnesses yourself. It is psychologically desirable to let them hear your voice and for you to hear theirs, so that you won't be strangers when you meet in court. If possible, persuade a witness to write his story in his own handwriting, or get his affidavit. If that is impossible, at least get his statement in the presence of two people. If you can't do this personally, employ investigators to do it for you. In the end preparation will pay off and success will be no accident. Practically speaking, preparation will bring success and success will bring you more clients and more cases to prepare.

Be accessible; vanity greases the skids to swift failure.

Never depend upon someone else to look up a case for you. I personally always read all the law I intend to use in court.

Honesty in a lawyer is a personal matter with him. He may fool others; he can't fool himself. Whether he is a counsel for a corporation or an individual, he knows whether or not his integrity is sullied, even if no one else knows.

Never get the idea that you're the only one who can do your job, whether it is private, professional or official. Plenty of others as good as you—maybe better than you—are waiting to take your place. The cemetery at the edge of the city is crowded with people who thought the world couldn't go on without them.

I feel strongly that a man who is in danger of the death penalty deserves to have a lawyer who feels his responsibility so deeply that in a sort of transference he takes the possibility of his client's guilt upon himself. The jury stares at the client because he is the defendant. As his attorney, it is up to you to make them stare at you and to concentrate upon listening to you. Your client is not doing any talking except what he may testify on the witness stand. It is your job to talk for him and reason for him. After all, you're handling for him both the direct and the cross-examination which he is not allowed to do.

Care should be taken to prepare a client for the contingency that the other side will prove its case. If the opposition does that, all is not over. There are still defense measures which can be taken.

And I always advise young lawyers that they must be prepared for a surprise in a trial and must school themselves to remain calm if one comes. I also assure them earnestly that the truth is never harmful. The truth may overthrow the opponent's case too.

29

My Courtroom Tactics

Although some of my most important victories have resulted from appeals to higher courts, I haven't touched upon that subject very much for fear that the average reader would find it dull going and too legalistic. The fact is that I try to make sure that my briefs are minutely detailed, carefully prepared and closely reasoned. Sometimes they are voluminous; even so, it is my hope they are scholarly. No matter what the subject may be, I read every case I mention in my brief before I cite it.

In my lifetime I have been lucky enough to do a number of things that I am proud of, but I'm proudest of all of some of the legal points I have researched which have thereafter become the law of the state. Among the first of these was the point of law I raised in the Pantages case concerning the questioning of a girl who claimed to have been raped, about her previous chastity or unchastity.

I also helped make the law which applies to the question of the custody of a child by its mother. The case in which I brought this up had to do with a mother who was guilty of misconduct with men while away from her home. Her children were not with her when her misconduct occurred, but because of it her former husband came into court and said, "My wife is no fit custodian of our children." Then and there I prepared a brief for the court which held that the wife's misconduct did not constitute sufficient grounds for revoking custody. What was determined was that no one can come into court and say that a mother is unfit to have custody of her children because she chooses to stay with men in hotels. The court held that even if this was true it did not constitute "unfit conduct," *because the children had no knowledge of her acts and therefore could not be influenced by them.*

I fight when I think it's needed—even if I do my fighting quietly and courteously. I have never made a bombastic address to a jury. I start out humbly. I tell the jury that it is an honor to be a juror. I tell them that they have great power over their fellow man and that theirs is a grave responsibility. There is nothing phony about this. I honestly believe it.

I tell them that the number twelve is not peculiar to juries alone, that it goes back to the twelve tribes of Israel and that it continued down through the twelve Apostles, until our present jury system evolved, based upon the foundation stone of that numeral. From this opening I build up gradually—gaining strength, I hope—until my voice is not quite so quiet and subdued. I do not have an orator's voice, nor do I make an orator's gestures, but I think I can put force into what I say. And I can be untiring. In one case I talked to a jury for a day and a half. At the close of that talk I asked the jury's permission to check my notes to make sure I hadn't forgotten anything, because, as I told them, I felt that my responsibility was tremendous. Having received their permission, I sat down in front of them and the clock ticked off fifteen minutes while I checked my notes. During that time not one word was said.

If it was dramatic, if it impressed the jury with my thoroughness, my sincerity and my determination to present all of the facts, those things were helpful by-products, but I didn't do it for those reasons. There *is* a heavy burden of responsibility which weighs upon a conscientious legal defender when a man's life is at stake. The only way anyone can realize that responsibility is to experience it himself.

I must admit that fire flares in my soul when the opposing attorney does something that I think is unfair. If that happens, I make sure of placing his unfairness on the record. But I would be ashamed to be the kind of trial lawyer who always bickers with the judge. That is not only bad manners, it is a disservice to a client.

I never attack a witness belligerently or with bullying force, particularly a woman witness. I try to make cross-examination a series of rapier thrusts rather than bludgeon blows.

My voice is naturally soft, so I take no credit for being soft-spoken. However, a number of people remember me as a fighter, even if I don't raise my voice in noisy courtroom oratory. In fact, it has been claimed that my quietness and soft way of talking are carefully calculated to lull opposing witnesses into a false sense of security. I don't do it for that reason, of course. It is just that my court manners have always been self-effacing and unobtrusive.

If I pretend not to understand an answer and I ask the same question again and even again, it is not to give the effect that I have been inattentive or that I am dozing. My repetition is an effort to have something repeated that I particularly want emphasized. If the point is one I want emphasized strongly, I may ask a witness to repeat his answer as many as three times. Some of those who read this may wonder why a judge will consent to let me pursue such a monotonous questioning technique. The reason is this: Most judges who know me know that I do not ask such questions idly, so they go along with me. They know that if I do it there is a reason for it.

In many newspaper accounts of my so-called legal machinations I have read that I questioned witnesses softly and quietly in order to lure them into lowering their guard. I do question them in that way, but not for that reason. As much as anything else it represents an effort to keep my own emotions and tensions under control. It may not generally be known about me, but, in spite of my quiet ways and my soft voice, emotion builds up inside of me until I let it escape by pounding the edge of the jury box with such force that I have broken bones in both my hands. The first time that happened I didn't believe it until my X-ray pictures were read. The second time I didn't need X-rays to tell me what had happened. My hands are small-boned. For all I know the bones may be abnormally brittle. I do know this: If I enter into an argument too spiritedly and try to emphasize a point too vociferously I'm likely to end with a broken bone or two.

Both of the times I broke my hands I continued my argument as if nothing had happened. I was mentally and emotionally so geared up that I didn't feel the pain until I had finished my argument and had cooled down. Then the next day I appeared with my hand in plaster of Paris.

I never attack unless I know I have enough ammunition to back me up. To do otherwise would weaken my position and leave me vulnerable. I never bluff. In other words, I never attack a witness for the other side unless I know I've got what it takes to win.

Those who have written about Earl Rogers have mentioned their amazement that as if by magic Mr. Rogers was able to switch things around until the plaintiff seemed to be on trial, instead of the accused. No one admired Mr. Rogers more than I did, but it is not unusual for a defense lawyer in a criminal case to achieve that kind of switch. If given the opportunity, almost any defense lawyer will do it. I can do it and I have done it. It is a very useful maneuver. I managed to do it in the Charlie Chaplin case, the Pantages case and the Errol Flynn case. In all of those I really put the complainants on trial.

I was extremely fortunate that things broke the way they did in the Flynn case. It is a wonderful feeling for a defense lawyer when the breaks begin to go his way. Even one break can make or lose a case, depending on how vital it is. Almost anyone would have given me any odds that I would not secure Flynn's acquittal; it was a break that came in the last moment of the last day of that trial that did it—when the D.A. called to the witness stand the one man I had prayed he would call.

My point is that Earl Rogers had no vested right in the technique of reversing the roles played by the plaintiff and the defendant. I have no vested right in it either, and I suspect that I copied the idea from him.

At least one reporter has noted that before the D.A. says a word, I seem to have a foreknowledge of what he will say, and that in my opening address I have even been known to outline the tactics and strategy the prosecutor will use before I mention my own defense. I don't know why it should surprise anyone that a defense lawyer should be armed with advance knowledge concerning such matters. That should be largely a matter of proper preparation on my part. Through the legitimate use of investigators it is even possible to form an advance mental picture of each member of the jury.

My mentor, Earl Rogers, went so far as to study psychology (including the works of William James), believing that it would make him a better defense advocate. This is not surprising, because it was Rogers' idea that a lawyer should know more about psychology than any witness he might face. He knew considerably more than the average layman about such things as medicine and religious dogma too.

I have tried to emulate Rogers in these matters. It is of course impossible for me to be as deeply versed in medical lore as a witness who has a doctor's degree, but I would regard myself as stupid if I didn't take the trouble to arm myself with as much medical lore as my head will hold about any medical point I think might arise in a case. It is possible to tutor yourself for this purpose in two ways. The first is by selective reading. The second, and more useful, method is to ask doctors you know for the information you need.

Intuition is supposed to be exclusively a feminine characteristic, but, while I am thoroughly male, I possess some of that female characteristic too. And upon occasion I have shown an intuitive ability to pick out the flaws in a case. I have even done that when someone from my office is in the courtroom reporting to me by telephone and I am not in the courtroom at all. I'll say, "Just a minute. Let's think this over. . . . No, I don't think you'd better do that. That's a mistake." And more often than not it turns out that it would have been a mistake. Sometimes I have said, "I suggest we do this," and my hunch has turned out to be right.

Although I've defended hundreds of cases, I've never yet reached the point of telling my associates, "I'll handle this alone. I don't need to discuss it with anyone." I invariably sit with them and ask, "What do *you* think? How do *you* like the last witness? How does the jury look to you? What do you think about calling this witness? Should we or shouldn't we?" And what they say in reply helps me make up my mind.

One of my former associates was kind enough to say that during the past nineteen years I have shown an uncanny ability, even over the telephone, to put a finger on the right moves to make, the right questions to ask. Even if this is exaggerated, it is gratifying.

This same associate and I were trying a murder case once, and while we were preparing our argument I said, "If you get any ideas, call me." He didn't call me. When I saw him the next morning, I asked him why.

"When I finished my notes it was two o'clock," he said. "I did have a couple of ideas, but I thought it too late to call you."

I told him, "It's never too late to call me when we're trying a case. Call me, even if it's three or four in the morning."

I once won a very hard case not because of anything I did but because the D.A. made the mistake of changing his pace. I don't want to mention his name, for he's still living in southern California, but it was a very important case, one of the really big ones I've described in these memoirs.

Before we went into court I knew that this D.A. was the fighting type. He was ready to go at the drop of a hint and he preferred chewing tenpenny nails to eating tenderloin steak. To my great and almost stupefying surprise, when we tangled in court he was a completely changed man. He was trying his best to be polite and nice. Not only that, but he kept it up. I couldn't understand it. Since I was just being normal, we were like the famous French bowers and scrapers, Alphonse and Gaston. The big difference was, in his case, that it meant he had lost his punch. The fire and brimstone which had given him his stock in trade were suddenly changed to velvet and lubricating oil.

I won that case, and while I might have won it anyway, it was clear to me that I had won it because overnight my opponent had changed into a Caspar Milquetoast who was trying to step on no one's toes and whose dearest desire was that everyone should be happy, including me and my client.

Someone asked him afterward, "Why did you change that way?" and he said, "I made a mistake. I talked to a newspaperman before the trial and he said, 'Jerry's always been very courteous and very quiet. Why don't you be the same way? Stop being yourself and do the same thing he does.'" He said he was sorry he had followed that advice, for whatever it was that made him successful wasn't there any more.

In trying a criminal case, I make it a policy not to defend but to attack. I am just as determined about this as I am in refusing to let one of my clients run his case for me. A defense attorney must attack even while the prosecution presents its case. He must know more about the witnesses than the prosecution knows. He must, if it is humanly possible, bring forth information about things the prosecution may not even have heard of. Not only are these sound, necessary legal tactics, they are stimulating and fun.

In my policy of always attacking rather than defending as the prosecution produces its witnesses, I sometimes engage in what I call silent cross-examination: When a prosecution witness is testifying about something important, and I have no information in my files that will help me attack him, I make a show of busying myself with other matters and of paying very little attention to what he is saying. When he is through, I announce very casually, "No questions."

The effect of this sometimes is to convey the impression to the jury that the testimony I have been busily ignoring couldn't have been very important or I wouldn't have been so uninterested in it. This helps that evidence to fly over the heads of the jury, and some of its impact is lost.

I have read the books called *Oneupmanship* and *Gamesmanship* written by the wryly ironical British humorist Stephen Potter, and I think he would be interested in this "ploy" I have just described. Perhaps one day Mr. Potter will get around to writing a book called "Defenselawyermanship." If he does he may mention the Giesler inactive or reverse attack upon a witness, meaning that the lawyer for the defense hasn't been sufficiently interested in what the prosecution's witness has just said even to ask him his name.

And of course there is the opportunity for a defense lawyer to attack by using two kinds of character evidence. One kind will vouch for your defendant's good character. I always put such witnesses on first, before the case really begins to roll. The other kind of character evidence is about the bad character of some of the prosecution's witnesses—if possible, its key witnesses. I take the position that if the jury doesn't believe the defendant I have no choice but to attack the credibility of the prosecution's witnesses whenever such an attack promises to bring results.

It is the nature of prosecution that in many cases the witnesses it uses are open to serious attack because of their unsavory background or doubtful reputation or both, or even because they hope to be granted special favors by the D.A. in the way of forgiveness for their sins in payment for their testimony. I always keep this in mind, and if a witness has testified who is personally connected with the case in question, but has not been prosecuted, I ask, "Have you been arrested or prosecuted in connection with this case?" If his answer is no, I ask him, "Well, have you had any discussion with the district attorney which might make you think that if you testify you won't be prosecuted?" Witnesses invariably reply No to this one too, but by that time the jury is usually beginning to have a few qualms about the string of pious and self-righteous No's emanating from the witness's lips.

In the past I have fought for and successfully contended for the right to ask a further question: "At least you are probably hoping that you won't be prosecuted, are you not?" It is pretty well established law now that I have a right to ask that, and most judges allow the witnesses to answer. This leaves them hanging precariously in mid-air. If they say No the jury doesn't quite believe them. If they say Yes, it helps discredit them as a witness. Like the question "When did you stop beating your wife?" this question cuts both ways.

I'd like to put into this story some of the philosophical aspects of practicing criminal law as I see them, as well as a little of the thinking behind some of my cases. I cannot broadcast those things which my clients have confided in me, but the reasoning which has gone on in my mind as I've defended them is for me to tell or not to tell, as I like.

One psychological factor a criminal lawyer should keep in mind when he's cross-examining a witness is that a jury invariably pays more attention to what a witness says on cross-examination than to what he says on direct examination. This is true because, since it is ordinarily based on an unfriendly relationship, cross-examination is more absorbing. It shapes up as a contest between lawyer and witness, a battle of wits. In such a situation my policy is this: If I ask a question and the opposing lawyer objects to it, I immediately withdraw it before the court has a chance to rule on the objection. That way the objection remains hanging in the air, and the jury becomes abnormally interested in both the question and the fact that it has been unanswered.

I may ask a second question along the same line, and once more when my opponent utters the words "I object" I say, "I withdraw it," before the judge has ruled.

Now the jury is really eager, really up on its toes. At this point I throw in still another query on the same subject, the difference being that this time I've made sure in advance it is a question phrased so that no one can possibly object to it. There is no objection, or, if there is, the judge says, "You may answer." The result is that my question has three times the impact it would have had if it had been asked and answered the first time around.

If I seem to be setting myself up as an authority on forensic tactics and strategy, that is not what I have in mind. What I am really trying to do is to present my own personal psychological approach as best I can, based on the fact that, since I have had more years of experience than I like to recall, there may be something I have learned in those years which may be helpful to the legal neophyte just hanging out his shingle.

If I have succeeded in making this point convincing, then perhaps one more sample of my trial philosophy will not be taken amiss. If I am more or less sure what a witness's answer is going to be, or if I don't care, I go right after it. But if I have no way of knowing what a witness may say, I skirt around the edges of his answer.

What I am trying to say is that I never seek the perfect answer. If I get an answer from a witness which scores a fraction of a point for my client, I'll settle for that. I don't pursue it further, trying for a more telling reply. If I were fool enough to do that, any smart opposition witness would soon realize what I was after and try to hedge his previous answer with a "Perhaps what I've just told you may not be completely accurate after all."

Another thing I am wary about is this: Points may come up which are favorable to my cause but which may also go over the jury's head. I try to spot those points, and once I have spotted them I make sure that they don't go over the heads of the jury when I present my closing argument.

My system of attacking rather than defending also shows inconsistencies on the part of the prosecution's witnesses. If I feel that they are trying to gloss over details I see to it that they go into them more deeply. My attack may very well begin in the preliminary hearing; I'm a great believer in memorizing each detail of the prosecution's testimony set forth at the preliminary hearing, for during the actual trial itself that testimony is apt to be contrary to what has been said before. For some reason, witnesses seldom take the trouble to read the transcript of their preliminary testimony, and they are quite likely to stray from it the second time around. This gives a defense attorney a chance to attack the credibility of the prosecution's witnesses, because the statements they make on the witness stand that are inconsistent with their previous testimony can always be made to damage their cause.

I don't know how other attorneys feel about it, but I myself always avoid asking a witness the question "Why?" If I do that it opens the way for a wide latitude of replies, over which I would have no control. A California court decision is that the question "Why?" may be answered on the basis of fact, fiction or suspicion, and if you don't like the answer you get you can't move to have it stricken.

A whole chapter in any book on cross-examination should be devoted to the art of *not* asking that one question too many. The trick is to stop at exactly the right point. I've already given a prime example of that in my story of the Paul Wright "white flame" case.

One of the things which helps me with a hostile jury is that I am careful never to adopt the attitude that I know more than the jury knows. I try not to make it seem too obvious a failing on my part, but I always know less about most things than anyone else in the courtroom. Witnesses always have to explain things to me. When a firearm is involved, I have to have its workings explained to me. In fact, I am likely to call bullets shells and shells bullets.

In questioning witnesses, particularly expert witnesses, I play down whatever special knowledge I possess, although I always make it a point to arm myself with as much special knowledge as I can. I don't use big words. I sometimes ask a witness to explain the simplest things to me. Some members of the jury may not know the answer either, and that makes me one with the jury. Together we are thirteen, instead of twelve, people who are not all-wise and all-knowing.

One of my former associates has been kind enough to contribute to this story a couple of examples of what he generously says is my ability to call the shots in cases even if I'm not actually in the courtroom. Such an incident occurred during one of the first cases he ever tried for me. We represented two defendants who were accused of selling liquor stolen in one of the biggest liquor burglaries in Los Angeles history. Thousands of cases of alcoholic beverages had been filched from the basement of a Los Angeles hotel, the Town House. The stolen booze had been taken away in Army trucks, and our two defendants had been accused of selling it at so much per case with the Town House labels still on the bottles. The charge against them was that they had used their garage as a retail outlet store for the stolen wet goods. Their defense (and I must say that it seemed a fairly balmy one to me) was that they didn't know the liquor they were selling was missing from the Town House. They said they had bought it without knowing that it was stolen.

Five liquor thieves were involved; all of them admitted burglary and all five of them testified against my two clients as "receivers of stolen goods." But somehow, somewhere, my associate managed to dig up character witnesses for our two clients. There was only one catch—during the trial he discovered that one of our clients had a police record. He called me on the telephone and said, "If we use character witnesses for both of our clients, the D.A. will bury them both, because one of them has a bad past-performance history. What do I do now?"

"Call the character witnesses for the fellow who has no record," I said. "Then go on to something else. Perhaps in the jury's mind the good character of one will rub off onto the other."

He did that, and, after accepting their story that they didn't know that the stolen goods they were selling had been burglarized, the jury acquitted the defendants. As I've said, theirs seemed an unlikely tale to me, but if the twelve good people and true on a jury decided they were innocent, what were my doubts against so many?

After that case was over the prosecutor told my associate, "If you had called character witnesses for that other defendant of yours we would have ruined you. We had his record and were loaded for him."

He makes much of the fact that after a moment's consideration on the telephone, I sensed that the jury would let the unchallenged good character of our first one lap over onto our second client and cover him with undeserved respectability.

Another example this same associate offers is that of a woman client who was accused of shooting her brother's girl friend at close range with a high-powered shotgun. The shooting was done indoors. She had told the girl to get out of the house; when the girl didn't leave, the sister had loaded a shotgun and brought it into the room, and, as she later said, the gun had gone off because it bumped against a table. That too seemed unlikely to me, but if her story was true the shooting was accidental and she had a right to the benefit of the doubt.

That case was tried twice. The first trial went on for two weeks, until a juror failed to show up. Once the absence of that juror was established, Judge Fricke, who was trying the case, called my associate and the D.A.'s deputy into chambers and said, "One of the jurors is not here. Her doctor has just called up and has told me that she has a psychopathic history and she shouldn't have been on the jury panel in the first place. She's had a recurrence of her psychopathic condition because you were firing off a shotgun in the courtroom yesterday, and the noise of those shots finally brought it

317

home to her cloudy mind that it was a murder case she was being asked to decide!"

It was true that my associate had fired a shell—with the court's permission—to demonstrate that a sharp knock of the shotgun in question against the floor or some other object would set it off.

After his session in chambers with the judge, he called me and said, "We have a choice. We can finish the case with eleven jurors"—the law permits that if both sides consent—"or we can take a mistrial and be thrown out of this court and into another court."

I asked a number of questions, among them: "How does the jury look to you? How many men and how many women are there on it? What are their occupations? What witnesses have been called? What has been said? What seems to be the judge's attitude?"

He told me that the judge's attitude seemed to be that we had no defense, that even if the gun had gone off accidentally it was at least second-degree murder, because our client had deliberately left the room to load the gun and had then brought the loaded gun back.

I told him, "You do what you think best, of course, but if I were you I would refuse to accept eleven jurors as a whole jury, take a mistrial and get out of there."

He followed my advice and the trial was dismissed.

After the dismissal, my associate had James Leahan check the discharged jurors in the corridor outside the courtroom, and he found that they had all been against us. This made him swear that I possessed second sight, or, to be up to date, extrasensory perception.

For that second trial I suggested that a table be set up in court, just as it had been at the time of the shooting, even with the same dishes on it. I further suggested that my associate stand where the defendant testified she had stood, that he pretend that her brother had made a grab for the gun, and that he then back into the table and let the court see whether the weapon—which was loaded with a blank shell—fired on contact or not. If it didn't fire, she would be convicted. If it did fire, she might not be. I insisted that we take that chance. The gun fired. The woman was acquitted.

One of the ironclad rules I've set for myself is to try a case for the trial jury and *not for a court of appeal.* I don't go ahead on the premise that a case is sure to go to a higher court. I try each case on its merits before the jury chosen to decide upon it. I keep a careful record of the times the court overrules my objections and on what grounds, but first and foremost I hope to win an acquittal from the original jury.

The most serious question a lawyer faces—and a deadly serious question it is—is this: *Shall I put my defendant on the stand?* Making such a decision carries tremendous responsibility. In the case of my client Frankie Carbo, I decided not to put him on the stand and he was not convicted.

In making such a decision I follow this philosophy: If I think that there's a chance I may not use my defendant as a witness, I am careful not to let on that I may not put him on the stand. I wait until the last possible minute to decide whether the prosecution has established a case to go to the jury with, and whether it will result in a conviction if it does go to a jury, and, finally, whether it will stand up under appeal if a conviction is obtained. Then and not until then do I make up my mind.

If I make up my mind that I'm not going to put the defendant on that stand, I put on no defense at all. The reason for this is that if I put any witnesses other than the defendant on the stand it seems to be an indication that I am afraid of exposing my defendant to the shafts the prosecution will hurl at him. On the other hand, if I put nobody at all on I am taking the strong position that the prosecution has produced nothing important enough to make me want to counteract it. In effect I am saying that the prosecution has produced a nullity, so why should I burden the jury with further testimony?

If this *is* my line, however, it is important that the prosecution should not know what I'm going to do. The reason for this is simple. If the prosecutor suspects that I'm not going to put any witnesses on, he will load everything he has into his case in chief as early in the proceedings as he can. Most prosecutors—both state and Federal—hold back some of their fire for what they loosely call their rebuttal. I use the word "loosely" because much of it is not legally rebuttal at all, but is in reality a part of their case in chief which they've held in reserve.

Recently in a Federal case the question of whether we should let our defendant testify arose. I was busy with another lawsuit, so I had asked one of my associates to handle the case for me and to consult with me if any problems arose in connection with it.

We knew that our client had held certain conversations with Federal agents which the prosecution hadn't mentioned, but if we put our defendant on the stand he would have to explain those conversations. He would also have to tell about a number of financial transactions he had had which might be difficult for him to explain. I therefore suggested that we follow the procedure of subpoenaing all of our defense witnesses and seeing to it that they were all on hand in the court during the last two days of the government's case. This was done. Then, when the government rested and the judge asked, "How long will the defense need to put on its case?" my associate rose and said calmly, "If *this* is all the government has in the way of a case, the defense rests too."

The government was flabbergasted. It had no less than four F.B.I. witnesses ready to tear our defendant to shreds, but they never got the chance. The judge said, "There'll be no rebuttals."

That is one example of that particular courtroom tactic paying off. The prosecution had held some of its heaviest artillery in reserve to blow our defense witnesses to smithereens but when we said, "The defense rests," and the judge said, "There'll be no rebuttals," the prosecution was through, done, washed up. What's more, our defendant was acquitted.

30

More of the Same

WHEN A CASE is finished, when the evidence is in and the arguments have been made, there comes a time in any jury case when the judge instructs the jury concerning the law as he thinks it applies to the facts they are about to consider. He may instruct them how to measure the amount of reasonable doubt involved, if any. He may tell them how to weigh the evidence. He may instruct them about such things as what constitutes a corroborating witness and an accomplice.

In a murder case the judge has to describe the degrees of murder and give the jurors the rules as to what constitutes what degree. He may tell the jury that in the state of California a conviction may be had upon either direct or circumstantial evidence. In a rape case he has to tell the jury that if it brings in a conviction it also has the right to recommend a sentence in the county jail instead of the state prison. In a murder case it has a right to fix the penalty. In other words, before they begin their deliberations the jurors wait for the judge to tell them the law to apply to the facts.

It will come as no news to anyone who has read *Anatomy of a Murder* that attorneys also suggest instructions to be read to a jury by a judge. But for those who haven't read that book, let me say that a lawyer is permitted to submit suggestions about the points of law he would like to have the judge mention to the jury when he delivers his final instructions.

The instructions a defense attorney submits to the court embody points of law he feels the jury should know to guide their deliberations and help them weigh the evidence. These legal points are based on decisions the defense lawyer has looked up in his law library. They are what he believes the law in the case should be. Naturally the district attorney submits his instructions too. Sometimes these two sets of suggestions conflict, and the layman may wonder how, if they were looked up in the same lawbooks, they can conflict.

They conflict in this way: If you're defending a person charged with murder and you're relying on "necessary self-defense" as your reply to the murder charge, whether self-defense was necessary or not might depend on who was the first aggressor, the decedent or the defendant. In this case the prosecution may ask the court to instruct the jury to this effect: "If, from the evidence, you believe that the defendant was the first aggressor, then he would, under the law, have no right to defend himself and take the life of the decedent, because he wasn't acting in the necessary self-defense as the first aggressor."

The defense may ask the court to offer this instruction: "On the contrary, if the jury believes from the evidence that the decedent was the first aggressor, then the accused had a right to stand his ground and defend himself. He was not obligated to retreat from the assault."

The instructions may conflict to that extent, but to be scrupulously fair a judge might give both sets of instructions to the jury. In my opinion, if he is going to give either he should give both, but it is possible that he may accept only the instructions from the prosecution and reject the instructions submitted by the defense. In that case and if the defendant is convicted, the defense can make an appeal, urging omission as an error on the part of the trial court. He will urge as his reason that if the court instructs only on the theory held to by the prosecution, and not from the theory adopted by the defense, it may convince the jury that in the judge's opinion the prosecution's theory is right and the defense theory is wrong, whereas the judge should be scrupulously impartial.

To make this easier for those involved, we now have a book in the state of California containing a numbered list of instructions which are applicable to criminal trials. As a result, many lawyers follow the easy practice of simply putting the name of a case on a sheet of paper, then jotting down numbers under that name. I do not do it that way. It is still my practice to write out meticulously each suggested instruction. I avoid the number-jotting method because it is lazy and sloppy. All suggested instructions prepared in my office are cross-indexed and filed, and there have been times when, in preparing instructions, I've picked from our old files instructions written in the handwriting of Clarence Darrow.

I prepare my instructions this way for two reasons. The first, of course, is to inform the jury of the way the defense hopes it will view the evidence; the second is to establish grounds for appeal if a judge refuses one of my suggested instructions which is demonstrably proper.

In my early days I once worked for days preparing a list of suggested instructions. Then I handed them in only to see the judge tear them up and throw them into his wastebasket. That in itself was an error. A judge has to rule on each instruction suggested to him. I'll never forget that judge glancing at the instructions I had slaved on and saying, "I don't like them," then tossing them into his wastebasket like confetti. However, I stood my ground and demanded my rights, and in the end that judge had to fish those pieces out of the wastebasket, paste them back together again and rule on each one of them.

Actually I know many cases where the defense lawyer has bothered to submit no instruction at all. This means that he's too lazy to prepare them. A proper preparation of instructions requires a burning of the midnight oil. To represent his client adequately a defense lawyer must spend long hours preparing his suggested instructions, but some lawyers take the position that the judge is obligated to instruct the jury upon the law, whether the opposing attorneys submit any suggested instructions or not, and if the instructions he gives are against them they feel it's the judge's fault, not theirs.

That book with its numbered list of suggested instructions is symptomatic of a factor which has crept into the practice of law since I began. The idea seems to have taken root, grown and blossomed that substitutes for hard work are hot stuff. No one has more respect for money than I have. I recall a passage from Holy Writ about the laborer being worthy of his hire, but that labor and that hire have been altered by the years. Time was when a young man going through one of our law schools wanted to become a trial lawyer. To him that was the stimulating, the challenging, even, to use a soggy word, the "glamorous" thing to be.

The softer and more pleasurable things of life, the country club, the luncheon club, the trips to the Bahamas, the "small" fifty-foot motor cruiser for weekends, the running over to Europe, the collecting of Renoirs and Van Goghs, the garageful of foreign sports cars for hacking about in, plus of course the large purring finny American monster with the armrests which lets down in the back seat and the windows which go up by pushing a button—all of those things seem much easier to attain to the young man in law school these days if he trains himself for corporate law or tax law rather than for the grueling give and take of the courtroom frays.

Mind you, this is just my opinion—or, rather, it is my opinion and that of a few others whose judgment I respect.

If more of those who teach in our law schools would tell the young men who sit at their feet that the duty of an attorney lies in court as well as in a law library or behind a big, fancy desk with a private tie line to a corporation, it would be better for the legal profession and for the public too.

Judging by the questions students ask me and the comments they make, only about one in thirty or forty of those who pass through a law school come out wanting to practice criminal law. If they do get into a courtroom, it is usually in connection with a civil case, such as a personal-injury or domestic-relations case.

Although that is necessary, of course, there is so much more to practicing law than that. I am admittedly prejudiced—but to me "lawyer" means a trial lawyer, and to be a trial lawyer a lawyer must try criminal cases. It is essential that there be advocates representing either the plaintiff or the defendant who try personal-injury cases which involve such things as mutilation or injury, but in such cases there is only one thing involved, liability; and there is only one thought, whether money will be awarded as damages or not awarded as damages. Divorce cases are a part of civil court-room work too, but they are in essence misery for one side or the other. Nobody wins.

To try a criminal case it is needful to talk about a man's liberty or his life or his reputation (which may be even more valuable to him than his life), and to me that is a spur which drives a man to day-and-night effort to do right by his client.

I like to think that a sense of duty is the incentive which inspires an attorney to such soul-trying efforts, but there's no denying that in addition it is an exciting challenge. To be truthful, I know of none more stimulating. This may explain why, when once a man has had a taste of criminal law, he will settle for nothing less, and other categories of the law will seem dull and flat even though not as much money comes his way in criminal law as in civil law.

It's also my belief that a young lawyer should be eager to try a criminal case whenever he gets the opportunity because he can enlarge his legal muscles much more quickly on criminal cases than on any other kind. It's an educational experience for a young-ster just starting out to be up against an old hand in the D.A.'s office.

On the other hand—and in all fairness—after having put in al-most half a century as a criminal lawyer I want to warn the young who are thinking of entering that field that it means that they will live and work under constant intense nervous and physical strain. The criminal advocate carries his client's life and liberty on his neck like a yoke, and life and liberty are two pretty heavy responsi-bilities.

And once more I'd like to remind a young law student that prac-ticing civil law usually makes more money for a lawyer than the criminal law. This is especially true today; it was not so true before big Federal income taxes. When the New York criminal lawyer Max Steuer died he left five million dollars, but he not only did some of the work in a day when there was no income tax and he could put it all away, he also charged large fees. His reputation was such that his fees didn't frighten the rich and important who flocked to his door. In fact, his large fees could have helped build his reputation as a desirable lawyer to have.

Not that many young lawyers today are in any doubt about where the big money lies. This is especially true since the public-defender system has come into being. The first public defender's office was in Los Angeles, and today the Los Angeles public defender's office is almost as large as the district attorney's office. It employs thirty or forty deputies. It has its own investigating department. As a result there are not as many criminal cases available to young lawyers to cut their teeth on, or to use as stepping stones, as there used to be.

I try to stress another fact to young lawyers. It's easy for a man who defends criminal cases to become too intimate, away from the courtroom, with the person he defends. Not only is that wrong common-sensewise, it is dangerous to play it any other way than cool, detached and objective.

In my time I have defended some nationally known hoods, but my name is never associated with them except during their trials. If I hadn't kept myself scrupulously clean in that respect, I wouldn't have been given a position of responsibility in the California State Bar Association as a member of its board of governors and I certainly would never have been elected president of the Beverly Hills Bar Association. You are not given such honors if a gamey odor clings to you.

31

My Life Now

I N THIS STORY I have been thinking and talking about Jerry Giesler, lawyer for the defense, rather than Jerry Giesler, husband and father. If the public wants anything of me, I'm sure it's the lawyer Giesler they want. Still, I'd like to talk about that other Giesler a little, even if only sketchily.

I am married to the former Ruth Stevens of Chicago, who was (and still is) one of the most beautiful women I've ever known. I've had two marriages. The first one, which began in 1918, when I was thirty-two, ended in divorce in 1928. I have a daughter, who is now living on the West Coast, from that first marriage.

I married my present wife in 1931. She dropped in to ask me for some legal advice. I took her out to lunch and dinner. She could have got a job in pictures, but we drifted together and she stopped thinking of a film job.

We have two children, a boy and a girl—Michael and Jerry Lee. Michael served a three-year hitch with the Marines He's in my office now doing investigative work.

When the present Mrs. Giesler and I were married, we had very little money. The depression was in full swing, and I had financial obligations arising out of my divorce. I'll never forget one night when I took her out to dinner and we had only enough money for one order of fish. Fortunately hard rolls were served free and the bus boy served two pats of butter. I ordered one order of fillet of sole, and that, with the rolls and butter, was our dinner.

We've had a lot of fun together. We've never had dull times—at least I haven't. We are of opposite types. I'm quiet and reserved. She loves gaiety. But at times our marriage has been trying to Mrs. Giesler, who occasionally remarks that I am married not only to her but also to my work. Being a wise wife, she doesn't say that resentfully. She mentions it as an established fact. However, she does put up with things other wives wouldn't. Not having vacations is one of them.

She gives my morale a tremendous lift by sitting up with me no matter what time it is, until I go to bed. I may work on a case until two o'clock or four o'clock in the morning—sometimes even five. Often I have had as little as two hours' sleep during the night, but she's always there to see if there's anything she can do for my comfort or to give me a fight talk if I need one.

One night while I was preparing for the third Busby Berkeley trial I thought, "It's too hard. I can't do it." Without realizing it, I said those things out loud as I paced the floor.

"What can't you do?" my wife asked me. "You can do anything if you put your mind to it. You've won harder cases. Impossible cases." True or not, it gave me the courage I needed.

When the Alexander Pantages case was over, we moved a little closer to Easy Street. After the Pantages trial I got more important cases and we moved from our flat to a beautiful apartment at Sycamore and Beverly. Mrs. Giesler did the decorating herself and it was exquisite.

From there we moved to a house on Ridgedale with eighteen rooms. There we put in our first swimming pool. However, that house was too big. By that time we had two children, but even the four of us rattled around. Our solution was to buy the one we live in now, which is more manageable.

Mrs. Giesler also decorated my suite of law offices. She has a remarkable knack for doing such things. My office has a quiet, muted atmosphere, enhanced by dark-green walls and pinpoint spotlights concealed in the ceiling. She had enlargements made of a small photograph of Mr. Darrow and a small photograph of Mr. Rogers and had them matted and framed to harmonize with each other.

Then she hung them on the wall behind my chair, so that my own face appears between their two likenesses.

If you talk to her, she'll tell you that I have certain pluses and minuses. She says that one plus is that I have infinite patience. But she'll say that when it comes to business matters I'm not so good. "I'm his business manager. He needs one." She is convinced that I am a soft touch, an easy mark, and she tells a story to prove she's right:

One Saturday night the front doorbell rang. Mrs. Giesler and I were propped up in bed watching television. She put on her robe, went to the front door, opened the peephole in it and asked, "What is it?"

A man's voice asked, "Is Jerry home?"

"You mean Mr. Giesler?" she asked. "What is it in reference to?"

"I must see him," the man said. "It's important."

"I'm sorry," Mrs. Giesler said "but Mr. Giesler doesn't see anyone on Saturdays and Sundays. You'll have to call him at his office Monday morning."

The man was persistent. He kept saying, "It's very urgent. I have to see him." And Mrs. Giesler kept saying, "I'm sorry, but you can't."

Finally the man said, "I'll go over to the Beverly Hills Hotel and call him from there."

He did go over to the hotel and he did call me. He said that he was desperately in need of money, and he asked if I could lend him a little to tide him over. What burned Mrs. Giesler was that I'd never seen the fellow in my life. He'd got my address from the phone book. But although I knew nothing about him, I was soft-hearted enough to say I would lend him money. When Mrs. Giesler heard me say that she excused herself and disappeared downstairs.

I was fumbling in my pockets to see how much cash I could find when the doorbell rang. Mrs. Giesler went to the door and said through the peephole, "What do you think this is, a loan company? Get out of here fast or I'll call the police! And it takes the Beverly Hills police only two minutes to get here!" Our maid saw the stranger run like a deer past the kitchen window.

Mrs. Giesler wasn't likely to let me forget this story in a hurry. "If you're that soft," she told me, "I think I'll make a few touches around here myself."

She has been a help to me in many other ways too. I used her as a mobile model in trying to work out in my mind just how things had happened in a case that another lawyer had tried and lost and I was asked to retry. It involved an Italian triangle. My Italian client was charged with killing his wife and her lover when he came home and found them in the bedroom.

I wasn't worried about defending my client for shooting the lover he had found in his own bed with his wife. There is no law which permits shooting under such circumstances, but it is only human nature to regard such a situation as extreme provocation. However, when it comes to shooting a wife under the same circumstances juries are apt to be more difficult.

My client, who had shot the lover as the latter tried to flee through a doorway, claimed that his wife, attempting to get out through the same doorway, had been hit accidentally by one of the bullets he had fired at the home wrecker. The only thing wrong with his story was that she had fallen facing her husband.

At home with Mrs. Giesler I tried to re-enact that scene in the way my client said it happened. Hour after hour I placed my wife by a door, took an unloaded gun, pointed it at her, had her try to go through the door; then I pretended to fire. Finally it came to me. What had happened was the same thing that happens when a hunter hits a deer with a high-powered rifle. If you hit a deer in the shoulder when it's running away from you, the force of your bullet is apt to spin him around. When her husband's bullet struck her, my client's wife whirled and fell back into the room, facing him. I used one of my associates to demonstrate this in the courtroom for the jury, and they found the husband not guilty.

I have been described by the press as "dressing well," whatever that means. If that description is true, it's because Mrs. Giesler selects my clothes. She has a tailor come to our house for fittings, and she chooses the fabrics. She even buys my shoes. I take her word for all these things. She insists on laying out at night the clothes that

I'm going to wear the next morning, including my shirt and tie, and she does all my mending. The truth is, she takes care of me like a baby.

There was a time when I'd answer my phone any time, day or night, but Mrs. Giesler has made me cut down on that. If someone needs me for something really important she doesn't object, but most of the people who call merely want to yap about a case or are worried or nervous and want someone to soothe them. When such calls come Mrs. Giesler has a system to help me get a few hours' rest. She answers the telephone and says, "I'm a maid in the household, and I've been given instructions not to awaken Mr. Giesler."

She says she can always tell whether a call is really urgent or not. If it's not, she says, "You can call him in the morning at his office, after nine o'clock." Most of the time they never call back, and she says, "You see! They're just people who *imagined* they needed you."

The few times that I've tried to take a vacation I've been very unhappy. If I must go out of town on business, I'm never out of touch with my office. If I'm in New York, I call my office at least twice a day and ask my secretary, Mrs. Fitzpatrick, to read me the mail or tell me what telephone calls have come in.

One year my wife persuaded me to go to Palm Springs with her. She thought that I should cut myself off from my office and have a complete rest. After making sure that it had no telephone, she rented a house near the springs.

I tried to fall in with her idea, but I couldn't stand it. I managed to get into Palm Springs three or four times a day to call my office. The Friday before Easter I called Mrs. Fitzpatrick and said, "I wish you'd drive down here and bring my mail and any messages." When she arrived, I said, "Perhaps you'd better stay over the weekend. I think I'll drive back with you Monday." With me, work is a compulsion. It is necessary to me for happiness.

I've been asked if I ever plan to retire. Mrs. Giesler puts it this way: "Every once in a while Jerry says that he might retire and take it easy; but I don't really believe it, not him!"

There are people who are foolish enough to try to act as their own lawyers in a criminal court. As a youngster, I was in court one day when one of those do-it-yourself defenders was having his day in the sun. The judge was patiently waiting to sentence him, but the defendant had spent the morning making motion after motion, although they had all been denied. Finally it neared noon and the judge asked wearily, "Have you any further motions before I pronounce sentence?"

"Yes, your honor," the defendant said hurriedly. "I move we adjourn."

Even the judge couldn't help laughing. But he didn't adjourn. He proceeded with the sentencing.

Right now I feel the way that young do-it-yourself defender must have felt. On my own behalf I'll say, "I move we adjourn."

Index

Adlon Hotel, Berlin, 208
Agabeg Occult Temple, Los Angeles, 217
Albany, Calif., 229
Alderman, Myrl, *see* Snyder case
Allen, Edward, 271
Allen, Giesler and Richardson, 271
Alto Nido Apartments, Los Angeles, 138
American Encyclopedia of Evidence, 273
American Humane Society, 215
A.S.P.C.A., 231
Anatomy of a Murder (Traver), 295, 321
Anderson Hotel, San Luis Obispo, Calif., 83
Angel's Flight Hill, Los Angeles, 266, 270, 271, 278
Anna Christie (film), 205
Appel, Horace, 11
Appelate Court of California, 281
Arborata Street, Los Angeles, 212
The Art of Advocacy (Stryker), 11; Giesler's review of, 11-12
assassination of Governor Steunenberg, 268
Avalon, Calif., 95

Bel Air, Calif., 94, 96, 101, 143, 146
Bergman, Ingrid, 260, 261
Berkeley, Busby, 2, 4, 9, 182, 249-255; *see also* Berkeley case
Berkeley case, 249-255; transcript of testimony in, 250, 251, 252
Berry, Joan, 182-190; *see also* Chaplin case
"Blue and Gray Series" (Otis), 264
Boise, Idaho, 218
Borah, William E., 268
Boyer, Lynne, 99
Brazil, A. H., 79ff., 93
Brice, Fanny, 215
Brice, Lew, 215-218
"The Brighter Side" (Runyon), *quoted*, 230-231
Broadway Department Store, Los Angeles, 213
Bruneman, Les, *see* Bruneman case
Bruneman case, 148-158, 175; transcript of testimony in, 150-156
Bryan, William Jennings, 85
Buchalter, Louis (Lepke), 236

Buck, Morrison, 269
Builders' Supply Company, Los Angeles, 267
Bull, Ingall W., judge in Wright case, 175
Burgess, Willard (attorney for Frankie Carbo), 240
Burnell, Judge, 250, 251, 252
Burns, William J., 274, 286, 287

Calhoun, John C., 274
Calhoun, Patrick, 274, 275-277
California Boxing Commission, 230
California Horse Racing Board, 229
California Supreme Court, 80, 134
California weather, 270
Canfield case, 269
Carbo, Frankie, 236-242, 319
Caress, E. L. (Zeke), see Bruneman case
"The Case of the Curious Commissioner," 228-229
"The Case of the Fleeced Foreigner," 215-218; legal responsibility for gambling debts in, 218
"The Case of the Missing Stomach," 232-235
"The Case of the Perjured Witness," see Dazey case
Castleman, Frank, "Frank Series," 264
Catalina Island, Calif., 95
Cathcart-Jones, Owen, 135-140
Central Jail, Los Angeles, 279

Central Park, Los Angeles, see Pershing Square
Chaplin, Charles, 2, 5, 182-190; see also Chaplin case
Chaplin case, 182-190, 309; Mann Act in, 184-190; Los Angeles Times quoted on, 185-186
Chaplin Studios, 185
Chicago Tribune, 194
Choate, Rufus, 279
Christie, Agatha, 47
Ciro's, Hollywood, Calif., 177, 178
Clifton, Henry Talbot Devers, 215-218
Cline, Herman (detective), 55
Cochran, Thomas W., 95ff.; see also Flynn case
Coleman, David, 250, 251
"the Colonel," see Snyder, Martin
Connolly, Bobby, 251
Coolidge, Calvin, 275
corpus delicti, legal aspects of, 288-289, 290
Costello, Deputy District Attorney, 43; see also Oesterreich-Sanhuber case
County Lunacy Commission, Los Angeles, 174
cross-examination, techniques of, 291-293
Culver City, Calif., 205

Daniels, Earl M., 29
Darrow, Clarence, 6, 11, 85, 268, 270; trial for bribery, 285-288

Darrow, Ruby (Mrs. Clarence Darrow), 286
Davis, Le Compte, 11
Dazey, Dr. George K., *see* Dazey case
Dazey, Mrs. George K., *see* Dazey case
Dazey case, 219-224
Diary of Anne Frank (film), 260
DiMaggio, Joe, 4
District Court of Appeals, Calif., 148, 157, 158, 204, 278, 280, 281
Dockweiler, John F., 242
Doherty, Frank, 296
Dominguez, Frank, 11, 50
Doolen, Jimmy, *see* Gatewood, James
Dunave, Nicholas, 27, 29, 37
Durante, Jimmy, 178

Eagan, Rexford, 82, 83, 84, 88-90, 91, 244, 245
Eau Claire, Wisc., 266
Eddy, Guy, 283, 284
Elementary Law (Robinson), 278
Etting, Ruth, 191-204; *see also* Snyder case

Facts on File Yearbook (1947), quoted, 240
Farrell, Glenda, 251
Federal Building, Los Angeles, 5
Federal court, Los Angeles, 188, 189
Fidler, Jimmy, 196

Fifth Amendment in Oesterreich-Sanhuber case, 53
Fitts, Buron, 51, 216; *see also* Pantages case
Fitzgerald, Barry, 299
Fitzpatrick, Mrs. Helen, 83, 90, 290, 331
Flynn, Errol, 2, 96-147, 150; *see also* Flynn case
Flynn case, 96-147, 150, 309; transcript of testimony in, 96-100, 101-109, 110-131, 133, 134, 136-139, 142-143, 144-145
Ford, Henry, Sr., 214
Ford, Robert, 95
Ford, W. J., 16, 29
Ford factory, Detroit, 214
"Frank Merriwell on Carson's Ranch," 265
"Frank Series" (Castleman), 264
Fricke, Judge, 31, 158, 317

Gabor, Zsa Zsa, 4, 259; Gabor-Sanders divorce, 259
Gage, Henry T., 11
Gambling debts, legal responsibility for, 218
Gamesmanship (Potter), 312
Garbo, Greta, 205-209; *see also* Schratter case
Gardner, Erle Stanley, 215
Gassman, Vittorio, 4, 259-260
Gatewood, James, 148, 149, 157
"Get me Giesler!" 260, 261
Giesler, Henry (uncle of Jerry Giesler), 264

Giesler, Jerry (Harold Lee): advice to young lawyers, 291*ff*., 298-305, 325, 326; Berkeley case, 249-255; Brice case, 215-218; Bruneman case, 148-158; chairman, Calif., State Athletic Commission, 228-229; chairman, Horse Racing Board, 229-231; and Clarence Darrow, 285-288; Dazey case, 219-224; divorce cases, 258-262; early years, 263-268; first cases, 281-284; first murder case, 256-257; Flynn case, 96-147; and Garbo, 205-209; Mitchum case, 246-248; Oesterreich-Sanhuber case, 40-71; Pantages case, 14-39; present-day life; 327-332; Robinson case, 243-246; and Earl Rogers, 269-284, 285-288; Ryan case, 72-93; St. Cyr case, 177-181; Siegel case, 236-240; Snyder case, 191-204; tactics in courtroom, 306-320; Tokyo Club case, 225-227; Wright case, 159-176, 315
Giesler, Jerry Lee (daughter), 327
Giesler, Michael (son), 327
Giesler, Ruth Stevens (Mrs. Jerry Geisler), 327-331
Gilbert, W. I., 16, 26-27, 29, 262
Glendale, Calif., 163
Glendale city jail, 159
Glendale police station, 159
Golden Gate Turf Club, 229

Gösta Berling (film), 207
Gotch, Frank, 228
Gotham Hotel, Los Angeles, 299
Grand Hotel, Stockholm, 207
Grange, Red, 270
Grant, Cary, 4
Greenberg, Harry (Big Greenie), 236-242
Greener, Reverend Violet, 217, 218
Guinan, Texas, 215
Guinan, Tommy, 215-217
Gustafsson, Greta, *see* Garbo, Greta

Haas, Morris, 275
Hanford, Calif., 285, 286
Hansen, Betty, *see* Flynn case
Hansen, Mrs. Lars, 207
Hardy, Judge Carlos, 53
Hauptmann, Bruno, 5
Healy, Betty Hickman (Mrs. Ted Healy), 261-262
Healy, Ted, 261-262
Heney, Francis J., 274, 275, 276, 277
Heston, Willie, 266
Hill, Virginia, 240
Hollywood Athletic Club, 160
Hollywood Park-Santa Anita fight, 229
Hollywood police station, 155
Hollywood Boulevard and Vine Street, Los Angeles, 228, 237
Holy Rollers, 81
Hover, Herman, 179
Hunter, Katherine, 186
Hutton, Barbara, 4

Index

Industrial Workers of the World
(I.W.W.), 268
International Bank Building, Los
Angeles, 278

James, William, 310
Johnson, Hiram, 275
jury, how to select, 300-301
Juvenile Hall, 103, 145

Kibbee, Guy, 251, 252
Kimmel, John, see Wright case
King, Alexander (former Solici-
tor General of the U.S.), 276
Kinowaki (accessory in Tokyo
Club case), 226
Knapp, Armand, 101, 102, 105,
109
Knight, Goodwin (former Gov-
ernor of California), 228
Koenig, Ben, 251, 252
Krakower, Whitey, 240, 241

La Brea tar pits, Los Angeles, 49,
50, 71
Landis, Kenesaw Mountain, 230
Las Vegas, Nevada, 202, 259, 270
Laurel Canyon, Calif., 246
"The Lawsuit" (McCay), 297
Lawyers' Guild of Los Angeles,
296
Leahan, James, 9, 161, 221, 223,
233-235, 318
Leavy, J. Miller, 165
Leroy, Mervyn, 251
Lewis, George, 216-217

Lewis, Strangler, 229
Liebowitz, Samuel, 6
Lincoln, Nebraska, 101, 103
Linden Drive, Beverly Hills,
Calif., 240
Lindsay, Judge Ben, 174
Lindsay, Vachel, 5
Lindstrom, Dr. Peter, 260
"Little Fellow in the Attic" case,
see Oesterreich-Sanhuber
case
Lodi, Calif., 225
Long Beach, California, 149, 150,
153, 155-156, 157, 215-216
Loop district, Chicago, 194
Lopez Canyon ranch, 72
Los Angeles County Superior
Court, 53, 133, 246
Los Angeles General Hospital, 174
Los Angeles Times, quoted, Chap-
lin case, 185-186
Los Angeles Times Building, 285
Lundquist, Gerda, 208

McCay, Winsor, "The Lawsuit,"
297
McCoy, Kid, see Selby, Norman,
Selby case
McGinley, Walter, 151
McHugh, Frank, 251
MacMurray, Fred, 91
McNamara, James B., 285
McNamara, Joseph J., 285
Malibu Beach, Calif., 249
Mann Act, 184-190; see also
Chaplin case
Marigold Gardens, Chicago, 191
Martenson, Mona, 207

337

Masonic lodge, Oakley, Kans., 264
Milan, Italy, 259
Milwaukee, Wisc., 40, 41, 43, 55, 66, 69, 70, 162
Mitchum, Robert, 3, 243, 246-248
Mitchum case, 246-248
Monroe, Marilyn, 4
Morgan Park, Ill., 264
Morgan Park Academy, 264, 265, 266
Mors, Albert, 210; see also Selby case
Mors, Mrs. Albert, see Selby case
Muir, Florabel, 180
Murder, Inc., 236-242

Namba (victim in Tokyo Club case), 225-227
National Broadcasting Company studios, Los Angeles, 198
Neilan, Marshall, 47
New York University Law Review, 11
Norton, Mrs. Cora N., 43-47

Oakley, Kansas, 264
O'Brien, Pat, 249, 252
O'Connor, J. F. T., Federal judge in Chaplin case, 189
O'Dwyer, William (former mayor of N.Y.), 237, 238, 242
Oesterreich, Fred, see Oesterreich-Sanhuber case
Oesterreich, Raymond, 40, 41
Oesterreich, Mrs. Walburga, see Oesterreich-Sanhuber case

Oesterreich-Sanhuber case, 40-71; Fifth Amendment in, 53; statute of limitations in, 69; transcript of testimony in, 43-47, 53- 69
Ogilvie, Alex, 266
One-upmanship (Potter), 312
Otis, James, "Blue and Gray Series," 264

Page, Farmer, 151
Palm Springs, Calif., 270, 331
Pantages, Alexander, 2, 14-39; see also Pantages case
Pantages case, 14-39, 72, 134, 182, 243, 306, 309, 328; brief on statutory rape in, 33-35; transcript of testimony in, 16-27
Pantages Theater, Los Angeles, 14
Pearl Harbor, 234
Pecora, Ferdinand, 6
penal code, Section 995, 299
penal code, Section 1111, in Siegel defense, 239
People v. Weatherford decision, 80
Pershing Square, Los Angeles, 267
Piovera, Evasio Henry, 72ff.; see also Ryan case
Potter, Stephen: Gamesmanship, 312; One-upmanship, 312
Pringle, Eunice Irene, 243; see also Pantages case
"Professor Fourman": letter from Giesler, quoted, 265; reply, quoted, 265-266

Prospect Law and Collection Agency, 271

Quiet Birdmen, 160

Ray, Leonard Durvan, Jr., see Ryan case
Reed, Harry, 161, 162
Reinhardt, Max, 185
Reynolds, Jack, 216-217
Richardson, John, 271
Robinson, Edward G., Jr., 4, 243-246
Robinson, Edward G., Sr., 245
Robinson, Nancy (Mrs. Edward G., Jr.), 244
Robinson case, 243-246
Rogers, Earl, 2, 5, 11, 269-270, 272-277, 279-280, 281, 282, 283, 285-288, 291, 309, 310
Roll, Ernest, 165
The Roost (restaurant), 158
Rubirosa, Porfirio, 259
Ruef, Abraham, 274, 275
Runyon, Damon, 148, 214, quoted 230-231
Ryan, Mrs. Margaret, see Ryan case
Ryan, Tommy, 210
Ryan case, 72-93

St. Cyr, Lili, 5, 177-181, 182
St. Cyr case, 177-181
St. Francis Hotel, San Francisco, 275

St. Louis, Mo., 66, 69
St. Louis Post-Dispatch, story on Jerry Giesler, 2-3
Sanders, George, 4, 259
San Francisco, Calif., 274, 275, 277; San Francisco fire, 268
Sanhuber, Otto, see Oesterreich-Sanhuber case
Sanitary District Department, Chicago, 195
San Luis Obispo, Calif., 72, 79, 80ff., 86, 90, 91, 92
San Luis Obispo County grand jury, 79
San Quentin prison, 171, 214
Santa Anita race track, 229
Santa Fé railroad, 221, 222, 223
Santa Monica, Calif., 94, 219, 223, 244, 249, 262
San Vicente Boulevard, Hollywood, 178
Satterlee, Peggy La Rue, 95, 110ff., 135; see also Flynn case
Schachter, George H., see Greenberg, Harry
Schenck, Paul W., 11
Schratter, David, see Schratter case
Schratter case, 205-209
Schreibman, Paul, 217
Scopes trial, 85
Scott, A. A., Superior Judge, 239, 240
Seattle, Wash., 236, 241
Sebastian, Charles, 283
Security Bank, Los Angeles, 267
Selby, Norman (Kid McCoy), 4, 210-218; see also Selby case

Selby case, 210-218
"Shepardizing," 282
Siegel, Benjamin (Bugsy), 236-240
Sirocco (Errol Flynn's yacht), 95, 110, 134, 140-142, 145; see also Flynn case
Snyder, Edith, 192-194, 196, 201, 202, 204; see also Snyder case
Snyder, Martin (Moe, "The Gimp"), 2, 191-204; see also Snyder case
Snyder case, 191-204
Social Security for race-track employees, 229-230
Southern Pacific Railroad, 276
Stackpole, Peter, 110, 119
State Athletic Commission, Calif., 228
Steffens, Lincoln, 286
Stephens, Albert Lee, 271, 272
Steuer, Max, 6, 325, 326
Stevens, Ruth, see Giesler, Ruth Stevens
Stewart (chief deputy district attorney in Pantages case), 31
Still, Judge Leslie E., 133, 146-147
Stiller, Mauritz, 206, 208
Stork Club, New York, 186
Stralla, Tony Cornero, 149
Stryker, Lloyd Paul, 5, 11-12
Sunset Boulevard, Los Angeles, 267
Supreme Court of California, 36, 204, 282
Svenska Film Company, Sweden, 206, 207

Tannenbaum, Allie, 237, 238-239, 242
Thaw, Harry, 257
Third and Main Streets, Los Angeles, 285
3090 Lake Hollywood Drive (Etting house), 193
"Three Stooges," 261
Tip-Top Weekly (magazine), 265-266
"Toast to the Babies" (Mark Twain), 264
Tokyo Club, 225
Tokyo Club case, 225-227; judicial error in, 226, 227
Town House (hotel), Los Angeles, 316
Traver, Robert, Anatomy of a Murder, 295
Trianon Film Company, Berlin, 207, 208
Turf and Sports (magazine), 228
Twain, Mark, "Toast to the Babies," 264

United Railroads, San Francisco, 275
U.S. Army Medical College, Washington, D.C., 234
United States Department of Justice, 274; Bureau of Investigation, 274
U.C.L.A., 169
University of Iowa law school, 268
University of Michigan, 266
U.S.C. Law School, 270, 271
Urbana, Ill., 270

Index

Veitch, Deputy District Attorney, 150

Ventura, Calif., 252

Verdugo Vista Drive, Glendale, Calif., 162

Wakeman (lawyer for Otto San-huber), 56-63, 64-69

Waldorf-Astoria Hotel, New York, 184, 185, 186, 187

Walters, Judge Byron J., 95, 101, 132

Warner Brothers Studio, 253

Watts, Calif., 256

Webster, Daniel, 279

Wells, Robert Wesley, 227-228

Westgate Hotel, Los Angeles, 213

West Seventh Street, Los Angeles, 210, 211, 212

White, Stephen M., 11, 279

"White Flame" case, see Wright case

Wiles, Buster, 110, 120

Williss, Judge, 271

Wilshire Boulevard, Los Angeles, 10

Wilson, Emmett, Superior Judge, 217

Wilson, Woodrow, 276

Wilton Junction, Iowa (birthplace of Jerry Giesler), 263

Winters, Shelley, 4, 259-260

Winters-Gassman suit, 259-260

women on juries, 296

Woollcott, Alexander, 5

World War II, 230, 232; Pearl Harbor, 234

Wright, Mrs. Evelyn, see Wright case

Wright, Paul, 159-176, 203; see also Wright case

Wright case, 159-176, 315; issue of insanity in, 171-174; use of Bible by defense, 170-171

Yamatoda, Hideichi, 225-227

Ziegfeld Follies, 191

Zybysko, Stanislaus, 229

Michael A. Carella
255 West Santa Inez Ave.
Hillsborough, Calif.

About the Author

HAROLD L. "JERRY" GIESLER'S *early life was as remote from Hollywood's glitter and tinsel as it is possible to be. He was born in the little town of Wilton Junction, Iowa, in 1886, the elder son of a bank cashier. After the usual public-school education, he decided to enter the University of Michigan, because the football star, Willie Heston, played there. In 1905 after a summer-school make-up session in mathematics, his eyes gave out and a specialist advised him to take a year off to rest. He spent that year in Los Angeles, staying with the family of a school chum. He got a job driving a lumber wagon to support himself while he was attending the University of Southern California's law school. Two years later, in 1907, he passed the state bar examination and began his practice in the law offi* of Earl Rogers. He stayed with Rogers for several years, acting as attorney of record for some of Rogers' historic cases. Eventually, of course, Mr. Giesler branched out on his own, a d, after his successful defense of Alexander Pantages in 1929, is rise was meteoric.*

Mr. Giesler lives in Los Angeles with his wife, the former Ruth Stevens. They have two children, Michael and Jerry Lee.